POLITICS IN AFRICA
A New Beginning?

Carlene J. Edie
University of Massachusetts at Amherst

THOMSON LEARNING

**Australia • Canada • Mexico • Singapore •
Spain • United Kingdom • United States**

Executive Editor: David Tatom
Editorial Assistant: Dianna Long
Marketing Manager: Caroline Croley
Marketing Assistant: Mary Ho
Project Manager, Editorial Production:
Barrett Lackey
Print/Media Buyer: Robert King
Permissions Editor: Stephanie Keough-Hedges
Production Service: UG / GGS Information
Services, Inc.

Photo Researcher: Sandra Lord
Copy Editor: Steven Baker
Cover Designer: Sue Hart
Cover Image: Hulton / Archive / Getty Images
Cover Printer: Webcom Limited
Compositor: UG / GGS Information
Services, Inc.
Printer: Webcom Limited

Printed in Canada
1 2 3 4 5 6 7 06 05 04 03 02

For more information about our products,
contact us at:
**Thomson Learning Academic
Resource Center
1-800-423-0563**

For permission to use material from this
text, contact us by:
Phone: 1-800-730-2214
Fax: 1-800-730-2215
Web: http://www.thomsonrights.com

Library of Congress Control Number:
2002103458

ISBN 0-15-508460-7

Wadsworth/Thomson Learning
10 Davis Drive
Belmont, CA 94002-3098
USA

Asia
Thomson Learning
60 Albert Street, #15-01
Albert Complex
Singapore 189969

Australia
Nelson Thomson Learning
102 Dodds Street
South Melbourne, Victoria 3205
Australia

Canada
Nelson Thomson Learning
1120 Birchmount Road
Toronto, Ontario M1K 5G4
Canada

Europe/Middle East/Africa
Thomson Learning
Berkshire House
168-173 High Holborn
London WC1V 7AA
United Kingdom

Latin America
Thomson Learning
Seneca, 53
Colonia Polanco
11560 Mexico D.F.
Mexico

Spain
Paraninfo Thomson Learning
Calle/Magallanes, 25
28015 Madrid, Spain

Table of Contents

List of Tables

Acronyms

ACP	African, Caribbean, and Pacific
ACRI	African Crisis Response Initiative
ADEMA	Alliance for Democracy (Mali)
ADF	Allied Democratic Forces (Uganda)
ADFL	Alliance of Democratic Forces for the Liberation of Zaire
AFPRC	Armed Forces Provisional Ruling Council (The Gambia)
ALCP	All Liberian Coalition Party
ANC	African National Congress (South Africa)
APC	All People's Congress (Sierra Leone)
APRC	Alliance for Patriotic Reorientation and Construction (Gambia)
AREMA	Association for the Rebirth of Madagascar
ASP	Afro-Shirazi Party (Zanzibar)
AU	African Union
BDP	Botswana Democratic Party
BDS	Bloc Democratique Senegalais
BIP	Botswana Independence Party
BNF	Botswana National Front
CACEU	Central African Customs and Economic Union
CCM	Chama Cha Mapinduzi (Tanzania)
CD	Campaign for Democracy (Nigeria)
CDHR	Committee for the Defense of Human Rights (Nigeria)
CEAO	Communaute Economique de l'Afrique de l'Ouest
CEMAC	Communaute Economique et Monetaire de l'Afrique Centrale
CFA	Communaute Financiere Africaine
CIA	Central Intelligence Agency

CLO	Civil Liberties Organization (Nigeria)
CNDD	Conseil National pour la Defense de la Democracie (Burundi)
CNSAPAS	National Commission to Implement the Structural Adjustment Program (Benin)
COMESA	Common Market for Eastern and Southern Africa
COSATU	Congress of South African Trade Unions
CPDM	Cameroon People's Democratic Movement
CPP	Convention People's Party (Ghana)
DCA	Democratic Congress Alliance (Sudan)
DP	Democratic Party (Uganda)
DRC	Democratic Republic of the Congo
EAC	East African Community
EACU	East African Customs Union
ECA	Economic Commission for Africa
ECCAS	Economic Community of Central African States
ECOMOG	Economic Community of West African States Monitoring Group
ECOWAS	Economic Community of West African States
EEC	European Economic Community
ELF	Eritrean Liberation Front
EPGL	Economic Community of Countries in the Great Lakes
EPLF	Eritrean People's Liberation Front
EPRDF	Ethiopian People's Revolutionary Democratic Front
EC/EU	European Community/European Union
EO	Executive outcomes
FAR	Rwandan Armed Forces
FDD	Front for the Defense of Democracy
FIDES	Fonds D'Investissement et de Developpement Economique et Social
FNLA	National Front for the Liberation of Angola
FPR	Front Patriotique Rwandais
FRELIMO	Front for the Liberation of Mozambique
FRODEBU	Front Democratique du Burundi
GATT	General Agreement on Tariffs and Trade
GDP	Gross domestic product
GNP	Gross national product
GNU	Government of National Unity (South Africa)

GPP	Gambia People's Party
HDI	Human Development Index
ICRG	International Country Risk Guide
IFP	Inkata Freedom Party (South Africa)
IGAD	Intergovernmental Authority on Drought and Development
IGNU	Interim Government of National Unity (Liberia)
IMF	International Monetary Fund
INPFL	Independent National Patriotic Front of Liberia
KADU	Kenya African Democratic Union
KANU	Kenya African National Union
LCs	Local councils (Uganda)
LDCs	Less developed countries
LLDCs	Least less developed countries
MCP	Malawi Congress Party
MINURCA	(U.N.) Mission in the Central African Republic
MLPC	Movement for the Liberation of the Central African People
MLSTP-PSD	Movement for the Liberation of São Tomé and Principe-Social Democratic Party
MMD	Movement for Multiparty Democracy (Zambia)
MNC	Multinational corporation
MNRD	Movement National pour la Revolution et le Developpement (Rwanda)
MRU	Manus River Union
NAM	Nonaligned Movement
NCCK	National Council of Churches of Kenya
NCNC	National Council of Nigeria and the Cameroons
NCP	National Convention Party (The Gambia)
NDA	National Democratic Alliance (Sudan)
NDC	National Democratic Congress
NEMU	National Elections Monitoring Unit (Kenya)
NEPU	Northern Elements Progressive Union (Nigeria)
NGO	Nongovernmental organization
NIEO	New international economic order
NIF	National Islamic Front (Sudan)
NP	National Party (South Africa)

NPC	Northern Peoples Congress (Nigeria)
NPC	National People's Congress (Uganda)
NPFL	National Patriotic Front of Liberia
NPP	National Patriotic Party (Liberia)
NPRC	National Provisional Ruling Council (Sierra Leone)
NRM	National Resistance Movement (Uganda)
NRP	National Reconciliation Party
OAU	Organization of African Unity
OECD	Organization for Economic Cooperation and Development
OPEC	Organization of Petroleum Exporting Countries
PAICV	African Party for the Independence of Cape Verde
PAIGC	African Party for the Independence of Guinea-Bissau and Cape Verde
PALIPEHUTU	Party for the Liberation of the Hutu People (Burundi)
PDCI	Parti Democratique de la Côte d'Ivoire
PDOIS	Peoples Democratic Organization for Independence and Socialism (The Gambia)
PDG	Democratic Party of Guinea (Guinea-Conakry)
PDGE	Democratic Party for Equatorial Guinea
PDP	Peoples Democratic Party (The Gambia)
PDP	Peoples Democratic Party (Nigeria)
PFDJ	Peoples Front for Democracy and Justice
POLISARIO	People's Front for the Liberation of Saquiet el-Hamra and Rio de Oro
PNDC	Provisional National Defense Council (Ghana)
PPP	People's Progressive Party (The Gambia)
PTA	Preferential Trade Area
RCs	Resistance Councils (Uganda)
RCD	Congolese Union for Democracy
RENAMO	Resistencia Nacional Mocambicana
RND	Rassemblement National pour le Development (Comoros)
RPF	Rwanda Patriotic Front
RTP	Rally of the Togolese People
RUF	Revolutionary United Front (Sierra Leone)
SACU	Southern African Customs Union

SADC	Southern African Development Community
SADCC	Southern African Development Coordination Conference
SDP	Social Democratic Party
SLPP	Sierra Leone's People's Party
SPLA	Sudanese People's Liberation Army
SPLM	Sudanese People's Liberation Movement
SPPF	Seychelles Peoples Progressive Front
SNM	Somali National Movement
SWAPO	Southwest Africa People's Organization
TANU	Tanganyika (Tanzania) African National Union
TPLF	Tigrean Peoples Liberation Front (Ethiopia)
UC	Union Camerounaise
UDEAC	Union Douaniere et Economique de l'Afrique Central
UDF	United Democratic Front
UDP	United Democratic Party (The Gambia)
UEMOA	Union Economique et Monetaire Ouest Africaine
ULIMO	United Liberian Movement for Democracy in Liberia
UNCTAD	UN Conference on Trade and Development
UNIP	United National Independence Party (Zambia)
UNIRD	National Union of Independents for Democratic Revival (Niger)
UNITA	Uniao Nacional para a Independencia Total de Angola
UNITAF	United Nations Interim Task Force
UNOSOM	United Nations Operation in Somalia
UPC	Uganda Peoples Congress
UPRONA	Union for National Progress (Burundi)
USAID	United States Agency for International Development
WACU	West African Customs Union
WTO	World Trade Organization
ZANU	Zimbabwe African National Union
ZAPU	Zimbabwe African Peoples Union
ZCTU	Zambia Congress of Trade Unions

Map of Africa

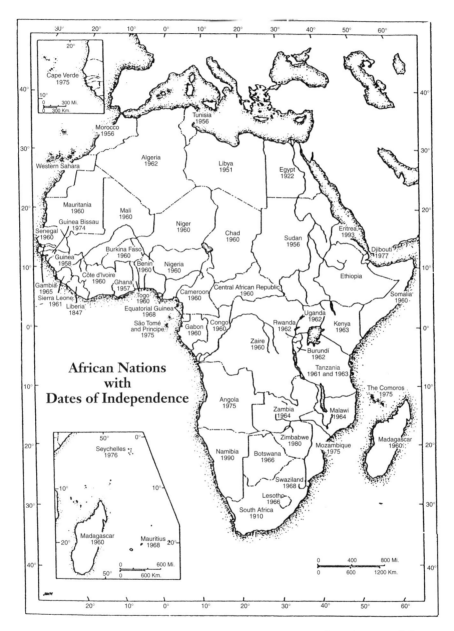

African Nations with Dates of Independence

Cape Verde 1975
Morocco 1956
Tunisia 1956
Western Sahara
Algeria 1962
Libya 1951
Egypt 1922
Mauritania 1960
Mali 1960
Guinea Bissau 1974
Niger 1960
Chad 1960
Sudan 1956
Eritrea 1993
Senegal 1960
Guinea 1958
Burkina Faso 1960
Benin 1960
Nigeria 1960
Djibouti 1977
Gambia 1965
Côte d'Ivoire 1960
Ghana 1957
Central African Republic 1960
Ethiopia
Sierra Leone 1961
Liberia 1847
Togo 1960
Equatorial Guinea 1968
Cameroon 1960
Somalia 1960
São Tomé and Principe 1975
Gabon 1960
Congo 1960
Uganda 1962
Rwanda 1962
Kenya 1963
Zaire 1960
Burundi 1962
Tanzania 1961 and 1963
The Comoros 1975
Angola 1975
Zambia 1964
Malawi 1964
Madagascar 1960
Zimbabwe 1980
Mozambique 1975
Namibia 1990
Botswana 1966
Swaziland 1968
Lesotho 1966
South Africa 1910
Seychelles 1976
Madagascar 1960
Mauritius 1968

0   300 Mi.
0   300 Km.

0   400   800 Mi.
0   600   1200 Km.

0   600 Mi.
0   600 Km.

JMcN

Preface and Acknowledgments

As a child growing up in Jamaica, I came to learn of Africa as a political entity through stories passed on to me by my maternal grandparents, about Jamaican hero Marcus Garvey. During my years in high school in Jamaica, I was first introduced to Africa as a part of a discussion of the impact of British imperialism on the West Indies. Living in the Jamaican multiethnic society, with an African majority but one in which race and class correlations placed that majority at the bottom of the society, I quickly became sensitive to the plight of the black poor at home as well as in the wider Caribbean, in the United States, and the rest of the world. In 1974, my last year of high school in Jamaica, I read Eric Williams's *Capitalism and Slavery* and Walter Rodney's *How Europe Underdeveloped Africa*. Those histories, together with the information I had gathered from the Rastafarians living in my community in Spanish Town, led to an intense desire for knowledge of Africa and solutions to the problems that plagued us as African people.

Although I was not interested in repatriation to Africa, I had a keen interest in visiting the African continent. In September 1974 I migrated to the United States and attended the University of California at Los Angeles (UCLA). At UCLA my undergraduate experience exposed me to African languages, literature, history, music, drama, and politics. Young, naive, and full of enthusiasm, I first visited Africa in 1978 as a graduate student. I went to Egypt for a year in an education abroad program attached to the American University in Cairo. From Egypt I visited The Sudan and Nigeria. I returned to Africa in the early 1990s (as a professor), when I conducted fieldwork in The Gambia and visited friends and relatives in Senegal and Guinea.

Apart from a personal interest in Africa, as a political science major at UCLA I developed an intellectual interest in African politics. My intellectual development has been heavily influenced by my training as a graduate student at UCLA, where I was exposed to the work on African politics of Richard Sklar, Michael Lofchie, and James Coleman, among others. My ideas about politics in developing nations, however, have been shaped mainly by C. L. R. James, Walter Rodney, Carl Stone, Archie Singham, George Beckford, Norman Girvan, Clive Thomas, Pierre-Michel Fontaine, and other scholars who had been members of the New World Group at the University of the West Indies at Mona, Kingston, Jamaica. My interest and work in Africa was informed by my earlier work on Caribbean politics. African colleagues who have helped me to understand politics in Africa include the late Boniface Obichere, Mazisi Kunene, Clement Udeze, Ladipo Adamolekun, Dunstan Wai, Akinsola Akiwowo, Ali Hersi, Ahmed Ahmed, Joao Da Costa, and Femi Badejo. My interest in African politics was also honed by my continuous interaction with Africans living in Los Angeles.

From the beginning of my graduate career at UCLA, I maintained an interest in both Caribbean and sub-Saharan African politics. I have always been intrigued by the similarities and differences in the political structures of Caribbean and former British colonies in Africa. My work on the functioning of the British-derived model of parliamentary democracy in Jamaica increased my interest in the same issue in former British colonies in Africa. I have done fieldwork in The Gambia, which at the time fit the model of uninterrupted multiparty electoral politics. However, with the 1994 coup d'etat that model fell apart. My interest then shifted to identifying the factors that accounted for both twenty-nine years of uninterrupted parliamentary democracy and that system's collapse. My work on Gambian politics joined the debate on fragile democratic transitions in post-1990 sub-Saharan Africa. Because of my work on The Gambia and my course offerings on African politics, the Series Editor, Howard Wiarda, approached me to write *Politics in Africa*. I thought this was a great opportunity for an up-to-date general book that surveyed the postindependence political experience in sub-Saharan Africa. This book should be of interest to beginning students of African politics, as well as students of the politics of developing nations in general.

From the time that I was approached to write this book and its actual completion, some significant debts were incurred. I thank the Wadsworth Publishing Company, whose patience with my delays in completing the book was often tested; the Series Editor, Howard Wiarda, for his comments on several drafts that improved the book considerably; Frank Holmquist, for his suggestions that led to a revised Chapter 8; Donna Dove, graduate secretary in the Department of Political Science at the University of Massachusetts at Amherst, whose preparation of my tables was invaluable; my daughter, Khadija, for her patience with me for the time spent away from her working on the book; and finally, to my beloved partner, Benjamin Oke, without whose patience, encouragement, good humor, and love, the book simply would not have been completed.

Carlene J. Edie

Amherst, Massachusetts
August 2001

1

Introduction

The aim of this book is to introduce the main issues of the politics and political economy of postindependence sub-Saharan Africa. In this book *Africa* refers to sub-Saharan Africa unless otherwise stated. A detailed study of the political economy of each of these countries will not be done. Rather, the purpose is to indicate the similarities among as well as the variety and complexity of political structures and economies of the African continent. Notwithstanding the unique differences among African countries, the region can be pulled together for interesting comparison, as many countries share similar obstacles to development as a result of colonization, history, politics, and the impact of the international economy.

The book incorporates useful insights from over four decades of studies of modern politics in Africa but will avoid a direct discussion of contending theoretical approaches. The book evaluates the postcolonial African state's management of power from the 1960s through the 1990s, indicating the extent to which domestic and external pressures of the 1990s have transformed state-society relations in African countries.

The model of development that emerged in postindependence sub-Saharan Africa in the 1960s has been one of external dependence and underdeveloped capitalism. Regardless of the colonizing power, African countries have functioned as marginalized countries from their colonization to the present. The effects of this are that the region has been largely a producer of raw materials for metropolitan countries; the economies of the region are extremely small and vulnerable and located on the periphery of the international economy; the region is heavily influenced by external actors; and power is extremely concentrated internally. The political component of this model has been a proliferation of military, civilian authoritarian, and one-party regimes that has denied broad political freedoms to the population. A small number of countries (Botswana, The Gambia, Senegal, Mauritius) maintained uninterrupted multiparty electoral systems for a relatively long period in the postindependence period, but even in those countries the majority of the population was excluded from political life.

Throughout the African continent, by the end of the 1980s, both the economic and the political situation had alienated the population. The economic crisis of the 1980s led to a total collapse of the postindependence model. This model came under pressure from a variety of domestic sources—wars, guerrilla movements, popular forces. In the case of Ethiopia, Somalia, Angola, Mozambique, Sierra Leone, Liberia, Rwanda, and Burundi, the costs of war contributed to the deepening of the economic crisis.

With the international system's restructuring as a result of communism's fall in the Soviet Union and Eastern Europe and with the end of the Cold War, Africa's political economy is being reshaped to fit the demands of a new era of globalization. The neoclassical liberal economic model touted by the United States has emerged as the dominant model of the new global economic order. Western-based multilateral lending agencies have argued that debt-ridden developing nations can achieve higher levels of development by shifting their economic development away from statism to market-oriented reforms. International factors have had an important role in democratizing political regimes across sub-Saharan Africa. With this shift in policy, the international environment no longer supported authoritarian regimes. Multiparty electoral politics became an issue in African politics, as domestic demands for greater participation in political and economic decision-making converged with international donor demands for "good governance" as a condition for economic aid. Authoritarian leaders were forced to embrace the concept of democratization (even if in a limited form) and moved toward instituting participatory structures.

Between 1989 and 1992 over thirty sub-Saharan African countries made a formal transition from the dominant single-party model to competitive elections and multiparty rule. Formal democratic institutions have been established in many countries, but many elected governments still display autocratic tendencies, such as the refusing to accept constitutionally-set term limits or placing restrictions on the opposition or the media. There have been some "reversals" where elected leaders were deposed by the military in Burundi (1993), The Gambia (1994), Niger (1996), Sierra Leone and Congo-Brazzaville (1997), and Cote D'Ivoire (1999). In Nigeria the military refused to accept the outcome of the 1993 elections and stayed in power until 1999. In Ghana, Niger, and The Gambia, military rulers have legitimized themselves through elections (two elections in the case of Ghana). In some countries with elected governments (e.g., Zambia and Kenya), symptoms of the countries' authoritarian legacy have surfaced continuously. In many countries, election results have led to dominant-party systems where one party won several consecutive elections and remains in power for several years (e.g., Botswana (four decades), South Africa (8 years)).

The new era of semiauthoritarian and semidemocratic politics, triggered by the transformation of many regimes to multiparty systems, has not yet produced a new African state capable of responding to the collective needs of the population. The process of economic liberalization, concurrent with democratization, has undermined the state's capacity to represent popular interests. These issues are often complicated by economic and social crises linked to the spread of AIDS and to corruption, crime, violence, and societal unraveling. In this context, is there any reason for optimism about a "new beginning" in African politics? This is the central question of the book's discussion of contemporary African political economy.

Plan of the Book

This book deals with post-1960s political and economic developments. The first chapter is a brief introduction identifying the aims and objectives of the book. The second chapter gives a background to the study of Africa, as well as basic facts on sub-Saharan Africa.

Chapter 3 examines aspects of sub-Saharan Africa's colonial legacy that are relevant to the authoritarian character of the postcolonial state. Several historical factors that are crucial to authoritarianism in the postindependence period are identified: the partition of Africa, centralized authoritarian bureaucratic structures, destruction or distortion of indigenous systems of governance, politicized ethnicity, racism, marginalized and dependent economies. The modern African authoritarian state is a consequence of these as well as contemporary political, economic, social, and cultural forces.

Chapter 4 examines the key strategy—clientelism—used by political elites to maintain dominance of the state over the African population. The chapter suggests a linkage between the clientelist political strategy of the educated middle classes who came to power at independence and the authoritarian state and statist economic policies that they implemented. The chapter discusses the various types of clientelism that can be found in Africa, using case studies from across sub-Saharan Africa. The international dimension of clientelism is also addressed with analyses of the reciprocal ties between African states and their international patrons. The state's dominance is linked to both its domestic and international clientelist base.

Chapter 5 identifies the main types of political regime that emerged in postindependence Africa. For the first three decades after independence, more than three-fourths of African countries developed authoritarian systems based on single-party, one-dominant-party, or military rule, and even in the one-fourth that had multiparty electoral systems the majority of the population has been excluded from political life and socioeconomic advancement. Factors accounting for this range are examined, linking the political patterns to the country's political history, level of material development, and linkage with the international economy.

Chapter 6 assesses the dominant political trends revealed in the transformation of the state in sub-Saharan Africa in the 1990s. In 1989–1991 antisystem domestic pressures converged with the post–Cold War goals of Western industrialized countries for political and economic liberalization. Broad sectors of the African population demanded a democracy embodying socioeconomic rights, while Western nations and international financial institutions under their control demanded multiparty elections and formal political rights. Despite differences in objectives, these two sets of pressures triggered a transformation of the domestic politics of authoritarian African states. The chapter focuses on the reconfiguration of state power in a semidemocratic and semiauthoritarian direction.

Antisystem demonstrations did not lead to multiparty elections and political reform everywhere in sub-Saharan Africa. Several subregions had political experiences that were in stark contrast to that dominant trend. The Horn of Africa (Sudan, Ethiopia, Eritrea, Somalia), the Great Lakes region (Burundi, Rwanda, Congo-Zaire, Congo-Brazzaville), Southern Africa (Angola), and West Africa (Liberia, Sierra Leone) saw the eruption of long festering as well as new conflicts leading to brutal wars. Chapter 7 analyzes the pressures on these states and describes the fragmentation, disintegration, and state collapse that occurred. The chapter also notes the strategies Africans have used to try to resolve these conflicts by themselves in the absence of the big powers' retreat from Africa at the end of the Cold War.

Chapter 8 reviews Africa's foreign relations from the 1960s through the 1990s, noting continuities and changes in response to domestic needs and the international environment. Africa's key international relations have been linked largely to the domestic interests of the state-controlling political elites (i.e., consolidation of power and the survival of their regimes). Development assistance and military and political support were sought from the major powers in exchange for ideological, political, and economic penetration of Africa. The chapter examines the varied ways in which African states, either individually or collectively, managed dependency relationships with states that were more powerful in the international system. Finally it assesses the challenges posed by the new post–Cold War world order and examines Africa's response to those challenges.

Chapter 9 concludes the book by exploring the prospects for a "new beginning" in African politics in the post–Cold War era. The constraints faced within African states themselves combined with those in the changing international environment are assessed. The question is raised as to whether a new African state has emerged capable of responding to the collective needs of its population. The discussion ends with a reflection on potential economic survival strategies: cooperation within Africa, south-south cooperation, reform of multilateral institutions, aid from industrialized countries, and the elimination of external debts.

2

Background and Setting

Overview

The African continent represents an amazing paradox. It is the oldest continent in the world and is the cradle of humankind. Discoveries of the remains of the earliest humans have been found in Olduvai Gorge in northeastern Tanzania (1.75 million years old) and at several sites near Lake Turkana in northern Kenya and southern Ethiopia (2.4 million years old). In the precolonial period, Africa boasted many ancient kingdoms and civilizations that were more technologically advanced than those in contemporary Europe.

Yet today the picture is a stark contrast. Sub-Saharan Africa is the most impoverished region in the world. The world views it as a place of famine, brutal dictatorships, recurrent economic crises, violation of human rights, and massacres of civilians by ruthless warlords. Africa's present condition is haunted by its past. As early as the eighth century, Africa was the victim of Arab slavery when Arabs transported African slaves from West, Central, East and South Central Africa to Arabia and the Middle East. From the fifteenth to the nineteenth centuries the Arabs were joined by the Europeans, who shipped African slaves across the Atlantic to the Americas.

Slavery was a principal source of wealth enriching Arab and European traders and African collaborators. European colonialism transformed Africa. This intrusion by European powers interrupted the original pattern of Africa's historical development. It severely altered political communities, complicated social systems, and linked the African continent to the margins of the international capitalist economy, where it has remained. By the 1880s, the continent was fully partitioned and divided among several European powers—France, Britain, Belgium, Spain, Italy, Germany, and Portugal (see Table 2.1). The exploitation of humans, minerals, and agricultural crops generated enormous wealth for the European powers, especially Britain. These past experiences do not alone explain Africa's contemporary condition, but they are a legacy from which Africa must recover.

The vast majority of African states gained their independence in the 1950s and 1960s and have continued to maintain close political and economic relationships with their former colonial masters. Since independence Africa has been ravaged by war, poverty, disease, political instability, social polarization and ethnic conflict, and economic crises. Some of these problems are related to Africa's physical environment, the legacy of colonialism, and the expediency of political elites and their foreign allies. The combined impact of these problems resulted in enduring political instability, social conflict, and economic underdevelopment.

Definition

The continent of Africa covers 11,677,240 square miles stretching from the Mediterranean Sea in the north to where the Atlantic and Indian Oceans meet in the south. Scholars often make a distinction between the North African states bordering the Mediterranean Sea and located north of the Sahara desert (Egypt, Libya, Tunisia, Algeria, and Morocco) and the rest of the continent to the south, known as sub-Saharan Africa. The perception has been that North Africa is totally separate and different from the rest of Africa and therefore warrants separate treatment. It is true that North Africa has been more heavily influenced by Islam in all aspects of life than the rest of the continent. However, for centuries there have been continuous linkages between North and sub-Saharan Africa despite the division of the continent by the Sahara Desert. This book will follow the conventional division in the literature and focus on sub-Saharan Africa, whose postindependence political histories scholars have grouped together because of parallel patterns in these countries' political evolutions.

TABLE 2.1   Colonial Powers in Africa

Country	Colonial Power	From	To
Algeria	France	1830	1962
Angola	Portugal	1482	1975
Benin	France	1892	1960
Botswana	Britain	1885	1966
Burundi	Germany	1985	
	Belgium*	1916	1962
Burkina Faso (formerly Upper Volta)	France	1896	1960
Cameroon	Germany	1884	
	Britain*	1916	1961
	France*	1916	1960
Cape Verde	Portugal	1600	1975
Central African Republic	France	1879	1960
Chad	France	1897	1960
Congo-Brazzaville	France	1839	1960
Comoros	France	1886	1975
Djibouti	France	1862	1977
Egypt	France	1798	1801
	Britain	1882	1922
Equatorial Guinea	Portugal	1472	
	Spain	1778	1968
Eritrea	Italy	1890	1941
Ethiopia	Italy	1935	1941
Gabon	France	1839	1960
The Gambia	Britain	1664	1965
Ghana	Netherlands	1637	
	Britain	1874	1957
Guinea	France	1898	1958
Guinea-Bissau	Portugal	1558	1973
Kenya	Britain	1885	1963
Lesotho	Britain	1867	1966
Libya	Italy	1912	1951
Madagascar	France	1885	1960
Malawi	Britain	1891	1964
Mali	France	1898	1960
Mauritania	France	1903	1960
Mauritius	Netherlands	1598	
	France	1715	
	Britain	1810	1968

TABLE 2.1 (Continued)

Country	Colonial Power	From	To
Morocco	Spain	1912	1956
	France	1912	1956
Mozambique	Portugal	1505	1975
Namibia	Germany	1884	
	South Africa*	1915	1990
Niger	France	1898	1960
Nigeria	Britain	1861	1960
Rwanda	Germany	1897	
	Belgium*	1916	1962
Western Sahara	Spain	1884	
	(Morocco)	1956	
Senegal	Britain	1783	
	France	1809	1960
Seychelles	France	1768	
	Britain	1794	1976
Sierra Leone	Britain	1787	1961
Somalia	Britain	1884	1960
Somalia	Italy	1889	1960
South Africa	Britain	1790s	1910
Sudan	Britain	1899	1956
Swaziland	Britain	1902	1968
Tanzania (Tanganyika)	Germany	1885	
	Britain	1918	1961
Tanzania (Zanzibar)	Britain	1890	1963
Togo	Germany	1884	
	France*	1914	1960
Tunisia	France	1881	1956
Uganda	Britain	1885	1963
Congo (Zaire)	Belgium	1885	1960
Zambia	Britain	1891	1964
Zimbabwe	Britain	1890	1980

* League of Nations trust and/or mandate

Source: Adapted from Hadjor, 1993: 73–78.

TABLE 2.2   Distribution of Country Size in Sub-Saharan Africa

Population	Number of Countries
Less than 2 million	13
2–5 million	9
6–10 million	12
11–19 million	7
20–29 million	3
30 million or more	3

Source: World Bank (1997).

Population

The African continent has about 700 million people, with two-thirds living in sub-Saharan Africa. As a result of migration, trade, and colonization, there is a mixed population of Africans, Arabs, and a small concentration of Asians (Indians) and Europeans. Arabs are found predominantly in North Africa; Europeans in a few countries in East and southern Africa; Asians in several countries in West, East, and southern Africa; and Africans throughout the continent. During the colonial and the postcolonial period, non-Africans have held privileged economic positions over Africans in many countries. In some parts of the continent this has led to social conflict, rebellions, wars, and political instability.

There is considerable variation in the size of the population in the forty-seven states of sub-Saharan Africa. The region has a large number of countries having small populations and a few having large populations (see Table 2.2).

Physical Environment

Africa is a continent of great variation in climate. The northern and southern edges of the continent have a Mediterranean climate, while areas of high elevation such as the Kenya Highlands have cooler temperatures. The rest of Africa (about 90 percent) lies between the Tropic of Cancer and the Tropic of Capricorn and is classified as having a tropical climate (the factor that distinguishes seasons in the tropics is precipitation, i.e., wet and dry seasons). The land beyond the tropics is extremely dry, including the Sahara Desert (which extends across most of northern and northwestern Africa) and the Kalahari Desert (which covers large portions of southwestern Africa).

The most powerful environmental impact on life and survival in sub-Saharan Africa is due to the movement of the intertropical convergence zone (ITCZ). The ITCZ marks the boundary between a moist, maritime air mass and a drier, continental one. The ITCZ shifts pronouncedly from June to January. When the ITCZ is stationed at its northward June position, the rainy season there should be on, and southern Africa is dry. The southward migration of the ITCZ signals rain for the south and the dry season for the north. Sometimes the ITCZ does not shift when or where it is normally expected to, bringing stress to the life of those who depend on it for farming and the raising of livestock. Trouble spots have been the semiarid Sahel and the East African desert (parts of Kenya, Somalia, Ethiopia), plagued by an unpredictable ITCZ and growing populations. The specter of mass starvation brought on by drought and desertification (and in some cases politics) in the semiarid regions of the Dry Savanna (Ethiopia, Somalia, Sudan) and the Sahelian region of West Africa (parts of Chad, Niger, Mali, Burkina Faso, and Senegal) has been prominent in the mass media.

Over 80 percent of the land of the African continent is not arable. Of the land that is arable, only 7 percent has naturally rich alluvial soils (Revell, 1976; Lewis and Berry, 1988; cited in Nyang'oro, 1996: 205). Arid and semiarid regions constitute more than 50 percent of tropical Africa and support more than 35 percent of its population (Skoupy, 1988: 30, cited in Nyang'oro 1996: 205). The drylands extend over twenty-four countries, among them Botswana, Cape Verde, Chad, Mauritania, Somalia (desert countries with more than 66 percent arid areas). Burkina Faso, Ethiopia, The Gambia, Mozambique, Senegal, Sudan, Tanzania, Zambia, and Zimbabwe all have between 30 and 66 percent arid areas. Angola, Benin, Nigeria, Cameroon, Madagascar, and Uganda have about 30 percent arid areas. Almost all of sub-Saharan Africa is marked by poor, infertile soils. The alluvial soils of the Inland Niger Delta between Segou and Timbuktu in Mali, the volcanically derived soils of Cameroon, and the Kenya Highlands' soils are the exception. South Africa also has good fertile soil, which was reserved for the white population under the apartheid regime. The greater productivity of the South African soil has supported the development of a diverse agricultural economy based on grain and livestock and relatively free of tropical diseases. Much of Africa's dryland cannot support sustained settlement, and that is the reason that the African continent has so many regions that are sparsely populated.

Impact of Language, Religion, and Ethnicity

Among Africans there are hundreds of different ethnic groups, each having its own language, religion, and culture (see Table 2.3). Of the known languages in the world, over eight hundred are spoken in Africa by hundreds of

TABLE 2.3   Main Ethnic Groups in Sub-Saharan Africa

Country	Ethnic Group	%	Country	Ethnic Group	%
Angola	Ovimbundu	37		Senoufon	11
	Mbundu	25		Kru	9
	Kongo	13		Lagoon	4
	European	1		Dan	3
Benin	Fon	25	Djibouti	Afar	44
	Yoruba	12		Issa (Somali)	30
	Bariba	12		Isaak, Gadabourse	24
	Goun	11	Eritrea	Tigrinya	50
	Adja	6		Tigre	30
	Fulani	6		Afar	4
	Aizo	5		Beni Amer	3
	Somba	4		Saho	3
	Banba	4	Ethiopia	Oromo	43
Botswana	Tswana	85		Amhara & Tigrean	30
	Kalanga	7		Sidama	9
	Bakgalagadi	5		Shankella	6
	Basawra	3	Gabon	Fang	34
Burkina Faso	Mossi	55		Non-Gabonese	18
	Peul, Tamajik,	19	Gambia	Mandingo	43
	Bellah	9		Fulani	13
	Gurumsi			Wolof	12
Burundi	Hutu	85		Jola	7
	Tutsi	15		Serahuli	6
Cameroon	Northerners	30		Aku	4
	Westerners	21	Ghana	Akan	44
Chad	Sara	28		Mole	16
	Sudanese/Arab	12		Dagbani	8
CAR	Baya	34		Ga-Adangbe	
	Banda	27		Ewe	6
	Mandjia	21		Guan	4
	Sara	10		Gurma	4
	Mboum	4	Guinea	Fulani	39
	Mbororo	2		Malinké	28
	Aka	1		Susu	16
Congo	Kongo	48		Kissi	6
	Teke	21		Kpelle	5
	M'Bouchi	14		Peuhl	1
Côte	Baule	23	Guinea-Bissau	Balante	28
d'Ivoire	Bete	18		Fulani	23
	Mandingo	16		Mandyako	14
	Agni	15		Malinke	13

TABLE 2.3   (Continued)

Country	Ethnic Group	%	Country	Ethnic Group	%
	Pepel	9		Malinke	7
	Dioula	5		Songhae	6
	Susu	5		Senoufo	6
	Felupe	3		Touareg	5
Kenya	Kikiyu	21		Marka	2
	Luhya	14		Dogon	1
	Luo	11	Mauritania	Maur-black mix	40
	Kalenjin	11		Maur	30
	Kamba	10	Mozambique	Makua-Lomwe	38
	Kisii	6	Namibia	Ovambo	46
	Meru	5		Damara	7
	Mijikenda	5		Herero	7
	Turkana	2		Kavango	7
	European	1		European	5
	Asians	1		Nama	4
Lesotho	Basotho	99		East Caprivan	3
Liberia	Kpelle	18		Bushmen	3
	Bassa	13		Coloured	3
	Dan	8		Basters	2
	Kru	8		North Sotho	7
	Grebo	7		South Sotho	7
	Ma	7		English	6
	Loma	6		Askan	3
	Krahn	5		Shangaan	3
	Americo-Liberian	5		Swazi	2
	Gola	4		Venda	2
	Mandingo	4		South Ndebele	1
	Kissi	3		North Ndebele	
	Vai	3	Niger	Hausa	5
	Gbandi	3		Djerma-Songhai	5
Madagascar	Merina	25		Tuareg	2
	Betsimisaraka	14		Peul (Fula)	3
	Betsileo	12		Kanouri (Beri Beri)	1
	Tsimihety	7			0
	Sakalava	6			9
	Antandroy	5			5
	Antaisaka	5	Nigeria	Hausa	2
Malawi	Chewa	35		Yoruba	1
	Nyanja	27		Ibo	2
	Lomwe	15		Fulani	0
Mali	Bambara	30		Kanuri	1
	Fulani	8		Ibibio	8

TABLE 2.3   Main Ethnic Groups in Sub-Saharan Africa (Continued)

Country	Ethnic Group	%	Country	Ethnic Group	%
	Tiv	1		Nueer	6
	Ijaw	2		Fur	6
		4		Nubian	2
		3		Beja	2
		3	Swaziland	Swazi	90
		2	Tanzania	Sukuma	12
Rwanda	Hutu	9		Nyamwezi	4
	Tusi	0		Makonde	4
		9		Haya	4
Senegal	Wolof	3		Chagga	4
	Fulani	6		Gogo	3
	Serer	1		Ha	3
	Toucouleur	7		Hehe	3
	Diola	1		Nyakusa	3
	Mandingo	7		Nyika	2
		9		Luguru	2
		9		Bena	2
		9		Turu	2
Sierra Leone	Mende	3		Sambaa	2
	Temne	0		Zaramo	2
	Luba	2		Asian	1
	Kono	1		European	0
	Sherbro	6			1
	Fulani	3	Togo	Ewe	45
	Loko	2		Moba	7
	Susu	2		Kokotoli	7
	Mandinka	2	Uganda	Baganda	16
	Kissi	2			12
		1		Karamojong	8
		1		Iteso	8
Somalia	Somail (Samaal)	8		Basoga	8
		5		Banynakore	
South Africa	Zulu	1		Bakiga	7
	Xhosa	9		Banyaruanda	6
	Coloured	1		Lango	6
	Afrikaaner	8		Bagisu	5
	Tswana	9		Acholi	4
		8		Lugbara	4
		8		Banyoro	3
Sudan	Arab	39		Batoro	3
	Dinka	11		European	1
	Nuba	9	Zaire		

TABLE 2.3   (Continued)

Country	Ethnic Group	%	Country	Ethnic Group	%
Zambia	Bemba	37		Lozi	3
	Tonga	19		European	1
	Lunda	12	Zimbabwe	Shona	75
	Nyanja	11		Ndebele	18
	Mambwe	8		European	1

Source: Taken from Fredland, 2002: 101-104.

African ethnic groups. In addition there are European "official" languages in most of sub-Saharan Africa; typically the former colony adopted the language spoken by its former colonial power. For example, French is the official language in Senegal, English in Nigeria, Portuguese in Angola, and German in Namibia. In the Belgian colonies of Congo, Rwanda, and Burundi, French is also the official language.

Islam, Christianity, and traditional African religions are the three major belief systems of the African continent. Native African religious practices permeate every facet of life of the African people, and Islam and Christianity have been grafted onto those religious beliefs. There are several hundred traditional African religions since each ethnic group practices its own religion. It is very difficult to numerically demarcate religious beliefs in Africa (see Table 2.4). This difficulty must be considered in looking at estimates that show the total number of Muslims at 215 million and the number of Christians at 250 million (Barrett, 1982: 8, 382).

Ethnic group solidarity became relevant in the postindependence political competition for control of the state. In choosing elected officials, rural Africans sought effective brokers between themselves and the government in the capital city that allocated desired resources. In this case, the important factor in selecting an official was not ethnicity but whether the person had the experience and other qualifications to become a successful intermediary. In urban areas, in contrast, ethnicity became a factor significant for the allocation of state resources. The ethnic group is often the primary basis of loyalty, and in periods of austerity when the state's resources decline, ethnic group leaders often replace the state as a provider of many services. "Tribalism" became an appeal that united large numbers of people who did not have other significant lines of division. Politicized ethnicity thus became a tool of the political elites in urban areas in the decolonization period before independence and continued to be so in the immediate postindependence period of multiparty politics.

TABLE 2.4   Religious Affiliation in Selected Sub-Saharan African
             Countries

State	Percent Christian*	Percent Muslim	Percent Traditional*
Angola	48 Catholic 8 Protestant	—— 12	—— ——
Benin	12 Catholic 3 Protestant	12	65
Botswana	15 African Independent Churches 15 Other	1	50
Burkina Faso	8 Catholic 2 Other	25	65
Burundi	50 Catholic 13 Other	1	35
Cameroon	35 Catholic 5 Protestant	20	39
CAR	20 Catholic 15 Protestant	5	60
Chad	6	44	40
Congo	20 African independent Churches 25 Catholic 10 Other	1	50
Côte d'Ivoire	12	23	65
Djibouti	3	94	——
Eritrea	——	90	——
Ethiopia	30 Ethiopian Orthodox Churches <1 Jewish (Falasha)	30	10
Gabon	60	<1	35
Gambia	10 Catholic	85	1
Ghana	43	12	40
Guinea	2	85	10
Guinea-Bissau	5 Catholic	30	60
Kenya	28 <1 Baha'i	6	26
Lesotho	44 Catholic 7 Anglican 29 Other	0	19
Liberia	75 Official	27	——
Madagascar	25 Catholic 25 Protestant	2	47
Malawi	35 (Catholic, Presbyterian)	20	45
Mali	2	70	20

Impact of Language, Religion, and Ethnicity   17

TABLE 2.4   (Continued)

State	Percent Christian*	Percent Muslim	Percent Traditional*
Mauritania	<1	99 Official	——
Mozambique	12	13	60
Namibia	85 (Lutheran, Catholic, etc.)	——	15
Niger	<1	95	5
Nigeria	21 Catholic 21 Other	52	6
Rwanda	38 Catholic 10 Other	1	48
Senegal	5 Catholic	85	10
Sierra Leone	10	40	50
Somalia	——	99 Official	——
South Africa+	80 Dutch Reformed, Methodist, Anglican, African Independent Churches [White Population 3 Jewish]	20 of Asians [80% of Asians are Hindu]	17
Sudan	15 <1 Baha'i 1 Hindu	75 Official 65	10 ——
Swaziland	80	——	20
Tanzania	20 Catholic 10 Other	35	35
Togo	17 Catholic 5 Other	10	58
Uganda	33 Catholic 30 Anglican	5	30
Zaire	44 Catholic 10 Protestant	1	45
Zambia	35 Catholic 37 Other	1	27
Zimbabwe	8 Protestant 7 Catholic 7 African Independent Churches	——	40

* The dividing lines between traditional African religious practices and Christianity in Africa is often blurred, as in many Christian churches local leaders integrate elements of Christianity with African traditional practices and beliefs.

Sources: *Worldmark Encyclopedia of Nations: Africa*, 1988; *Africa South of the Sahara*, 1987, cited in Fredland, 2001: 112–113.

Resources

The resource base of sub-Saharan Africa is rich and has been a powerful attraction for European exploiters. Africa contains several categories of industrial raw materials and minerals on which the economies of Western industrialized nations depend (see Table 2.5).

The copper zone on the borders of Zambia and Congo (Zaire) accounts for 7 percent of the world's output of copper and makes it the fourth-ranked production region in the world, following Chile, the United States, and Canada. Congo and Zambia account for about half of the world's output of cobalt (a ferroalloy in jet and rocket engines) and provide the United States with over one-third of its cobalt needs ([CRB] *Commodity Yearbook*, 1994).

Other important resource producers are Guinea, second to Australia in bauxite production for aluminum. South Africa and Zimbabwe together provide nearly 30 percent of the global output of chromite (crucial to steel manufacturing in the Western industrialized countries). Nigeria is among the top five exporters of crude oil to the United States and is Africa's top producer of petroleum, ahead of Algeria and Libya (United Nations, 1994: 180–181). Although rich in metallic ores, sub-Saharan Africa has had to import most of its energy. Only a few favored fossil fuels—petroleum and coal—are found in Africa. The notable exceptions are the Niger River Delta (in Nigeria), Gabon, Angola (petroleum), and South Africa (coal).

Waterpower exists in great potential abundance and sub-Saharan Africa has the greatest hydroelectric potential of any continent. The sites of this potential are where major rivers experience impressive drops in elevation (at rapids and falls) in their escape from the continent's interior. Electricity generation at these sites could enhance economic development over large regions. Projects completed with this objective are the Nile Aswan High Dam in Egypt, the Zambezi River's Kariba Dam, shared by Zimbabwe and Zambia, and the Volta's Akosombo Dam in Ghana. This particular component of Africa's resource base remains greatly underexploited for an economic reason: lack of markets.

Economy

There are long-term colonial-historical factors that have determined Africa's present economic condition. Africa's colonial history left it with monocrop and import-dependent production structures. European colonial powers brought African economies into world capitalism as suppliers of primary commodities without any effort at structural diversification. Examples of primary commodities include coffee, cotton, sugarcane, sorghum, yam, corn, cassava, groundnuts, rice, sesame, beans, millet, pineapples, and palm-oil

TABLE 2.5   African Sources of EEC Mineral Imports

Metal	Country	Percentage
Aluminum	Ghana	3
	Cameroon	3
Antimony	South Africa	9
Asbestos	South Africa	13
	Swaziland	2
Bauxite	Guinea	18
	Ghana	4
	Sierra Leone	4
Cadmium	Zaire	4
Chromium	South Africa	31
	Mozambique	5
Cobalt	Zambia	33
	Zaire	24
	South Africa	7
Columbium	Nigeria	2
Copper	Zambia	19
	Zaire	20
	South Africa & Namibia	4.5
Iron Ore	Liberia	1.6
	Mauritania	6.5
Lead	Morocco	6
	South Africa	4
Manganese	South Africa	52
	Gabon	24
Nickel	South Africa	5
Phosphate	Morocco	44
	Togo	13
	Tunisia	4
Platinum Group	South Africa	24
Tin	Zaire	6.5
	Nigeria	6
	Rwanda	2
Tungsten	Rwanda	3
Uranium	N/A	N/A
Vanadium	South Africa	42
Zinc	South Africa	2
Zirconium	South Africa	2

Source: Cornell, 1981: 80.

products, among others. Later, mineral export industries developed around natural resources such as bauxite, oil, copper, diamonds and gold. Twenty-eight sub-Saharan African countries in 1998 were identified as relying on primary commodities for their main source of export earnings. Monocrop dependence makes African economies vulnerable to world market demand and other exogenous changes. If copper prices plunge and the terms of trade deteriorate because of rising import prices, countries such as Zambia and Congo, which depend heavily on copper, are forced to borrow. Every monocrop-dependent economy is vulnerable in this way.

During the colonial period, African countries supplied cheap raw materials and were captive markets for manufacturing imports from Europe. Manufactured goods such as textiles, vehicles, pharmaceuticals, household goods, and farming equipment were sold to Africans at huge profits for Europe. Those imported items had to be purchased with foreign exchange, most of which was earned through exporting primary commodities. Europe left Africa with an economy that negatively impacted independent Africa's economic future.

Since the 1960s, when most of sub-Saharan Africa gained its independence, the region has remained the most economically underdeveloped in the world. Its continuous economic problems have affected all aspects of development. Economic growth has faltered, averaging about 3 percent since 1961, with variations across the region. Poverty, income inequality, and unemployment levels have all increased. Population growth has also exceeded economic growth causing a decline in the gross national product (GNP) per capita.

Between 1960 and 1972 per capita income increased, and there was a net positive inflow of foreign investment and assistance. After the 1973 increase in oil prices by the Organization of Petroleum Exporting Countries (OPEC), all the non-oil-producing states of Africa experienced economic difficulties as they depleted their foreign exchange reserves to maintain petroleum imports necessary for development programs. The oil crisis was compounded by a severe drought in the Sahel that led to a decline in agricultural production and the death of huge numbers of livestock. This calamity led to an increase in imported food that put an additional burden on foreign exchange reserves and increased African indebtedness to international financial agencies and foreign governments. In 1979 a similar crisis occurred with another increase in the price of oil coupled with declining world prices for Africa's primary commodity exports. Inappropriate domestic policies exacerbated the problem, leading to further economic decline in the 1980s through the early 1990s. Estimates of annual GNP-per-capita growth from 1980 to 1993 vary from –0.8 percent to –1.8 percent (World Bank, 1995b: 163; United Nations Development Program (UNDP), 1995: 195).

Today Africa is in the depths of an economic crisis. This crisis is characterized by weak agricultural growth, declining industrial output, poor export production, disintegrating productive and infrastructural activities, deteriorating social indicators and institutions, and increasing debt and destruction of the environment. The standard of living of most Africans has declined in recent years and there is increased poverty throughout the continent.

Political Culture

The term *political culture* has been defined in various ways since it was first adopted in the comparative politics literature five decades ago. It generally refers to the "collective political attitudes, values, feelings, information, and skills in a society" (Almond and Powell, 1966: 43).

As the foregoing sections indicate, sub-Saharan African societies are heterogeneous. It is therefore possible to find numerous political subcultures among different social groups such as the military, farmers, urban traders, professionals, or the political elite.

The values of the political elite and the mass public were similar during the nationalist movements for independence. However, by the end of the 1960s, in most sub-Saharan African countries elite values and those of the masses that they governed diverged sharply. At that point, the democratic values shared in the nationalist movement and the period of decolonization collapsed. The political elite no longer viewed the existence of representative institutions (political parties, labor unions, the media) as in their best interest and so consolidated their power through domination of the state and clientelistic allocation of its resources to favored groups. There was no deep commitment to the inherited Western representative institutions, so within the first decade after independence they gave way to authoritarian single-party and military regimes throughout sub-Saharan Africa (with the exception of The Gambia, Botswana, Mauritius, Zimbabwe). Even in the handful of countries where representative institutions remained uninterrupted, there was no deep commitment to political and economic democracy, and in most cases the population had a cynical view of democracy, viewing it as a façade for authoritarian elite rule.

Historians have traced the undemocratic political culture that has prevailed throughout sub-Saharan Africa since independence to colonial roots. The most prevalent view among historians of Africa is that European colonialism was a major and decisive turning point in Africa's history, ushering in changes that were both fundamental and irreversible (Rodney, 1972). Colonialism incorporated Africa into the world economy and international capitalism through the slave trade, mercantilism, and world capitalist investment. The colonial impact has also been decisive in that boundaries arbitrarily drawn in Africa by European powers in the late nineteenth century formed the basis for Africa's integration into the world system of nation-states. These colonial boundaries have been stubbornly defended by the African political elite and have been at the heart of major conflicts in places like Nigeria, Congo, Rwanda, Burundi, and Somalia.

Colonization led to greater economic complexity in African societies, even in some instances to incipient industrialization. Under the imposed colonial boundaries multiple ethnic communities were forced to share a new national collective identity. The polarization of the ethnic base in postindependence sub-Saharan Africa led to politicized ethnicity as each ethnic group competed for scarce resources controlled by the state. Within each ethnic group there were also different levels of advantage and prosperity. This added the dimension of class to some of Africa's ethnic conflicts.

African political cultures have changed since 1945. In the decolonization period (approximately 1945–1960 for the majority of sub-Saharan Africa) the elites and the mass population, motivated by nationalism, shared political loyalties as a result of the colonial impact. They jointly fought against European subjugation and shared a broad awareness of belonging to an African continent united by a Pan-African identity. Within a decade after independence, the political culture shifted as the transition from nationalism to nationhood occurred (Mazrui and Tidy, 1984). Competition among different ethnic groups for scarce resources destroyed previous solidarity between the elites and the mass population, as well as within the latter.

In the post–Cold War period beginning in the early 1990s, most authoritarian governments in sub-Saharan Africa have been removed through internal and external pressures. However, the political culture still contains antidemocratic seeds. Fragmentation still occurs on the basis of ethnicity, class, religion, clientelism, and political corruption. There is optimism that elite and popular beliefs in a democratic political culture can now develop and be sustained with the removal of the authoritarian governments. Elite cooperation and respect for democratic procedures would need to be accompanied by broad citizen participation in political and economic decision making. This will be difficult to achieve despite international pressures designed to force such an outcome. The African population still believes politicians (military and civilian) are corrupt. They remain illegitimate in the eyes of the population because they have been unable to deliver economic benefits to the vast majority. The development of democratic values again in the political culture of sub-Saharan Africa is not impossible but is perhaps unlikely to happen very soon.

Brief Profiles of the Countries of Sub-Saharan Africa

Angola

After winning its independence from Portugal in 1975 through armed struggle, Angola has been under the rule of the Popular Movement for the Liberation of Angola (MPLA) for the past two and a half decades. A single party

TABLE 2.6   Sub-Saharan Africa in Comparative Perspective

	Year	All LDC's	SSSA	SSA + SoAf	South Asia	East Asia	Latin Am.
Population (millions)	1992	4,610	503	543	1,178	1,689	453
Population Growth	1980–92	1.9%	3.1%	3.0%	2.2%	1.6%	2.0
Per-Capita GNP	1992	$1,040	$350	$530	$310	$760	$2,690
Per-Capita GNP Growth	1960–70	3.3%	0.6%	——	1.4%	3.6%	2.5%
	1970–80	3.0%	0.9%	——	1.1%	4.6%	3.1%
	1980–82	0.9%	−1.2%	−0.8%	3.0%	6.1%	−0.2%
Projected	1990–00	2.9%	0.3%	——	3.1%	5.7%	2.2%
Agricultural Growth	1980–92	3.1%	——	1.7%	3.3%	4.4%	2.0%
Industrial Growth	1980–92	3.6%	——	1.2%	6.4%	9.4%	1.3%
Life Expectancy	1960	46 yrs	40	43	43	47	56
	1992	64	51	52	60	68	68
Literacy	1970	46%	27%	——	31%	——	73%
	1990	64%	50	——	56	76%	85%
IMR	1960	136	151	——	147	128	108
	1992	65	104	99	85	39	44
Population with Safe Water	1990 all (rural)	72% 65	—— ——	44% 37	80% 78	71% 65	80% 57
Population per Physician	1990	4,810	23,540	19,690	2,930	6,170	1,180
Daily Calories per Capital	1965	2,108	2,074	——	1,992	1,939	2,445
	1989	2,523	2,122	——	2,215	2,617	2,721
Population below Poverty Line	1985	30.5%	47.6%	——	51.8%	13.2%	22.4%
	1990	29.7%	47.8	——	49.0	11.3	25.5
	2000	24.1%	49.7	——	36.9	4.2	24.9

LDCs: Less Developed countries; SSA + SoAF: Sub-Saharan Africa + South Africa; IMR: Infant Mortality Rate per 1000 live births.

Source: World Bank, 1992, 1993, 1994: appendix tables; UNICEF, 1993, 1994; cited in Stryker and Ndegwa, 1995: 376.

TABLE 2.7   Sub-Saharan Countries and Resources

Country	Population est. (1992) (thousands)[1]	Area (square miles)[2]	GNP (1992 current $) (billions)[3]	GNP ($) per capital (1992)[4]
Nigeria	115,660	356,669	32.94	320
Egypt	55,163	385,229	34.51	630
Ethiopia	53,110	436,349	6.20	110
Zaire	39,880	905,365	8.84	260
South Africa	39,820	471,445	106.01	2,670
Tanzania	27,830	364,900	2.56	110
Sudan	26,660	967,500	10.10	400
Algeria	26,350	919,595	48.32	1,830
Morocco*	26,320	274,461	27.21	1,030
Kenya	25,700	224,081	8.45	330
Uganda	18,670	93,104	2.94	170
Ghana	15,960	92,100	7.06	450
Mozambique	15,730	308,641	1.03	60
Côte d'Ivoire	12,910	124,503	8.65	670
Madagascar	12,830	226,658	2.80	230
Cameroon	12,200	183,569	10.00	820
Zimbabwe	10,580	150,873	5.89	570
Malawi	10,360	45,747	1.89	210
Angola	10,020	481,354	6.01	620
Mali	9,820	478,841	2.73	300
Burkina Faso	9,490	105,870	2.90	290
Somalia	9,200	246,201	1.03	170
Zambia	8,640	290,586	2.58	290
Tunisia	8,400	63,170	14.61	1,740
Niger	8,250	489,191	2.46	300
Senegal	7,740	75,955	6.12	780
Rwanda	7,530	10,169	1.81	250
Chad	5,960	495,800	1.26	220
Burundi	5,780	10,747	1.19	210
Guinea	5,600	94,926	3.10	510
Benin	5,050	43,484	2.05	410
Libya	4,870	679,359	22.97	5,310
Sierra Leone	4,380	27,699	0.72	170
Togo	3,760	21,925	1.57	400
Central African Republic	3,170	240,535	1.30	410

TABLE 2.7   (Continued)

Country	Population est. (1992) (thousands)[1]	Area (square miles)[2]	GNP (1992 current $) (billions)[3]	GNP ($) per capital (1992)[4]
Liberia	2,580	37,743	<u>1.05</u>	<u>450</u>
Congo	2,370	132,047	2.50	1,030
Mauritania	2,140	397,950	1.10	530
Eritrea	<u>2,000</u>	46,774	N/A	N/A
Lesotho	1,840	11,720	1.09	590
Namibia	1,530	318,261	2.50	1,610
Botswana	1,370	224,711	3.79	2,790
Gabon	1,240	103,347	5.34	4,450
Mauritius	1,080	788	2.96	2,700
Guinea-Bissau	943	13,948	0.21	210
The Gambia	880	4,361	0.36	390
Swaziland	820	6,704	0.93	1,080
The Comoros	580	863	0.26	510
Djibouti	470	8,958	<u>0.15</u>	<u>480</u>
Cape Verde	380	1,557	0.33	850
Equatorial Guinea	370	10,830	0.14	330
São Tomé and Principe	<u>116</u>	372	0.04	370
Seychelles	<u>70</u>	175	0.37	5,480

Figures underlined are for years other than 1992.

* International statistics for Morocco include the disputed territory of Western Sahara.

1. Sources: International Monetary Fund, *International Financial Statistics: July 1994* (Washington, DC, 1994); *Africa South of the Sahara*, 1994, 23rd ed. (London: Europa Publications, 1994).

2. Sources: *Africa South of the Sahara*, 1994.

3. Sources: *The World Bank Atlas*, 1994 (Washington, DC: The World Bank, 1993); *Africa at a Glance, 1992: Facts and Figures* (Pretoria: Africa Institute of South Africa, 1992); *Africa South of the Sahara*, 1994.

4. Sources: *The World Bank Atlas*, 1994; *Africa at a Glance, 1992: Facts and Figures*; *Africa South of the Sahara*, 1994.

Source: Martin and O'Meara, 1995: 15–16.

TABLE 2.8   Postindependence Name Changes, Sub-Saharan
             African Countries

Current Name	Former Name(s)	Date(s) of Change
Benin	Dahomey	1975
Burkina Faso	Upper Volta	1984
Central African Republic	Central African Empire	1975 (short-lived name change)
Côte d'Ivoire	Ivory Coast	*Ivory Coast* was taken at independence and revised in 1988.
Democratic Republic of the Congo	Congo-Leopoldville Zaire	1971 1997
Eritrea, Ethiopia	Ethiopia	1993 (Eritrea was separated from Ethiopia after gaining independence.)
Ghana	Gold Coast	1957
Namibia	South West Africa	1976–1993
Republic of South Africa	Union of South Africa	1961 (left the Commonwealth)
Tanzania	Tanganyika, Zanzibar	1964 (Merger)
Zimbabwe	Rhodesia	1965–1975

Source: Adapted from Fredland, 2000: 15.

system existed from 1975 to 1992; however, the incumbent MPLA defeated the National Union for the Total Independence of Angola (UNITA) in the 1992 multiparty elections and remained in power. Despite Angola's abundant natural resources (petroleum, diamonds, iron ore, phosphates, copper, gold, bauxite, uranium, manganese), the country's economy is in disarray because of over two decades of continuous warfare between the MPLA and opposition forces, especially the Jonas Savimbi–led UNITA.

Benin

Following independence in 1960, Benin experienced significant political instability under several civilian and military governments from 1960 to 1972. From 1972 until 1991, the government was under the military dictatorship of (General) President Mathieu Kerekou's People's Revolutionary Party of

Benin. Antigovernment dissatisfaction erupted in the country in 1989, and a broad-based democratic movement forced the government to call a national conference. This resulted in multiparty elections in 1991, and Mathieu Kerekou was defeated by a former World Bank official, Nicephore Soglo. Kerekou was returned to power after being reelected in the second elections, conducted in 1996. Political change has not led to significant socioeconomic progress. Benin is largely dependent on agricultural exports (palm oil products, cotton, corn, yam, cassava, cocoa, coffee, groundnuts). It remains among the least developed of sub-Saharan African countries, with a per-capita GNP of $250 (a $1.1 billion total GNP).

Botswana

Since Britain granted it independence in 1966, Botswana has maintained an uninterrupted multiparty political system and adopted capitalist development strategies. The major political parties have been the Botswana Democratic Party (BDP), the Botswana National Front (BNF), the Botswana People's Party (BPP), and the Botswana Independence Party (BIP). There has been one-party domination since independence, with the state-controlling BDP winning every election. The country's industries are developed around its natural resources, including diamonds, copper, nickel, salt, soda ash, potash, and coal. The mining and cattle industries are the most significant aspects of the economy, but agricultural exports (corn, sorghum, millet, cowpeas and beans) are also important to the economy. Having a per-capita income of $920 (total GNP, $900 million) and high levels of economic growth since independence, Botswana is often held up as a symbol of peace and prosperity in southern Africa.

Burkina Faso

Burkina Faso has had both civilian and military governments in the postindependence period. After independence in 1960 Thomas Sankara, the country's best known leader, came to power in a military coup in 1983. He promoted populist and anti-imperialist policies that made him popular at home. In 1987 he was killed by military officers, his government was overthrown, and Captain Blaise Compaora became the new head of state. Multiparty elections were reintroduced in the 1990s, for the first time in over three decades since independence, but did not result in any changes in government. Having few natural resources, the country is largely dependent on agricultural exports (e.g., millet, sorghum, corn, rice, peanuts, sugarcane, cotton, sesame). Many Burkinabe workers are migrant laborers in other parts of West Africa, especially in Côte d'Ivoire.

Burundi

Postindependence politics in Burundi have centered on political conflicts between the country's two main ethnic groups, the Hutu and the Tutsi, struggling for power since the country's independence from Belgium in 1962. Politicized ethnicity introduced by German and Belgian colonial powers has continued in the postindependence period. Under single-party domination by the Union for National Progress (UPRONA) and military rule, the minority Tutsi (making up 15 percent of the population) have wielded control over the Hutu (the other 85 percent of the population). Unsuccessful Hutu attempts to capture state power in 1972, 1988, and 1992 led to widespread bloodshed and tensions in the country. Multiparty elections held in 1993 led to the country's first Hutu president, Melchior Ndadaye, who was assassinated soon after the elections by members of the military. His appointed successor, Cyprien Ntaryama, was killed several months later in a mysterious plane crash along with the president of Rwanda. In 1996, Pierre Buyoya, defeated in the 1993 elections, seized power in a bloodless coup d'etat. Political instability has devastated the country, stymied economic growth, and created an enormous refugee problem in Burundi as well as in neighboring countries Rwanda, Uganda, the Democratic Republic of the Congo, and Tanzania. Burundi's natural resources include nickel, uranium, cobalt, copper, and platinum. Export revenues come almost entirely from agricultural products such as coffee, tea, cotton, and food crops.

Cameroon

Cameroon was first colonized by Germany, but after World War I the area was divided between Britain and France. An independent Cameroon Republic was established with Ahmadou Ahidjo as the first president in 1960. In 1961 French Cameroun and British Cameroon were united in the Cameroon Federal Republic after a UN supervised referendum. The new constitution created a unitary state in 1972. Cameroon's oil resources and favorable agricultural conditions make it one of the best-endowed primary commodity economies in sub-Saharan Africa. However, it remains plagued by economic problems common to the region. The country was under the rule of a single party, the Cameroon Peoples Democratic Movement (CPDM), from 1966 until the 1990s, when multiparty elections were held. These elections did not lead to a change in the government.

Cape Verde

The Republic of Cape Verde is an archipelago located in the North Atlantic about four hundred miles off the coast of West Africa. Having limited industry and no known natural resources, the economy of the country is service oriented, with commerce, transportation, and public services accounting for most of the country's revenues. Between 1963 and 1974 the African Party for Independence of Guinea-Bissau and Cape Verde (PAIGC), under the leadership of Amilcar Cabral, organized a successful liberation struggle against the Portuguese in Guinea-Bissau that was ultimately instrumental in bringing about the independence of both countries. From independence in 1975 until 1981 the two countries were ruled separately by a united PAIGC. After a 1980 coup d'etat in Guinea-Bissau, the party divided along national lines, and in 1981 the Cape Verdean PAIGC formally renounced its Guinean links and became the PAICV (African Party for the Independence of Cape Verde). Multiparty politics was launched in Cape Verde in 1991, and a new government replaced the PAICV. Economic reforms launched by the new government are aimed at developing the private sector and attracting foreign investment.

Central African Republic

The Central African Republic was under single-party rule from 1966 to 1993. The infamous (emperor) Jean-Bedel Bokassa came to power in a coup d'etat in 1966, and his dictatorial rule lasted until 1979, when he was overthrown while outside the country. Under Bokassa's rule, all democratic institutions were abolished as he monopolized the wealth of the country, crowning himself in a lavish ceremony in 1976. His sanctioning of the massacre of one hundred young people jailed after demonstrating against school uniforms sparked an international outcry against his regime. Politics in the post-Bokassa era remained authoritarian. But, in 1985, prodded by opposition forces demanding changes, a new government was formed that included civilians. In 1993 a multiparty political system was established, and the government is presently controlled by the Movement for the Liberation of the Central African People (MLPC). The MLPC has been under attack from rebel military groups over pay issues, living conditions, and lack of opposition party representation in the government. Peacekeeping operations by African countries in 1997 and the UN Mission in the Central African Republic (MINURCA) in 1998 have tried to restore order. The agricultural sector is the backbone of the economy, but the diamond industry accounted for almost 54 percent of the country's GDP in 1999.

Chad

Chad was a relatively unknown country in Africa until 1983, when its internal war became internationalized. The Hissene Habre government, the United States, and France were on one side, and Libyan-backed troops of Ouiddi Goukoumi on the other. Behind the war were long-standing regional, political, economic, and cultural conflicts. Like Sudan and other countries in the region, Chad is plagued by north-south divisions created and exacerbated by colonialism. European colonialists arbitrarily forced northerners (mixed farmers, herders, Arabic-speaking Muslims) and southerners (agriculturalists growing cotton for export, French-educated Christians, leaders in government and the army at independence) into one nation. There has been a continuing contest for control of the state as various factions fight for control of political power and socioeconomic opportunities.

Comoros

The Federal Islamic Republic of the Comoros consists of a group of three islands off the coast of southern Africa between northern Madagascar and northern Mozambique. Since it was granted independence from France in 1975, the Comoros has endured eighteen coups or attempted coups. The islands of Anjvuan and Moheli declared their independence from Comoros in 1997, and government attempts to reestablish control have failed. A two-party system was established in 1996, and the Rassemblement National pour le Development (RND) is the current ruling party. With few natural resources, the country is dependent on agricultural exports. Rice, its staple food, accounts for the bulk of its imports. One of the world's poorest countries, the economy of the Comoros is extremely dependent on foreign grants and technical assistance.

The Congo (Democratic Republic of the Congo; formerly Zaire until 1997)

The Congo had brief constitutional government under the leadership of President Joseph Kasavubu and Prime Minister Patrice Lumumba (1960–1961). Amidst disorder caused by an army mutiny, in 1961 Patrice Lumumba was assassinated, and the U.S. Central Intelligence Agency (CIA) was implicated. In 1965 Joseph Mobutu Sese Seko led a military coup d'état, set up a military single-party state, and held power until he was forced out in 1997.

Power had been centralized under Mobutu: he controlled the party generally, and he controlled the Central Committee, the key institutions of power. And the country's institutions all came under the party's jurisdiction. Corruption and kleptocratic behavior were taken to the fullest. State expansionist policies were pursued under an ideology of "authenticity," where Mobutu replaced the European names of cities and the country itself (Congo to Zaire in 1971), as well as his own name (Joseph Mobutu to Mobutu Sese Seko), while accumulating most of the state's wealth. Mobutu had economic, political, and military support from Western countries, especially the United States, France, and Belgium. After many years of struggle against his regime, opposition forces overthrew it in 1997 as external support was withdrawn.

Rebel leader Laurent Kabila then became head of state. He was assassinated in 2000 and was succeeded by his son. The political situation remains fluid.

Congo-Brazzaville (Republic of the Congo)

Granted independence from France in 1960, the country, after three decades of single-party and military rule, returned to multiparty politics with the election of Pascal Lissouba as president in 1997. Civil war erupted in that year and the president was deposed. When the war ended in October 1997 Denis Sasson-Ngueso became president. Slumping oil prices in 1998 and the resumption of armed conflict in December 1998 worsened the deteriorating economic situation.

Côte d'Ivoire

From 1960 Côte d'Ivoire was under the single-party rule of President Felix Houphouet-Boigny's Democratic Party of Côte d'Ivoire (PDCI), until it was removed by the military in 1999. Côte d'Ivoire has been one of the most productive countries in West Africa; based on revenues from its agricultural exports, from 1960 to 1970 it had one of the highest growth rates in sub-Saharan Africa under capitalist development policies. Côte d'Ivoire is the world's largest producer of cocoa and the third largest producer of coffee. Coffee is one of the principal sources of income for the 2.5 million Ivorians who farm and provide services for the industry. Other industries include food and lumber processing, oil refining, textile manufacturing, soap making, and automobile assembly. Its per-capita income of $1,000 and GNP of $56 billion suggest relative prosperity in sub-Saharan Africa. The French expatriate community and the Ivorian planter class have benefited the most from Côte d'Ivoire's postindependence development.

Djibouti

Djibouti was granted its independence in 1977 and since then has been under the single-party rule of the Peoples Progressive Assembly. The country has few natural resources and little industry. The economy is based on service activities the country provides as a transit port for the Horn of Africa and an international transshipment and refueling center. The country is currently experiencing economic difficulties and struggling with foreign debt and is affected by the renewed fighting between Ethiopia and Eritrea.

Equatorial Guinea

Since Spain granted its independence in 1968, Equatorial Guinea has been governed by authoritarian regimes. Under the notorious government of

Macias Nguema (1968–1979) all public and private enterprises collapsed, thousands of people were murdered, many were put into forced labor, and at least one-third of the population went into exile. The post-Nguema era remained authoritarian, but the country's human rights record and economic situation reportedly improved. Multiparty politics was reintroduced in 1996, but the same authoritarian leaders remained in power under a new party, the Democratic Party for Equatorial Guinea (PDGE). Oil, forestry, farming, and fishing are the major components of the GDP. Agriculture-led growth has diminished under successive brutal regimes. The discovery and exploitation of large oil reserves contributed to dramatic economic growth in the 1990s.

Eritrea

Eritrea is sub-Saharan Africa's newest state, winning its independence from Ethiopia in 1993 after three decades of armed struggle. Eritrea was an Italian colony from the nineteenth century until 1941, when it became a British protectorate. In 1952 it was federated with the Ethiopian empire and granted a high degree of autonomy. But in 1962 Ethiopian emperor Haile Selassie absorbed Eritrea into the Ethiopian empire as a province. This led to decades of armed resistance. The Eritrean Liberation Front (ELF) began guerrilla operations in 1963. A breakaway faction, the Eritrean Peoples Liberation Front (EPLF) was established and soon became the dominant group challenging the Ethiopian state. The war continued until the Mengistu regime in Addis Ababa collapsed in May 1991. Eritrea immediately declared its independence, which was confirmed in a popular referendum on April 25, 1993.

The EPLF transformed itself into a political party, the Peoples Front for Democracy and Justice (PFDJ), and is governing the country today under the leadership of President Isaias Afworki. The Eritrean economy is largely based on subsistence agriculture, with over 70 percent of the population involved in farming and herding. Government revenues come from customs duties and taxes on income and sales. Eritrea has long-term prospects for revenues based on the development of off-shore oil, off-shore fishing, and tourism. The possible expansion of the hostilities that erupted in 1999 between Eritrea and Ethiopia represents the most immediate threat to the economy.

Ethiopia

Ethiopia has the unique distinction in sub-Saharan Africa of not having been subjected to extensive European colonization. For that reason Ethiopia served as a model of resistance against the Italians in the colonial period. Emperor Haile Selassie ruled Ethiopia for most of the twentieth century, until he was removed from power in a military coup d'état in 1974. Led by Haile Mariam Mengistu, the coup leaders then declared Ethiopia a Marxist-Leninist state. In 1991 the Tigrean People's Liberation Front (TPLF) forced Mengistu from power. In 1995 President Negaso Gidado became the first democratically elected leader. Melas Zerawi, who is now prime minister in President Gidado's government, had served as transitional president from 1991 to 1995. Successive Ethiopian leaders have had a long struggle with ethnic minorities (e.g., Eritrean, Somali) that object to incorporation within the Ethiopian state. After more than thirty years of war, Eritrea finally won its independence in 1993, but hostilities broke out between the two countries in 1999. Ethiopia's economy is based largely on agriculture centered on coffee and tea. Its natural resources include potash, salt, gold, copper, and platinum. There is very little economic development in Ethiopia today, partly as a result of the feudal legacy of the Selassie period and subsequent mismanagement during the period of Mengistu's rule.

Gabon

The Gabonese Democratic Party (GDP), led by Omar Bongo, was in power from independence in 1960 until 1992 under a single-party system. Multiparty elections were held in 1992, Bongo was reelected, and the GDP remained in power. Largely because of its oil wealth, Gabon enjoys a per-capita income four times that of most nations of sub-Saharan Africa. Yet inequality persists. Like most other countries in the region, Gabon has been plagued by problems of economic mismanagement and political corruption. Gabon continues to face fluctuating prices for its oil, timber, manganese, and uranium exports.

The Gambia

The Gambia is one of Africa's smallest countries, with an area of 11,295 square kilometers (smaller than Connecticut). It is surrounded on three sides by Senegal, with whom it entered into a confederation (Senegambia) from 1982 to 1987. The Gambia was under the control of the Peoples Progressive Party (PPP), led by Dawda Jawara, from 1965 to 1994. The PPP was overthrown in 1994 by a military coup d'état led by Yahya Jammeh. As a result of external pressures from international donors, civilian rule was restored in January 1997. Jammeh remained president, and most of the old leaders from the military interlude are still in power. The Gambia's natural resources are limited and include fish, ilmenite, zircon, and rutile. Its cash crops are those typically found in West Africa—groundnuts, rice, cotton, millet, sorghum, palm kernels. Light industries exist, including soft drinks, agricultural machinery, clothing, and tourism (which has grown significantly since the

1980s). The Gambia is one of Africa's poorest countries; in 1999 the World Bank estimated its per-capita income to be $275 and GNP, $179 million. The country is presently dealing with economic liberalization and donor-driven political reform. The political transition is still fragile, and The Gambia's future is uncertain.

Ghana

Ghana's first postindependence president, Kwame Nkrumah, is known around the world. He founded the Convention People's Party (CPP) and ruled Ghana from its independence from Britain in 1957 until his overthrow by the military in 1968. Since then, Ghana has had both military and civilian governments, experiencing a number of coups and countercoups. Its economic difficulties during the postindependence period have often been linked to the statist policies of the Nkrumah era. Ghana is currently under civilian rule led by President (and retired captain) Jerry Rawlings. Multiparty politics have been restored since 1992, with a second set of elections held in 1996. The Rawlings regime has been working under IMF structural adjustment programs for more than a decade. Ghana's per-capita income is $390; its GNP, $4.7 billion. Yet international lending agencies are encouraged by Ghana's economic policy changes and its performance. Ghana's natural resources include diamonds, gold, bauxite, manganese, fish, timber, and oil. Its agricultural staples are cocoa, coconuts, coffee, rubber, and subsistence crops. Industries include mining, lumber, light manufacturing, fishing, and aluminum manufacturing.

Guinea

In a 1958 referendum, alone among France's West African colonies, Guineans voted to leave the community of self-governing states in West Africa established by France. French retaliation led to a withdrawal of all aid, personnel, and equipment from the country. Guinea, led by President Ahmed Sekou Touré, became isolated from the Western industrialized countries, and close ties were subsequently developed with Eastern European communist bloc countries. For most of the 1960s and 1970s Sekou Touré's Guinea maintained a socialist government under one-party rule. Following Sekou Touré's death in 1984, a military government was installed under President Lansana Conté. Multiparty elections were held in 1993, and President Conté remained in power under his Party for Unity and Progress. The post–Sekou Touré era has been characterized by a shift away from socialism toward capitalist free market development strategies and a reintegration of the Guinean economy into Western European capitalism. Among Guinea's natural resources are bauxite (Guinea possesses over 25 percent of the world's bauxite reserves and is the second largest producer), iron ore, gold, uranium, hydropower, and diamonds. The mining sector accounted for 75 percent of its exports in 1998. Bauxite and agricultural exports (rice, millet, cassava, corn, coffee, beans, pineapples, palm oil products) contribute the most revenues to the economy.

Guinea-Bissau

Guinea-Bissau is well known for its liberation struggle against the Portuguese colonial government between 1962 and 1973. Amilcar Cabral and his PAIGC's use of guerrilla warfare became a model of resistance against colonialism around the world that others have followed. The PAIGC ruled the country from independence in 1973 until 1994 under a single-party system. The PAIGC's Joao Vieira assumed power in 1980, won the multiparty elections of 1994 and 1999, and has remained in power. Explorations have revealed major sources of oil, bauxite, and phosphates, but they have not yet been exploited. One of the poorest countries in the world, Guinea-Bissau depends mainly on farming and fishing. The bulk of the country's revenues come from groundnuts, palm kernels, and timber. The country is currently under an IMF-sponsored structural adjustment program. The tightening of monetary policy and the development of the private sector are expected to reinvigorate the economy.

Kenya

British colonial rulers gave African land in Kenya to white settlers from Britain, leaving the majority of Africans landless and subservient to the Europeans. Acute landlessness led to an African peasant rebellion in the 1950s (referred to as the Mau Mau rebellion), which aimed to regain African land and to end inequality between white settlers and Kenyans. After the rebellion, Britain was forced to grant Kenya its independence in 1963. Kenya was under one-party rule under Jomo Kenyatta (1964–1978) and Daniel arap Moi (1978–1992). External economic pressures forced the government to hold multiparty elections in 1992, which it managed to win, and the ruling Kenya African National Union (KANU) remained in power under arap Moi. Kenya's cash crops are varied and extensive: corn, wheat, rice, sugarcane, coffee, sisal, tea, and pyrethrum. Tourism is one of its largest industries, contributing significant revenues to the economy. Kenya is currently facing a declining economy and political instability.

Lesotho

Lesotho has had a long-established hereditary monarchy dating back to the precolonial period. The 1993 constitution reduced the power of the monarchy, giving it only a symbolic role with no legislative or executive powers. Since the last elections in 1998 the government has been controlled by the Lesotho Congress for Democracy. The economy is based on subsistence agriculture, livestock, and remittances from miners employed in South Africa, the country's largest trading partner. Water is Lesotho's most important natural resource. Sale of water to South Africa generated royalties that have become an important source of revenues for the government.

Liberia

Liberia was established by free American Blacks in 1822, and in 1847 became sub-Saharan Africa's first republic. Americo-Liberian rule of Liberia was terminated when military leader Samuel Doe overthrew the Tubman regime in 1980. Doe's brutal dictatorship was subsequently overthrown in 1989, and since then the country has experienced almost continuous warfare. The war between 1989 and 1997 destroyed much of Liberia's economy. Former rebel leader Charles Taylor won the multiparty elections held in 1997, and his National Patriotic Party (NPP) controlled the government. The NPP government faced the challenges of paying down the massive international debts it inherited and restoring infrastructure and raising incomes in the war-ravaged economy. Agricultural exports include rubber, rice, palm oil products, cassava, coffee, sugar, and cocoa. Natural resources include timber, diamonds, iron ore, and rubber.

Madagascar

Madagascar is the world's fourth largest island, located off the coast of southern Africa in the Indian Ocean, in a strategic location in the Mozambique Channel. Granted its independence from France in 1960, Madagascar remained under a civilian government led by President Philbert Tsiranana's Social Democratic Party (SDP) from 1960 to 1972. A military coup in 1972 led to the fall of the Tsiranana government and the first Malagasy Republic. After much political disturbance, the military installed Didier Ratsiraka as president in 1975. From 1975 to 1992 Madagascar had a socialist one-party government under the National Front for the Defense of the Socialist Malagasy Revolution. Multiparty elections were held in 1992, and President Ratsiraka's Association for the Rebirth of Madagascar (AREMA) has since controlled the government. Economic growth has been impeded by antigovernment strikes and demonstrations and a decline in world coffee demand over the 1990s. Agriculture (e.g., coffee, vanilla, sugarcane, cloves, beans, cassava) is the mainstay of the economy, accounting in 1997 for 32 percent of the GDP and 70 percent of export earnings.

Malawi

Following independence in 1964, Malawi was under the authoritarian single-party government of Hastings Banda until 1994. Malawi's political stability for three decades was based on political repression by the secret police and militia of the ruling Malawi Congress Party (MCP), as well as through allocation of resources from the agricultural sector (tobacco, tea, sugarcane, cotton, potatoes, cassava, sorghum, livestock) to a small group of favored elite clients. In 1992 antigovernment unrest led to broad-based opposition movements, most notably the southern-based United Democratic Front (UDF) and the northern-based Alliance for Democracy (AFORD). In the 1994 multiparty elections, the UDF defeated the MCP. Bakili Muluzi was elected president and was narrowly reelected in 1999. Neoliberal economic reforms implemented since the mid-1980s have been insufficient to overcome the impoverishment of the rural population. Migrant labor has been an economic opportunity for many Malawians, but these opportunities have been declining in South Africa and Zimbabwe.

Mali

Mali's first postindependence president was Modibo Keita of the Union Soudanaise Party, who ruled until he was overthrown in a 1968 coup d'état, after which the country was largely under military rule. In 1992, multiparty elections were held and Alpha Oumar Konore was elected president; since then the Alliance for Democracy (ADEMA) has been in control of government. In 1997 Konore was reelected in elections that were denounced both internally and by international observers. Mali remains one of the poorest countries in the world, with 65 percent of its land area desert. Economic activity is largely centered on the riverine area irrigated by the Niger. About 80 percent of the labor force is engaged in agriculture, especially in cotton, the country's main export. The government implemented structural adjustment programs in 1997 that have led to economic growth, as well as attracting some foreign investment. Multinational corporations increased gold-mining operations in 1996–1998, and the Mali government is optimistic that the country will become a major sub-Saharan gold exporter in the near future.

Mauritania

Since independence in 1960, Mauritania has had both civilian (Moktar Ould Daddah, 1960–1978) and military (1978–present) governments. Like Chad and Sudan, Mauritania has had long-existing hostilities between northerners and southerners that threaten political stability. The government has unsuccessfully attempted to use Islam to foster national unity. In 1979 Mauritania renounced sovereignty over any part of the Western Sahara (on the country's northern border) and recognized the POLISARIO (People's Front for the Liberation of Saquiet el-Hamra and Rio de Oro), the liberation movement of the Western Sahara. The war of the POLISARIO for independence from Morocco continues. The Western Sahara issue continues to affect Mauritania's relationships with Morocco, POLISARIO, and other African states. Mauritania is mostly desert with few natural resources. Most employed Mauritanians work in Tazadit iron ore mines in the northern desert. Iron ore provides 70–85 percent of the country's exports and foreign exchange earnings.

Mauritius

Mauritius is a small island located east of Madagascar in the Indian Ocean. Mauritius was originally a colony of France but was taken over by Britain in the late nineteenth century. Britain granted it independence in 1968. From the colonial period until now, the island has been dominated by the sugarcane industry, but other cash crops include tea and tobacco. In addition to sugar, the tourism industry is also a large contributor to the economy. Since 1886 Mauritius has maintained an uninterrupted record of parliamentary-style democracy, although the majority of the island population received the right to vote only after World War II. Ethnic divisions play an important political role, reflected in voting patterns. However, ethnic constituency building has not led to ethnic polarization. Class and ideology have also been important in shaping the character of political allegiance. All postindependence governments have been formed by coalitions of the major parties (the Mauritian Labor Party, Mauritian Militant Movement, Mauritian Socialist Party, and others). There is high unemployment in the country, largely caused by dependence on the sugar industry, which can provide only seasonal employment. By regional standards, Mauritius has been doing well, with a per-capita income of $1,240 and GNP of $957 million.

Mozambique

Following several years of armed struggle, Mozambique won its independence from Portugal in 1975. Since then the Marxist-Leninist Front for the Liberation of Mozambique (FRELIMO) government ruled the country but was under attack from 1975 to 1992 by the opposition rebel group Resistancia Naçional Moçambiçana (RENAMO), sustained by external support from the apartheid regime in South Africa. Multiparty elections were held in the 1990s, returning the incumbent FRELIMO to power. With moderate natural resources (coal, iron ore, tantalite, timber) and typical African cash crops (cotton, tobacco, cashews, sugarcane, tea, sisal), Mozambique had begun to show signs of economic recovery until cyclones in 1999, which devastated the eastern part of the country, set it back.

Namibia

Namibia was a German colony until after World War I, when it was made a mandate of the League of Nations. It was subsequently illegally annexed by South Africa and was dominated through policies of apartheid. The Southwest Africa Peoples Organization (SWAPO) fought a long liberation struggle against Afrikaner domination and control and South African occupation of Namibia. South Africa controlled it illegally until the 1990s, when SWAPO defeated the Afrikaners; Namibia was formally granted its independence in 1996. Namibia's natural resources include diamonds, copper, lead, zinc, uranium, silver, coal, and possibly oil reserves. Its cash crops include sorghum, millet, and corn.

Niger

Following independence in 1960, Niger had a constitutional government under President Hamani Diori until 1974. It was replaced by a military government in that year, and military rule continued until 1996, when a military-turned-civilian government came to power after the July 1996 multiparty elections were held. The National Union of Independents for Democratic Revival (UNIRD) is currently in control of the government. President (Colonel) Ibrahim Barre Mainassara ousted the elected president Mohamed Ousmane in a coup on January 27, 1996, and subsequently defeated him in the flawed multiparty election of July 1996. President Mainassara was assassinated on April 9, 1999. The economy centers on subsistence agriculture, animal husbandry, a reexport trade, and uranium (its major export since the 1970s). The government is heavily dependent on bilateral and multilateral aid for its development budget. The country has established IMF and World Bank–approved structural adjustment programs.

Nigeria

Nigeria is Africa's most populous country, with population recently estimated at 120 million. One in four sub-Saharan Africans is a Nigerian. More than 250 languages are spoken and are recognized by the Nigerian government. Nigeria is oil rich, making it potentially one of Africa's most prosperous countries. Britain granted Nigeria its independence in 1960. Its four decades of independence have included twenty-nine years of military rule, a bloody civil war, interethnic violence, and three civilian republics. Nigeria's foreign policy has been aggressive, supporting liberation struggles in southern Africa and economic integration in West Africa (embodied in the Economic Community of West African States [ECOWAS]), and it has taken a lead in solving regional conflicts (Economic Community of West African States Monitoring Group [ECOMOG]) and regional issues such as the dumping of toxic wastes in Africa. Despite Nigeria's oil wealth, corrupt regimes, both military and civilian, have plundered the economy, and Nigerians have a relatively low standard of living in sub-Saharan Africa. After decades of military rule, multiparty elections were held in 1999 after numerous delays by intransigent military leaders such as Ibrahim Babanginda and Sani Abacha. Olusegun Obasanjo, a former military ruler (1979–1983), was elected president in 1999 and remains in power.

Rwanda

Rwanda is the most densely populated country in sub-Saharan Africa, covering an area of 26,340 square kilometers, with a population of approximately 8.1 million. It is landlocked and has few natural resources and minimal industry. Its primary exports are coffee and tea, and other agricultural products include pyrethrum, bananas, beans, sorghum, and potatoes.

As in Burundi, politicized ethnicity under colonial rule (Germany and then Belgium) led to the notorious Hutu-Tutsi conflict (the population is 80 percent Hutu, 19 percent Tutsi, and 1 percent Twa), which has ravaged the country and created a huge refugee problem in the Great Lakes region. The Tutsi minority was favored in education and employment under colonial rule. In 1959 the Hutus overthrew the ruling Tutsi monarch. The Hutus killed hundreds of Tutsis and drove thousands into exile in neighboring countries. The children of these exiles later formed the Rwanda Patriotic Front (RPF) and began a war in October 1990. The war culminated in the April 1994 genocide of roughly 800,000 Tutsis and moderate Hutus. The Tutsi rebels defeated the Hutu regime and ended the genocide on July 1994, but approximately two million Hutu refugees fled to neighboring countries.

The 1994 constitution provided for multiparty elections. President Juvénal Habyarimana was elected in the 1994 multiparty elections but was subsequently killed in a mysterious plane crash on April 6, 1994, which ignited the genocide. He was replaced by President Pasteur Bizimungu, whom military forces of the RPF installed in July 1994. The country is now at peace, but members of the former regime continue to destabilize the northwest part of the country through a low-intensity insurgency. With constant political instability and a refugee crisis, there has been little economic development.

São Tomé and Principe

São Tomé and Principe are islands located off the west coast of Africa in the Gulf of Guinea, west of Gabon. For most of its history after gaining its independence from Portugal in 1975, São Tomé was under single-party rule. São Tomé and Principe were among a few countries in Africa to have held second multiparty elections in the 1990s. The Movement for the Liberation of São Tomé and Principe–Social Democratic Party (MLSTP-PSD) controls the government. The economy is dependent on cocoa, but cocoa production has declined, resulting in a persistent balance-of-payments problem. The islands are dependent on imports of fuel, consumer and manufactured goods, and significant amounts of food. External debt is high, and the country is dependent on concessional aid and debt rescheduling. The government is optimistic that the fledgling tourist industry and petroleum discoveries will lead to economic growth.

Senegal

Senegal is located on the west coast of Africa, at the closest point between the African continent and the United States. During the colonial period, this location allowed the French, Dutch, and English to use Senegal as an important distribution center for the Atlantic slave trade. Since it was granted independence from France in 1960, Senegal has maintained close economic, diplomatic, and military ties with its former colonial ruler. Senegal has had relative political stability in the postindependence period under a one-party-dominant system. The Socialist Party had control of the government under Leopold Senghor (1960–1980), who was succeeded by Abdou Diouf (1980–2000). President Diouf was defeated in the elections of March 2000 by Abdoulaye Wade, who captured more than 60 percent of the vote as the head of a coalition of opposition parties. Senegal and The Gambia formed the short-lived Senegambia Federation, from 1982–1987. Senegal's economy has been based on cash crops (millet, sorghum, manioc, rice, cotton, and groundnuts). Within the region its economic performance has been moderate. Its per-capita income is $380; GNP, $2.4 billion. Senegal has had relative political stability, with internal conflicts in its Cassemance province, near Mauritania.

Seychelles

Colonized by France and then Britain, Seychelles was granted its independence in 1976. Since then it has been ruled by the Seychelles People's Progressive Front (SPPF). Multiparty elections were held in the 1990s but did not lead to a change in government. The economy has been dependent on tourism (which provides more than 70 percent of hard currency and employs about 30 percent of the labor force) and tuna fishing (which accounted for 70 percent of GDP in 1996–1997). The government has recently promoted farming, fishing, and small-scale manufacturing, attempting to reduce the country's dependence on the vulnerable tourist industry.

Sierra Leone

Sierra Leone has had a unique colonial history. Freetown, its capital city, was founded by waves of former black slaves brought there by the British from Britain and the New World. The first wave (known as the "Black Poor") was brought from England (where they were living) to Sierra Leone in 1787. Former slaves from Jamaica and Nova Scotia (Canada) arrived shortly thereafter. The descendants of these settlers blended British and African ways and were called creole because of their mixed heritage.

Granted independence from Britain in 1961, the Sierra Leone People's Party (SLPP) controlled the postindependence government until 1967. After 1967 the All People's Congress (APC) won control and became the only recognized party in 1978. Siaka Stevens, leader of the APC, was president for seventeen years until he stepped down in 1985 for his chosen successor, General Joseph Mommoh. The Mommoh government was removed in 1992 in a coup led by Captain Valentine Strasser. Since then Foday Sankoh's Revolutionary United Front (RUF) and the central government have clashed over control of the country's eastern region, where diamond deposits are located. Multiparty elections were held in 1996; Alhaji Tejan Kabbah of the SLPP was elected president, subsequently overthrown, and reinstated in 1998 with the help of ECOMOG. Sierra Leone's natural resources include diamonds, bauxite, rutile, chromite, and iron ore. Its cash crops are coffee, piassava, cocoa, ginger, and rice. The country has not seen much economic development in its recent unstable political history. Its per-capita income and GNP are among the lowest in the region: $232 and $1 billion, respectively.

Somalia

Colonial policies divide the Somali people; for seventy-five years the north was governed by Britain, while the south and east were subjected to Italian rule. This experience contributed to postindependence secessionist movements in the north (the Ogaden War), as well as Somali irredentism. Somalia was under single-party and military rule from 1969 to 1992. Siyad Barre seized power in 1969 and was the longest-serving ruler until he was overthrown in 1992. In the 1970s Somalia and Ethiopia became pawns in the superpower conflict between the Soviet Union and the United States, with both providing military support for the two countries. Since Siyad Barre was deposed, Somalia has been in a state of anarchy. Except for a brief period of humanitarian intervention from 1992 to 1994, the United States has maintained its distance from Somalia. The Somali state collapsed in 1992, and since then no internationally recognizable government has been formed.

South Africa

South Africa is perceived to be the wealthiest country in Africa, boasting a per-capita income of $4,000 and GNP of $112 billion, comparable to many western European countries. Its natural resources include gold, diamonds, mineral ores, uranium, and fish. Its varied cash crops include corn, wheat, wool, sugarcane, and tobacco. South Africa's wealth and economic prosperity has been built on the exploitation of the African majority for decades under a vicious system of racial segregation (called apartheid in South Africa) based on the legal subordination of Africans, Coloureds (mixed races), and Indians.

The country's first multiracial multiparty elections were held in 1994. Nelson Mandela (jailed for twenty-seven years for fighting against the apartheid system) was released from jail in 1993, was elected president in 1994, and led the transition process from white to black rule. The country's "democratic transition" remains fragile as economic resources are still racially distributed and remain concentrated in the hands of white South Africans.

The Sudan

The Sudan is the largest country in Africa, with a land area of approximately 2,504,530 square kilometers (about one-fourth the size of the United States). Since independence was granted in 1956, an internal war has threatened the state's survival. About four-fifths of the people in Sudan are Muslims. They live in the north, center, and west of the country, and most of them speak Arabic. The remaining one-fifth of the population lives in the south. Few are Muslim; many are Christian and speak Dinka, Nuer, Shilluk, and other languages. The British colonial system divided Arabic-speaking northerners from the people in the south. The development of the south was neglected. At independence the Muslim Sudanese inherited the state that the colonial power left, with all its economic resources. Since then, southern Sudanese have been fighting against northern domination by the central government in Khartoum. Rebels (the Sudanese Peoples Liberation Army/Movement) have received support from neighbors such as Ethiopia and Libya.

Between 1956 and 1969 Sudan had constitutional government, but since 1969 the country has been under single-party and military rule. Sudan's most noted postindependence dictator, Jafar Numeiri (1969–1985), consolidated his power by eliminating challenges to his government from both the Islamic right and the communist left. The present National Islamic Front (NIF) government, led by President Omer Hassan Ahmed Al-Bashir (1989–) has been seen by the United States as supporting anti-U.S. terrorist organizations in the Middle East. A 1999 U.S. bombing of a pharmaceutical building in Sudan (suspected by the United States to be a storage facility for bombs and other weapons) confirmed the current hostile relationship between the two countries.

Swaziland

Granted its independence from Britain in 1968, Swaziland remained an autocratic hereditary monarchy with no suffrage until September 1993. The monarch is the head of state; he appoints the prime minister and confirms the cabinet recommended by the prime minister. Judges of the high court and court of appeal are all appointed by the monarch. Political parties are banned (by the last constitution, of October 1978), but a host of illegal parties exist, including the Peoples United Democratic Movement (PUDEMO); Swaziland Youth Congress (SWAYOCO), Swaziland Communist Party (SWACOPA), Swaziland Liberation Front (FROLISA), Swaziland Democratic Alliance (which represents key opposition parties), and Swaziland Federation of Trade Unions (SFTU). The main hard currency earners in Swaziland are soft drink concentrates, sugar, and wood pulp. Swaziland is heavily dependent on South Africa, from which it receives nearly all of its imports and to which it sends more than half of its exports. Remittances from Swazi workers in South African mines supplement domestic incomes.

Tanzania

Tanzania was originally a German colony; then it was taken over by Britain after World War II. Britain granted its independence in 1961. For most of the postindependence period, it has been under single-party rule (of the Tanganyika African National Union [TANU] and later the Chama Cha Mapinduzi [CCM]). Julius Nyerere, TANU's founder and president of Tanzania from 1961 until his retirement from politics in 1985, ruled Tanzania under a single-party socialist government. In the 1970s Tanzania was a model for a noncapitalist path to development among Third World countries, with its *ujamaa* (Swahili word—refers to "Socialism in villages") experiment carried out by Tanzania in the 1970s. Although ujamaa failed and was abandoned by the mid-1980s, it generated a huge literature on development and attracted socialists from the Caribbean, other parts of Africa, Britain, Sweden, and Denmark. Nyerere was one of postindependence

Africa's most respected leaders, playing many leadership roles in regional issues, especially in the liberation struggles in southern Africa. The CCM is still in power, having won the 1996 multiparty elections (the first held since independence). The performance of Tanzania's economy has been relatively weak. Its per-capita income is $200, and GNP $4.1. billion. Its chief cash crops are cotton, coffee, sisal, tea, tobacco, and wheat. The 1990s brought an upward turn in the economy. Political reform and economic liberalization have both been attempted and are believed to have contributed to the improvements in the economy.

Togo

Togo has been under single-party and military rule for most of its postindependence history. A multiparty constitution was adopted by public referendum in 1992. Two elections were held in the 1990s. Authoritarian president Gnassingbe Eyadema (in power since 1967) won both presidential elections and remained in power under the new political party, Rally of the Togolese People (RTP). The Togolese economy is heavily dependent on agriculture (e.g., cotton, coffee, and cocoa), which provides employment for 65 percent of the labor force and 30 percent of its export earnings. Phosphate mining is important in the industrial sector, but world prices have recently collapsed, and foreign competition has increased. Economic reform measures encouraged by IMF and World Bank donors have recently stalled as a result of the government's inability to pay arrears as well as its failure to meet the donor's requirements for free multiparty elections.

Uganda

Uganda's first postindependence civilian government, of President Milton Obote, was overthrown in 1971 by General Idi Amin, who ruled until 1979, when he was overthrown by Tanzanian-backed exiled forces. Amin's rule was notorious for human rights violations, including torture, intimidation, and murder of dissenters. His expulsion of thousands of Asians underscored the policies of his dictatorial regime and brought him condemnation from Western nations and from Tanzania. His long feud with Tanzania's Julius Nyerere culminated with the Tanzania-assisted coup that removed him from power. Uganda has achieved relative political stability under President Yoweri Musuveni, and its economy is said to be performing remarkably well under economic liberalization. Political reform has also been attempted; elections have been held, but Musuveni has resisted the formation of competing political parties. There is a positive feeling that national reconstruction is now taking place. The country's natural resources include copper, and its cash crops are coffee, tea, cotton, and sisal.

Zambia

Zambia was under a single-party system led by Kenneth Kaunda for most of its postindependence history until 1991. Kaunda was well known for his philosophy of "humanism" with a socialist component. Along with Julius Nyerere, he was one of the most respected leaders in the region, with a progressive foreign policy supporting liberation movements in southern Africa and anti-imperialism struggles in general. He was defeated in the country's first multiparty elections in 1991 and acceded to the results. His successor, Frederick Chiluba, reelected in 1996 for a second five-year term, changed the constitution, banning him from running for president in Zambia again. The present government has adopted policies of economic liberalization and limited political reform. Zambia's natural resources include copper, zinc, lead, cobalt, and coal, and its cash crops include corn, sugarcane, tobacco, and cotton. The economy is centered around copper, performing moderately but subjected to the vagaries of dependence on one mineral.

Zimbabwe

Rhodesia (as Zimbabwe was then known) was a British colony until Ian Smith announced its Unilateral Declaration of Independence (UDI) in 1965. An apartheid regime was established under Smith, and the white minority ruled until 1980. After decades of armed struggle, in 1980 Africans in Rhodesia won their independence and the state of Zimbabwe was created. The country's natural resources are varied: gold, copper, chrome, coal, nickel, iron ore, silver, and asbestos. Its agricultural resources are tobacco, corn, sugar, cotton, and livestock. Its major industries are mining, steel, and textiles. Robert Mugabe's Zimbabwe African People's Union (ZAPU)/Patriotic Front (PF) government inherited the apartheid legacy of the Ian Smith regime. Formidable problems emerging from the racial concentration of power and resources in the hands of the minority white population remain. The one-party socialist state that existed since independence did not address these problems. Its major objective has been regime survival, largely through suppression of the opposition. The Mugabe regime is currently having serious problems, facing growing economic problems, escalating land crises resulting from African seizures of white farms and the killing of white farmers, and internal and external pressures to hold multiparty elections in the face of a diminishing support base. The situation in Zimbabwe is very volatile and could explode along racial lines.

3
—

The African State: Its Colonial Legacy

The state has been widely recognized as the primary force in politics and the economy in postindependence sub-Saharan Africa. Following independence in the late 1950s and early 1960s, the representative democratic model bequeathed by the former European colonial powers rapidly collapsed, and by the beginning of 1964 there were single-party authoritarian and military governments in two-thirds of independent Africa. Political life in many sub-Saharan African countries was often characterized by political repression, brutality, terror, military coups, countercoups, and intense intraelite competition for control of the postcolonial state, vacated by the departure of the European colonial powers. Expropriation of the state's resources by the few and immiseration of the masses have been the result. The state's coercive apparatus, often built with international support, guaranteed against challenges to the distribution of wealth and power in the society. Civil society has been weak; it is the state that dominates.

Why did such a violent and repressive form of the postcolonial state emerge? What is the origin of the modern African state form? The premise of this chapter is that the political and economic structures established under colonial rule, providing little experience in self-government and allowing little development of interest groups and political parties, are directly linked to the authoritarian postcolonial state form that emerged. The African state was created in response to both the internal and external needs of the colonial power. In all cases of colonial domination in Africa, indigenous authorities were either eliminated or neutralized and subordinated to the domination of the colonial power. The postcolonial state that emerged in the decade of the 1960s was organically linked to its predecessor, the colonial state. To gain a proper understanding of postindependence political developments, one must begin with the colonial state.

Political and Economic Structures: The Colonial Era

All colonial states in Africa had certain characteristics: they were conceived in violence and issued from conquest; they established imperial sovereignty on the conquered territories; they were all centralized and coercive; they all created an indigenous bureaucratic elite; they dominated economic activities; they employed racist ideologies; and they all sought to integrate the economy of the colony into the imperial economy (Chabal, 1992, 1994).

European colonization of Africa occurred in the late nineteenth century as a result of both political and economic factors. Nationalist rivalries and balance-of-power politics among the leading European nations heightened the desire for colonies. Colonization also answered the major industrial European powers' need to acquire and control new markets and sources of raw materials in underexploited areas of the globe. Many African nations resisted colonization, but with the exception of Liberia and Ethiopia they all ultimately succumbed to Europe's sophisticated military technology. The colonial powers justified their rule on the grounds of superiority. Whether the justification was given in terms of the "white man's burden," the spread of Christianity, the propagation of French "civilization," or British principles of law and government, colonialism was justified on grounds that one civilization was going to remake and impose a better order on a second (Crowder, 1968).

European conquest of Africa began much earlier than the partition of Africa at the Congress of Berlin in 1884–1885. By the seventeenth century, France had already begun its activities in the Senegambia region, establishing Saint Louis (along with Dakar, Goree and Rufisque, Saint Louis was one of three of the towns of Senegal where legally born residents had rights of French citizenship from the time of the French Revolution and were represented after 1848 in the French Chamber of Deputies). By 1830 France also seized Algeria. Britain established Sierra Leone in 1808, The Gambia in 1816, and in 1844 obtained a treaty with the Fante state that established its claim to the Gold Coast. In 1861 it gained Nigeria, made Lagos a crown colony, and established the Oil Rivers Protectorate (Marable, 1987). The Berlin Congress was convened by German chancellor Otto von Bismarck to make a final agreement on the carving up of those parts of Africa that remained uncolonized. The conference was attended by Austria-Hungary, Belgium, Britain, Denmark, Germany, Italy, Luxembourg, the Netherlands, Norway, Portugal, Russia, Spain, Sweden, Turkey, and the United States. The delegates at the conference recognized the King of Belgium's control of the Congo Free State (later called the Belgian Congo, then Zaire, and currently the Democratic Republic of the Congo) and the borders of the colonies of Britain, France, Spain, Germany, and Portugal. Within twenty-five years after the conference, only Liberia and Ethiopia remained independent states. With the partition at the Congress of Berlin, Africa was carved up into more than fifty states dominated by seven western European countries (Britain, France, Germany, Belgium, Portugal, Italy, and Spain).

Africa has hundreds of distinct ethnic groups (condescendingly referred to by many Westerners as "tribes"); they share language, history, cultural values, territory, economic and political institutions. They range in size from many millions, such as the Hausa, the Baganda, and the Ashanti, to the thousands, such as the Nzuma. Boundaries were drawn arbitrarily by the colonial powers, based solely on political and economic expediency, dividing ethnic and language groups among several colonies. In East Africa the Somali were divided among Ethiopia, Somalia, and Kenya; the Maasai between German Tanganyika and British Kenya; in West Africa the Akan split between Côte d'Ivoire and the Gold Coast (known today as Ghana); the Ewe between the Gold Coast and Togo; the Ibo between Nigeria and Cameroon; the Malinke, Yoruba, Fulani, and Ewe splintered between three or more colonial regimes; in Central Africa, the Hutus and Tutsis were spread across Rwanda, Burundi, Congo, Uganda, and Tanzania; in southern Africa, the Ovimbundu were spread across several colonial regimes. Hundreds of other ethnic groups across the continent were divided across two or more colonial regimes. Groups with traditional rivalries or histories of warfare were often included within a single state, such as the Ashanti and Brong in Ghana and the Yoruba and Hausa in Nigeria (Crowder, 1968). The colonial state arbitrarily defined the boundaries of the political community with little or no consideration of ethnic groups or the realities of African society. These artificial boundaries have created one of the greatest political problems in postindependence Africa and have led to several wars and conflicts, such as the Biafran War (Nigeria), the war in the Ogaden (Somalia-Ethiopia), and brutal conflicts in the Great Lakes region.

Having created these boundaries, the colonial powers did little to help foster a sense of national unity within them. Instead, they often used a divide-and-rule tactic, favoring one group over others, especially in education and employment. Colonial policy aimed to intensify ethnic competition and to stimulate insecurity and conflict. Groups close to original colonial settlements or administrative centers advanced more quickly into education, trade, civil service, and the professions. Some groups were regarded by the colonial powers as uniquely suited for military service and were recruited in large numbers and hence dominated the rank and file of the army. Very often the officers, if they were African, came from a different ethnic group. Some groups favored by colonial policy evolved with a politically dominant position in the national government (e.g., the Fulani emirs of northern Nigeria); others dominated the civil service. Ethnic tensions developed from these distinctions of power, status, and socioeconomic opportunities. It must be noted, however, that the vast majority of Africans live peacefully with their multiethnic neighbors. Where ethnicity has grown into violence, as in Nigeria, Sudan, Rwanda, Burundi, and Uganda, among others, it can be clearly linked to policies and constitutions constructed and left by colonial powers. In some cases, minorities were given greater advantage over other groups and then placed in a constitutional structure that either sustained or worsened the situation (Rothchild and Olorunsola, 1983).

A centralized authoritarian administrative structure was established to guarantee the colonial political order. A high degree of political authority was concentrated in a small number of administrators, merchants, and landlords who received their directives from London, Paris, Brussels, Lisbon, and other Western capitals. Whether it was under French, British, Belgian, or Portuguese control, the colonial state apparatus instituted a severe form of authoritarian control. Coercive methods were used to eliminate any democratic or popular access to political authority by broad sectors of the African population. Authority came from overseas (from the capitals of the metropole), and orders were distributed from the governor through the colonial hierarchy to the local chief. Colonial governors enjoyed very broad powers and were insulated from the African people at the bottom of the society. In many countries, the governor ruled by decree or proclamation, and his decision on policy was overriding even when he had an executive council that he appointed. Policy was made either in the metropole or by the Governor and implemented by his appointed officials with little or no participation by the governed. In British colonies legislative power was centralized at the governor's level; in French colonies, in Paris in the office of the minister of colonies and the president of the republic. Serious policies were made without consulting the indigenous population. The African people were never consulted, for example, when the policy was established for the immigration of large numbers of Asians and Lebanese in East and West Africa to fill commercial positions or for the compulsory development of cash cropping. The elites in control of the bureaucracy perceived themselves to be accountable not to the indigenous people of the colonies but to the colonial government (Crowder, 1968).

Africans had little opportunity to participate in the colonial state's governmental machinery until a few years before the end of colonial rule. There were a handful of elected Africans in local government in Nigeria, the Gold Coast, and Senegal before 1945. But generally in the British and French-controlled territories, preparation for taking over the colonial state's legislative, executive, and administrative organs by Africans began only after World War II. Further, colonial administrators destroyed or distorted the systems of local rule through which Africans might take collective action. Although colonial powers left some local organizations in Africa intact (e.g., peasant cooperatives, market associations, community improvement organizations, professional organizations, religious societies, labor unions), these organizations were not instituted through law but were left out of the formal political structure. Traditional authority operated in some British and French colonies where the colonial state relied upon traditional African rulers, chiefs, and religious authorities to help govern the vast population under its control. The British system of indirect rule permitted rulers and chiefs to govern certain areas under the careful supervision of the Europeans. The survival of traditional authorities did not change the fact that they were clearly subordinated to the colonial power structure and could be removed if they did not follow colonial policy. As long as they complied with the demands of the colonial power, local rulers retained a privileged position within the colonial system. The integration of chiefs as subordinates in the colonial bureaucracy, performing unpopular tasks such as collecting taxes and recruiting forced labor, undermined chiefly authority throughout much of Africa.

The centralizing, elitist practices and patterns of the colonial period have endured in the postindependence bureaucracy and in the population's view of it. Many leaders of the early postindependence period, when challenged by the people over policies they believed essential to stability and economic progress, have responded in much the same way as colonial governments have responded. Kwame Nkrumah of Ghana and Julius Nyerere of Tanzania, for example, acted to ban peasant purchasing of cooperatives in key cash crop areas when the cooperatives demanded pricing policies inconsistent with the government's. They were also acting to enhance their own personal power base. The institutional structure providing for continued centralization of power still exists, and African leaders in the postindependence period have used those structures to facilitate their own elitism. Centralization under colonialism predisposed independent African regimes toward centralized constitutions.

Colonial policy also reinforced centralization in the geographical legacy as well. A single city (usually the capital) generally has the administrative headquarters of the country and all the educational facilities, public utilities, consumer goods, and communication facilities. Most opportunities in paid employment, commerce, and the professions are also there. Africans who find a place in the city have far greater opportunities to advance. Thus began the development of a domestic African petty bourgeois and professional elite (Crowder, 1968). Under the European colonial system, to hold positions in the mission churches, the colonial bureaucracy, the professions, or the government, an African had to be educated in the metropole. Those who were able to do this had far greater opportunities to hold and exercise political power. After independence, interests of this educated elite became linked to maintaining a centralized, elite-oriented government.

The European powers used a host of coercive mechanisms to secure the colonial order that benefited them. Coercion was heavily used to discipline the laboring classes. Enormous political authority was concentrated in a small number of administrators, merchants, and landlords. As modern industries developed in some colonies, the elitist coercive orientation of the colonial state evolved. Coercive methods were used to eliminate any democratic or popular access to political authority by broad sectors of the African population. Coercion was used to subordinate peasants and workers in settler states in Southern Rhodesia, Kenya, Angola, and Mozambique. In Southern Rhodesia Africans were forcibly moved from vast territories to facilitate the development of white-owned farms.

The historical role of the colonial military was to suppress internal conflicts and local uprisings. The postcolonial army that the independent African nations inherited from the colonial government was predisposed toward intervention in domestic politics (Mbaku, 1994).

During colonial rule most African states were (and many still are) small and dependent agricultural economies. They depended on one or two major commodities for most of their export earnings and depended on the metropole to purchase the bulk of their production. Colonial policy prevented them from adding much value to those products in the production process (Rodney, 1972). Further, colonial policy decisions encouraged most African economies to develop with "enclaves" or dual sectors, where one urban or rural area was heavily involved in export and cash crop production or mining, and the rest of the country lagged far behind. The enclave area would have far higher incomes, enjoy greater access to education and other social services, and consume manufactured goods largely imported from overseas. The enclave sector had no linkages with any other sectors of the economy and as a result did not stimulate growth in the rest of the country (Crowder, 1968).

The colonies had to generate the revenues to pay for colonial state construction. In West Africa, trade in palm oil, textiles, and some other commodities provided modest customs revenues. In South Africa, diamond and gold mines provided the economic base for state construction, and African labor was exploited to provide revenues in some areas. Arbitrary regulations were passed, such as the Masters and Servants Ordinances, which specified periods of obligatory labor service at state-defined tasks. In some of the French colonies, there were plenary powers given to local administrators to impose penalties for disobedience (Young, 1988). Measures imposed to satisfy state revenue needs triggered revolts, as in Sierra Leone (the Hut Tax War in 1896) and Tanganyika (the Maji-Maji rebellion of 1906).

The colonial powers placed an excessive share of the fiscal burden on the rural population through export taxation and pricing policies. The roots of rural poverty in Africa lie in this policy. In the white settler colonies of East, Central, and southern Africa, the best land was taken from the African farmer, who was forced onto less fertile reserves to produce the cash crops that the colonial rulers required rather than those he needed. Through taxation, forced labor, compulsory crop cultivation, and in some cases physical coercion, the African farmer produced the crops that the big companies overseas required. This was often done at the risk of impoverishing his family and of famine. British taxation policies designed to increase cultivation of cotton and groundnuts took sometimes as much as 50 percent of a farmer's income and led to shortages of subsistence crops, which in turn led to famines (Shenton, 1987). After independence the state similarly used marketing boards created under colonialism as a means of taxing further the potential earnings of the farmer. The neglect and exploitation of the African farmer in the postcolonial period is a major legacy of colonial rule.

The colonial rulers did not operate the economy in the interests of their subjects. Profits were expatriated, not invested in local industries (which is similar to the present practice of self-interested African leaders siphoning funds from the treasury and investing them in safe banks in Switzerland). There was a lack of local industrial development, as manufactured goods were brought in from the metropolitan countries.

The colonial state played an aggressive role in creating the dependent economy that characterized sub-Saharan Africa. First, in order to expand cash crop economies in Kenya, Britain gave grants and loans for the establishment of African-owned farms under individual land titles. In this way, a successful group of stable rural capitalists and landowners directly tied to the state and the colonial economy was created. Second, the colonial state promoted the expansion of direct foreign investments and the growth of light industries in many areas. The reason was that post–World War II capitalism had moved from concentrating investments in raw materials and plantation production to manufacturing and extractive industries. This required huge increases in capital exports to the colonies. Colonial grants to new private capital rose from 0.4 million British pounds in 1946 to 9.5 million pounds in 1956, and private capital imports from 6.2 million pounds to 21.2 million pounds in 1953 (Marable, 1987: 43). Expanded capital investments led to the growth of a small industrial working class, which had a direct impact on all independence movements.

Third, through bureaucratic structures such as marketing boards, the colonial state directed production and trade. Colonial governments established marketing boards (A group of people employed by the state to maintain control over the internal and international marketing of goods.) and state monopolies to expand the production of agricultural goods, stabilize markets, and bring them under state control. As a result, the state was able to directly appropriate a very large part of the economic surplus and deploy it in bureaucratically directed economic activities in the name of promoting economic development (Alavi, 1972).

The Decolonization Process

The process of decolonization in the British colonies having few European settlers (e.g., Tanganyika, Uganda, Nigeria, Cameroon, Ghana) was more rapid, and self-government and independence were perceived by the colonial power more favorably. Where there were large numbers of settlers (as in Kenya and Northern and Southern Rhodesia), the process of decolonization was usually characterized by periods of violent conflict between Africans and Europeans. In those countries with few European settlers, the nationalist leaders who emerged to deal with the colonial authorities (e.g., Kwame Nkrumah in Ghana, Julius Nyerere in Tanzania, Dawda Jawara in The Gambia) represented both the elites and the masses of the population. The colonial government had little choice but to agree to begin negotiations for independence with the objective of handing over power to these "moderate" leaders, who they felt could preserve social and political order.

In countries with extensive white settler populations holding political power, the process was different. In Kenya, laws were enacted to give white settlers social, economic, and political advantages over Africans. Africans were deprived of their land and in large numbers forced to live in overcrowded and overcultivated reserves, and a pass system similar to that in apartheid South Africa was introduced to regulate population movements. In the post–World War II period, political tensions escalated, leading to a peasant rebellion by the Land and Freedom Army (also referred to as "Mau Mau"). This rebellion was ultimately defeated militarily by the British but set the stage for independence within a decade. As a result of this rebellion, Britain opted to support the African nationalists, who agreed to protect the rights of the European settlers and to allow foreign capitalist economic activities to continue. Under these terms Kenya was granted independence in 1963 with Jomo Kenyatta as prime minister.

In Southern Rhodesia (currently Zimbabwe) the settler population used its relatively powerful position in the economy to make a unilateral declaration of independence from British rule in 1965, under the leadership of Ian

Smith. International sanctions imposed by Britain and the United States, combined with almost two decades of armed struggle by the Zimbabwe African National Union (ZANU) and the Zimbabwe African Peoples Union (ZAPU), were efforts to force the rebellious Smith regime to allow for full African participation in government and politics. The internal and external pressures weakened the Smith regime. At the end of the 1970s, the British Commonwealth brokered a negotiated settlement that resulted in the election in 1980 of Robert Mugabe as Zimbabwe's first prime minister.

The French colonies, with the exception of Algeria (in North Africa), did not have substantial European settlement. In Algeria, a national liberation struggle erupted in the 1950s, and nationalists waged an effective guerrilla campaign that forced France in 1962 to abandon its plans to make Algeria its most prized overseas possession. The pattern in other French colonies, in West and equatorial Africa, was different. In 1958 a referendum was held in which African countries were asked to vote on whether they wanted to remain a part of the French community. The French colonial government believed that most colonies, recognizing their political weakness and economic vulnerability, would opt to remain French. Guinea was the only country that voted for independence in 1958, but by 1960 the other French colonies asked for and were granted independence. The French subsequently maintained close political and economic (and in some instances military) ties with most of their former African colonies.

Belgium's major colony in Africa, the Belgian Congo, had significant white settler involvement. As a result, Belgium only reluctantly dealt with the idea of African majority rule and independence in the late 1950s. Until then Africans had been involved in politics only through their affiliation with organizations established by European settlers. Belgium, like most colonizing powers, had convinced itself that it dominated Africans to benefit them more. The colonial bureaucracy, the Catholic Church, and foreign economic concerns all joined to support the colonial state in its domination of the African population. The colonial state regulated African social behavior. The Catholic missions "educated" many Africans, and many accepted the subordinate position accorded to them by the colonizers. Like other colonial powers, Belgium also cultivated an African petty bourgeoisie, educated in Belgian culture and supportive of the status quo. However, inspired by the nationalist struggles taking place in other parts of Africa and the world, African nationalist organizations began to spring up in the late 1950s. More than one hundred separate predominantly cultural and ethnic parties were established, but only Patrice Lumumba's National Congolese Movement (MNC) had a broad base of support. Pressured by African demands for political change, the Belgian government held a conference in Brussels in January 1960 to discuss the possibility of independence. Within six months, despite white settler protest, the Congo was granted independence. By 1962 Belgium's colonial adventure in

Africa ended, with independence granted also to its two final African colonies, Rwanda and Burundi (Mazrui and Tidy, 1984).

Portugal was the last major European power to give up its African possessions: Guinea-Bissau, Cape Verde, Mozambique, Angola, and São Tomé and Principe. The Portuguese government was a dictatorship; hence the same authoritarian structures at home were automatically transferred to the colonies. Ethnicism and class determined African peoples' life chances. They were kept in a state of near servitude with little opportunity for education or social advancement. The Portuguese government viewed its colonies as extensions or provinces of Portugal, and believed that its colonialism was both different and better than other colonialism. Since democratic freedoms were not allowed in Portugal, it was inconceivable (to the Portuguese colonial government) that the colonies could be set free and allowed to have those freedoms. Based on that reality, liberation movements began armed struggles for independence in Angola in 1961, in Guinea-Bissau in 1962, and in Mozambique in 1964. Ultimately, military pressure from African nationalists and the overthrow of the fascist Portuguese dictatorship and political instability at home combined to force Portugal to retreat from Africa. Guinea-Bissau secured independence in 1974, Mozambique and Angola in 1975, and Cape Verde and São Tomé and Principe in 1975. As in the former French, British, and Belgian colonies, the educated middle classes also assumed power in Angola. However, the presence of the colonial-imperial power was eliminated. The client state apparatus was missing as a result of the war of liberation. Colonially structured power relations were challenged by Marxist-Leninist governments formed in these countries after independence.

Economic Development during the Decolonization Period

At the same time that African colonies were preparing for independence and weakening political ties with Europe, they were increasing their economic dependence on Europe and the Western industrialized nations in general. Between 1945 and 1960 almost all sub-Saharan African countries underwent considerable growth, but their economic resources continued to be exploited, rather than developed, by Western companies. Africa continued as before to provide cheap raw materials for European and North American industry. Between the end of World War II and independence, colonial administrations granted concessions to Western companies for the working of African mineral, agricultural, and forest resources. In the absence of indigenous capitalists, foreign firms poured in to these countries. In Nigeria on the eve of independence the United Africa Company controlled about half of Nigeria's import trade. In Liberia many firms came to exploit the cheap labor that had already made huge profits for Firestone. Many American and Belgian companies also flocked to the Congo.

Britain and France made attempts to develop their African colonies after 1945 through developing agencies and marketing boards. These efforts had little success. The French government set up the Fonds d'Investissement et de Developpement Economique et Social (FIDES) in 1946. Between 1946 and 1947, FIDES invested more capital in the French West African colonies than the total estimated investment from both public and private sources from 1903 to 1946. Britain provided the first capital outlay to encourage foreign investment in its colonies through its Colonial Development and Welfare Acts of 1940 and 1945. The postwar investment did not seem to yield much to meet the people's development needs. The highest proportion of the development funds went to Western construction firms for improving infrastructure, transport, power plants, and other public works. Very little was invested in education, agriculture, or industry (Mazrui and Tidy, 1984).

The British set up marketing boards in its West African colonies to purchase cash crops from peasants through European middlemen and export the crops. Crops would be purchased from the peasants at a guaranteed price regardless of the state of the world market. The prices the boards paid for cocoa, groundnuts, and palm products between 1950 and 1958 were lower than world prices; the boards paid African peasant farmers a low fixed rate during many years when world prices were rising. The profits made by the boards were not held in reserve to support prices paid to farmers when world prices fell. Rather, the beneficiaries of the marketing board system were European trading companies acting as middlemen (e.g., the United Africa Company and John Holt); Britain's gold and dollar reserves, which increased; public works projects in West Africa; and the British and French governments, whose use of their colonies' foreign exchange earnings helped their postwar reconstruction. In 1952 Guinea earned France one billion francs in foreign exchange based on the sale of coffee, bananas, and bauxite (Mazrui and Tidy, 1984).

Between 1945 and 1960 African imports of Western manufactured goods increased. Although a small manufacturing industry emerged in a few centers (e.g., Dakar, Senegal, Accra, Ghana), colonial economic policy concentrated on economic growth through exports of minerals and cash crops and neglected developing an industrial base that would give impetus to genuine economic growth and development. The decolonization process left the colonial division of labor and its emphasis on primary commodity production and export specialization (agricultural crops and minerals) virtually unchanged. Decolonization led to minimal industrial development; forced trade and financial links with the metropole designed to reproduce the world market internally; immigration of foreign personnel to fill crucial executive positions in the upper echelons of the state and private sectors;

Cocoa: the more Africa produces, the less money it gets.

© John Marshall / Getty Images

and limited autonomy of local economic, political, and social institutions (Thomas, 1984).

The Transfer of Power: Impact on the State

World War II marked the beginning of the end of the colonial era and its autocratic rule. The war discredited the racist ideologies that had served to justify European colonialism. African participation in the war increased

Africans' aspirations for self-government by forcing them to question their subject status. The war weakened the will of the major colonial powers to maintain their overseas empires. At the same time, the governments of the European colonial powers came under the control of more liberal minded, anticolonial elites who were skeptical of the policies that their countries had been pursuing. In addition, the colonial powers were confronted with pressures for independence from all parts of the colonized world. France was confronted with pressures for independence in its colonies in Indochina and North Africa. Britain was similarly challenged in the Caribbean, the Middle East, and India. Belgium was involved in internal political turmoil over the status of the Belgian Congo. Throughout Europe the mood in the immediate postwar period regarding continued colonial rule was one of skepticism. This European climate combined with the push by African nationalists to set the stage for political decolonization.

Limited reforms within the framework of colonialism were extended to much of Africa after World War II. In 1945 all French African colonies were permitted to elect two representatives to the Constituent Assembly in Paris. The British enlarged Sierra Leone's Legislative Council and in 1951 held direct elections. In Uganda, Africans were first nominated to the Legislative Council in 1945, and the first direct elections were held in 1956. In the states with larger white settler populations, like Kenya, Southern Rhodesia, and Northern Rhodesia, electoral reforms were slower. Africans were not represented until 1954 in Kenya (whites won seats in 1937); in 1959 in Tanganyika ten seats were allotted to Africans; in 1958 in Northern Rhodesia eight Africans were elected to the Legislative Council; in 1957 in Southern Rhodesia, of the fifteen seats allotted for Africans, eight had to be selected by European settlers' votes. In the Belgian colonies, reforms were even slower. In 1960 in the Belgian Congo, only weeks before its independence, the first national elections were held. The Portuguese maintained extremely repressive regimes in their colonies, and no concessions were granted for political participation (Marable, 1987).

These limited reforms created some political space for the rise of nationalist mass parties. The mass parties were largely linked to trade unions or drew their primary electoral support from urban working classes or militant agricultural laborers in rural areas. Many former trade union activists later formed political parties: Siaka Stevens was general secretary of Sierra Leone's Mineworkers Union and later formed the All People's Congress; Joshua Nkomo, leading trade unionist in Southern Rhodesia, became president of Southern Rhodesia's African National Congress in 1957 and in 1961 head of the Zimbabwe African Peoples Union; Sekou Toure, trade unionist in Guinea, later joined Madeira Keita and Ray Autra to found the Democratic Party of Guinea (PDG), a section of the Rassemblement Developpement Africaine (RDA). In Tanzania dockworkers led successful strikes in 1947 and established an activist model of anticolonial struggle that directly contributed to the founding of the Tanganyika African National Union (TANU) in 1954.

The educated middle class consolidated its hold over the nationalist movements for independence, dominating the tiny industrial working class and the largely illiterate peasant class. For the most part, the leaders were all professionals or intellectuals: Ghana's Kwame Nkrumah and Kenya's Jomo Kenyatta were both college graduates; Senegal's Leopold Senghor, a Negritude poet; Sierra Leone's Milton Margai, a physician; Nigeria's Nnamdi Azikiwe, a college-educated businessman; Zambia's Kenneth Kaunda and Tanzania's Julius Nyerere, both school teachers; Zimbabwe's Robert Mugabe, a college graduate. Others started as petty entrepreneurs (e.g., Oginga Odinga of Kenya started the Luo Thrift and Trading Corporation). A few exceptions include Ahmadou Ahidjo, the first president of the Cameroon Republic and party leader of Union Camerounaise (UC), who began his political life as a telephone operator.

The experience of the anticolonial struggles influenced the complexion of African leadership for decades after independence. The colonial powers preferred to hand over power to "moderate" political elites with vested interests in maintaining a liberal democratic and capitalist order, rather than to "radicals" or grassroots activists among the working classes. With few exceptions in places like Angola, Cape Verde, Guinea-Bissau, Guinea, Mozambique, Namibia, and Zimbabwe, moderate members of the educated middle classes assumed the leadership of most of the nationalist movements. The moderate political leaders were often ready to compromise with past colonial institutions rather than transform them. Most of them agreed to continue to govern through the old autocratic colonial institutions with a degree of popular political mobilization. As political leadership distanced itself from the masses of the population, African leaders subsequently became more dependent on civil service bureaucrats and administrators for governing than on the population. The mass movement that had been key to the independence movement's success soon came to be perceived as a problem and mass participation as unnecessary.

Before long, the political elite united with state bureaucrats against the working classes. Many believe that the demise of the nationalist party that brought many African countries to independence was linked to its social composition, since it was dominated by the urbanized, educated middle classes. The teachers, civil servants, and other professionals of the colonial period became the politicians of the nationalist movement and the early postindependence period. As a social stratum, this group of political leaders, with a few exceptions, became primarily interested in acquiring access to state resources rather than forging social change (Hadjor, 1987). A majority of the nationalist leadership came to recognize that control of the state apparatus would provide access to a surplus that could be utilized for personal consumption and long-term accumulation. Once in charge of the administrative apparatus, the bureaucratic elites could promote its economic interests and those of its allies. Expatriates would be removed from the civil service, and public sector posts reallocated to friends and allies of the political elite. Administrative salaries would be expanded to meet class expectations. In Senegal, for example, 47.2 percent of the 1964–1965 budget was spent on administrative salaries alone; in the Central African Republic 58 percent was spent; in Dahomey 64.9 percent; in Kenya between 1963 and 1966 the salaries of Kenya members of Parliament were doubled to 1,210 pounds annually. Junior ministers received 2,260 pounds a year, and President Kenyatta was granted a tax free annual stipend of 15,000 pounds (Marable, 1987).

Although the colonial state machinery remained largely intact throughout Africa and broad sectors of the population were excluded from the transfer of power, political independence had real significance across the continent. The transition from colonial to postcolonial state structures involved a qualitative change. For instance, expansion of state functions and modifications in methods of rule were significant. The most important aspects of this expansion included the diversification of foreign relations and foreign trade (although economic and military agreements were often entered into with former colonial powers); state expansion into the rural sector through rural development projects, marketing boards, and the provision of electricity and piped water; promotion of import-substituting industrialization in alliance with foreign capital; creation of other national institutions; and the expansion of state property (Thomas, 1984). The emerging form was that of a postcolonial state that boldly and systematically intervened in the economy in areas that had formerly been the exclusive preserve of the metropole. However, the postcolonial state's capture of significant sectors of the economy did not necessarily mean that substantive changes were always made in the colonial nexus.

The postcolonial state was forced to try to build a nation on the foundations laid down by the colonial state. Europe transferred its own state system to Africa without considering whether a congruence existed between this system and the African nation—its social and ethnic groups—or even whether cultural similarities existed among the different units being ruled by the same colonial government. Most of the European countries that colonized Africa had achieved a coincidence between nationhood and statehood at home. In virtually every European country a single cultural group comprised more than half of the population and in many cases more than two-thirds. Highly fragmented countries like Yugoslavia were the exception rather than the rule. In Africa, by contrast, ethnically fragmented countries are the rule. Only in a small number of countries is there one ethnic group that comprises more than half of the population. It was very difficult for postcolonial political leaders, with no unified political tradition, to build a political community out of these ethnically fragmented states.

The colonial powers had tried to use ethnicity to divide the nationalist movements, and it remained a factor at independence. Some nationalist parties were able to resist ethnic divisions. In Senegal, Senghor's Bloc Democratique Senegalais (BDS), founded in 1948, campaigned against ethnic divisions. The party courted various class and ethnic blocs and had a catch-all coalition held together by patronage. The National Council of Nigeria and the Cameroons (NCNC), led by Nnamdi Azikiwe, was dominated by Ibos, but it attempted to project a multiethnic front against British colonialism; in Kenya, KANU included the nation's largest ethnic bloc, the Kikuyu, and Luo but also included smaller ethnic groups (Marable, 1987).

The development of ethnic politics between 1950 and 1960 tended to occur in states that had one or more of the following characteristics: several dominant ethnic groups possessed traditional hierarchical political structures, which in turn exercised local hegemony over other smaller ethnic communities; the transitional colonial state apparatus permitted or encouraged the growth of regional or local power centers led by traditional chiefs, rural entrepreneurs, or ethnically-oriented urban leaders; trade unions and other multiethnic associations were particularly weak. The 1951 MacPherson constitution, for example, divided Nigeria into three regions and encouraged ethnic minorities to create their own regional microparties: the AG (Western Action groups), the NCNC (east) and the NPC (Northern Peoples Congress). No single nationalist party with a significant cross section of the working classes, of many ethnic backgrounds, would ever emerge in Nigeria.

In British East Africa, except in Tanganyika, a similar process occurred. In Uganda the first political parties, formed in the early 1950s, represented Western-educated elites—the Democratic Party (DP), led by Catholic middle strata from the Buganda ethnic group, and the Protestant-oriented Uganda National Congress (UNC). Both organizations were soon superseded by two very different movements. Milton Obote led a fraction of former UNC radical nationalists to form a conservative, federalist state in Uganda that preserved political privileges won by the Buganda elites under British rule. In order to secure independence, Obote's Uganda Peoples Congress (UPC) and the traditionalist Kabaka Yekka, the ruling authority of the kingdom of Buganda, united temporarily, winning the 1962 elections. Obote's non-Baganda majority gradually eroded the political influence of the Kabaka and the traditional chiefs. Finally in 1966 Obote purged the government of his opponents and ordered the army to occupy the Kingdom of Buganda. The Kabaka Yekka was destroyed; later, all traditional kinship positions of the Ankole and other ethnic substates were also eliminated. Ethnicism was an important weapon used by the departing European colonial powers to guarantee continued social divisions within their former colonies. The colonial powers did not want to transfer power to mass parties with radical leaders in positions of state authority.

Reflecting the survival from the colonial value system of the tendency to elevate political leaders as if they were mythical figures, African political leaders were given enormous amounts of power by those they governed, allowing them the authority to carry out actions that were inconsistent with a democratic pluralist system of government. In most of the new postcolonial states, the administrative apparatus provided the context for any authoritarian impulses that bureaucratic elites may have developed. Many former French colonies (e.g., Senegal, Tunisia, Madagascar, Mauritania, Gabon, Guinea, Côte d'Ivoire, Niger) adopted constitutions patterned after the Gaullist constitution of the 1958 Fifth Republic, which gave supreme authority to the president, greatly curtailing the powers of the Parliament. Accordingly these constitutions provided for strong executives elected by universal suffrage. In former British territories the executive systems were more diverse. Tanzania used direct elections for the presidency; in Kenya the president was chosen by the House of Representatives; in Zambia the National Assembly elected the president. Other states created dual-executive parliamentary systems with a weak president as nominal head of state and a powerful prime minister (e.g., Sierra Leone, Nigeria, Uganda, The Gambia, Somalia).

Despite their range of constitutional variation, most postcolonial African regimes had several basic similarities that directly reflected their colonial government predecessors. First, all chief executives were granted extraordinary powers by their respective constitutions. They made all military and most civil appointments and issued decrees or ordinances; some (in former British colonies) named chief justices and all other Supreme Court judges; and many could declare a state of emergency, suspending civil and political liberties. The inevitable political by-product of a powerful executive system was the tendency toward a single party and the dominance of a single person over others; this in turn created a tendency for loyalty to center on single figures rather than party structures. Despite differences in ideology, this tendency was marked throughout postcolonial Africa (Kenyatta in Kenya, Sekou Toure in Guinea, Nyerere in Tanzania).

Conclusion

The foundation of modern African politics was partially established during the historical period of capitalist-colonial domination of Africa. In order to understand fully the politics of the postindependence state in Africa, one needs a clear understanding of the colonial state itself. The colonial state left a destructive legacy to postindependence Africa: centralized and coercive governance, arbitrary boundaries, arbitrary power unaccountable to those ruled, integration of African economies into European economies, a state-controlled economy, and the transformation of African indigenous structures to suit the interests of the metropolitan powers. Patrick Chabal (1992) correctly describes the colonial state as not just a political entity but the focal point of the drive for political and economic hegemony. Those who seek access to state power do so with the intent to use the state apparatus to gain hegemonic control of both political and economic resources. It is the mechanism by which hegemony is achieved that is explained in Chapter 4.

For Further Reading

Rodney, Walter (1972). *How Europe Underdeveloped Africa*. London: Bogle L'Ouverture.

Boahen, Adu (1987). *African Perspectives on Colonialism*. London: James Currey.

Young, Crawford (1988). "The African Colonial State and its Political Legacy," in Donald Rothchild and Naomi Chazan, eds., *The Precarious Balance: State and Society in Africa*. Boulder, Colo., and London: Westview Press. 25–66.

Chabal, Patrick (1992). *Power in Africa*. London: Macmillan.

Davidson, Basil (1994). *Modern Africa: A Social and Political History*. London and New York: Longman.

4
—
The Dominance of the State: Domestic and External Factors

The 1960s marked the advent of political independence for the vast majority of sub-Saharan African countries. The colonial state had the resources of the economic power centers of the world at its disposal. It accumulated capital on a global scale, and it integrated colonial economies into worldwide systems of exchange, trade, markets, investments, and profit generation. The state was assumed at independence to have preserved intact its ability to create, mobilize, and direct economies and social development in the same way as the colonial state. The African population expected the decolonized state that inherited power at independence to operate with the same administrative political capacity that existed under colonialism and to be able to deliver the benefits of independence and freedom. However, the decolonized state had a diminished resource base (e.g., insufficient university graduates to staff major positions, declining state revenues) and could not find adequate resources to direct rapid economic and social progress.

Despite these weaknesses vis-à-vis the colonial state, at independence the postcolonial state was the preeminent institution in society. It was the largest single employer of labor and had access to domestic

resources and investment funds from abroad. It was not only a political institution but the most powerful economic force in the society. With weak and
underdeveloped private sectors, economic success became linked to access to
the state's resources. Everyone soon realized that the only road to prosperity
was through access to the state. Civil servants and bureaucrats realized that
employment in the public sector gave them a privileged position over the distribution of resources: licenses, contracts, scholarships, and leases soon became important political tools. The state became so critical for sustaining the
rich that it became a battleground where elites competed for scarce resources.
For the elites the loss of influence over the state meant the loss of everything.
Losing an office meant losing not only political influence but also access to
economic resources. The state thus also held the power to determine the success or failure of economic actors. Political conflicts in sub-Saharan Africa
have played out within the state—the established public arena for the resolution or mediation of conflict. Because of its control of political and economic
power relative to other groups in the society the postcolonial state emerged as
the key to the structure of African politics.

This chapter seeks to identify the most general themes that describe the
"stuff" of African politics and indicate the reasons for the dominance of the
state in the postindependence period. The premise of the chapter is that
informal political institutions—most significantly clientelism—have had a
central role in African political life over the past four decades and have been
at the center of state-society relations. I have chosen clientelism for analysis
because I believe it is the most useful analytical tool in helping to explain
micropolitical behavior in sub-Saharan Africa. Further, clientelism is also
related to the macropolitical and economic environment within African
countries and in the international arena, whence most of the resources with
which they operate must come.

Clientelism

Clientelism is defined as a reciprocal exchange of goods and/or services on a
personal level between two unequal parties. A clientelistic political system is
based on the exchange of material rewards for political support. If the state
in which such a system operates functions as a competitive party system,
client aggregations will form voting blocs to support the patron in elections.

Clientelism is likely to flourish where there is inequality of wealth and
power, since those relations develop, by definition, between unequal parties.
But inequities in access to vital resources alone are not sufficient to promote
the expansion of patron-client ties. If this was the case, patron-client
ties would predominate everywhere. A necessary condition of patron-client

politics is the absence of institutional guarantees for an individual's security, status, and wealth (Stone, 1980a).

Clientelistic exchanges generally (but not always) arise in face-to-face relationships that create feelings of affection and trust between the partners. The clientelistic bond is often centered on a dyadic (two-person) relationship between a poor person and a more powerful political figure. The maintenance of this relationship is based upon repetition of specific acts of material exchange as well as the personal bond created between patron and client.

In Powell's definition (1970), patron-client relations are emphasized as two-person links. However, more complex forms do exist, such as multiperson patron-broker-client systems involving large numbers of people and sometimes an entire community. In the latter form, brokers (intermediaries) exist as connectors between aggregates of people and patrons and also as "interfaces" linking communities to the larger society (Scott, 1972). The basic function of the broker is to "relate community-oriented individuals who want to stabilize or improve their life-chances but who lack economic security and political connections with national-oriented individuals" (Wolf, 1971: 61). F. G. Bailey further describes the village broker as "the man who makes a profession of helping officials or politicians and peasants to communicate with one another, and is paid either directly or indirectly for doing so" (1971: 311). The characteristics of patron-client relationships and brokerage are similar: reciprocity, inequality, and face-to-face contact. Both two-person (patron-client dyad) and multiperson (patron-client pyramid) types of clientelistic relationships exist in Africa (Lemarchand, 1988).

The concepts *patron, broker, client, dyad, reciprocity,* and *exchange* are most relevant to the political systems of Africa where extreme inequality of access to power, wealth, property, and social opportunity created conditions conducive to clientelism. Informal social patterns of clientelism evolved in the precolonial and colonial social structures as privileged classes developed ties of mutual obligation with the poor by acting as patrons facilitating access to scarce resources. During the nationalist movement for independence, nationalist leaders built their authority on promises to deliver material advantages denied to ordinary people under colonialism. In the early years following independence, when competitive party politics existed in most sub-Saharan African countries, the new political leaders constructed personal networks through which they traded the goods and services of independence in return for political loyalty (Bratton, 1994). Competitive party politics extended, elaborated, and incorporated informal social patterns of clientelism as a central base of power in the political system (Stone, 1980a). With the collapse of competitive party politics in most sub-Saharan African countries within the first decade after independence, clientelistic loyalties survived in the new military, noncommunist single-party, and communist single-party systems.

It must be noted that clientelism is not unique to political systems of the developing nations of the world. The political structures of North America and western and southern Europe also contain considerable patron-client relationships. Machine politics (city boss politics), campaign contributions, interest group organization, electoral politics, hierarchies within legislatures and the bureaucracy, and even the court system, all involve patron-client relationships. The wealthier industrialized countries clearly still contain some clientelism but for the most part have moved beyond it. Patron-client relationships now occupy a less significant place in the politics of wealthier countries than in those of the poorer countries of the world. Individuals in the former can rise high in institutions or enter politics without personally exchanging goods and services with anyone. In the latter, it would be rare to find someone involved in politics who is not a part of a patron-client network. It is possible to receive substantial material rewards in the United States, for example, without involvement in a patron-client network. It is possible but much less likely in the world's poorer countries. The reason is that clientelism thrives in situations of scarce resources. Many developing countries have been ruled by clientelism and have not yet moved beyond it in the postindependence period, because the economic situation that perpetuates it still exists.

Forms of Clientelism in sub-Saharan Africa

Party Clientelism

Carl Stone argues that clientelism emerged in competitive party systems in Third World countries as a function of partisan competitiveness. In these systems the emphasis on material and social inducements in exchange for political support became institutionalized where competition for party loyalties sharpened in situations of severe social deprivation. By extension, modern forms of clientelism in poorer nations can be linked to the decolonization period, when competitive party politics were introduced under universal adult suffrage:

> Clientelism as a power structure usually emerges in Third World countries
> where imperialist interests disengage from the management of state power,
> handing over the machinery of government to the emerging politically-dominant
> petty bourgeois leaders. These leaders harness the state as a resource from which
> to establish a power structure that competes with and parallels the old and
> continuing power structure rooted in the ownership of the forces of production
> by local and foreign capitalist interests (Stone, 1980a: 93).

Decolonization accelerated the shift from traditional clientelism to political patronage by providing the conditions for popular participation in electoral politics. With the rise of nationalist party machines across sub-Saharan Africa (e.g., Kenya [KANU], Ghana [CPP], The Gambia [PPP] and Zambia [United National Independence Party (UNIP)]) the vote emerged as a critical political resource that was traded for material rewards (e.g., schools, piped water, jobs, scholarships, food, clothing). Party politicians supplanted the traditional patrons (e.g., chiefs, leaders of kinship groups, religious leaders) as the key recipients of patronage from the state's coffers. They became the new intermediaries between the state and the people at the local level.

The Gambia

Elite-mass clientelism was extensive only in those countries where electoral pressures and party competition existed and where the public sector was large enough to accommodate an extensive patronage system. The political leaders constructed personal networks through which they traded the goods and services of "development" in return for political loyalty. In The Gambia, a competitive party system existed for twenty-nine years (1965–1994) before it was overthrown by the military. During that period only one party, Dawda Jawara's Peoples Progressive Party (PPP) held state power. The opposition and its followers attributed clientelist political behavior as the major factor for PPP dominance of the state for almost three decades.

Party clientelism by the PPP government was facilitated by the 1970s policy of "Gambianization" of the economy. Gambianization refers to a process of indigenization whereby many Gambians were hired in civil service positions and the Gambian government took control of many sectors of the economy. Gambianization led to a 75 percent increase in total government employment over the 1975–1980 period: the civil service increased from 4,000 civil servants and 2,000 nonpermanent staff in 1975 to 10,700 civil servants and 5,000 nonpermanent staff in 1985. Public sector investment geared mainly to the urban areas increased rapidly from 21 million dalasi (D) in 1975–1976 to D45.3 million in 1976–1977 and D93.6 million in 1977–1978 (Hadjimichael,Rumbaugh, and Verreydt, 1992: 19). The middle and professional classes, living in the urban areas, benefited from civil service expansion and public sector investment.

Lower-income PPP supporters became absorbed into a party-based system financed by a public sector budget that reflected development expenditures totaling D350 million over the 1975–1980 period, as compared to the D175 million originally projected (Hadjimichael et al., 1992: 19). Patronage networks favoring PPP supporters have been noted by both PPP government officials and the opposition and its supporters. In urban areas opposition parties alleged "vote buying." Some PPP government officials conceded that they had heard of cases of people selling their voter cards or some other critical resources (Edie, 2000). In 1992 an opposition Member of Parliament (MP) confirmed this to me:

> During Presidential election campaigns, party activists dole out money to buy votes. People can buy voting cards. They take an opposition party card and confiscate it and offer that potential voter a sum of money. In this way, it is ensured that the opposition does not get the vote. Lots of inducements are offered during the election period (Edie, 2000: 15).

The poor were faced with the choice of selling their voters' cards or refusing resources needed for daily sustenance. Self-preservation under conditions of severe poverty seemed to be the most significant factor considered by many Gambians, as they accepted rice, money, and other resources from politicians in exchange for their votes. Vote buying was alleged in The Gambia even as far back as the 1962 elections, when the Muslim Congress Party leader I. Garba-Jahumpa believed he lost his seat to the United Party (UP) member because the UP paid for many of its votes (Rice, 1967).

In rural Gambia multiperson patronage networks flourished during PPP rule. Divisional commissioners, *alkalos* (village heads), *kabilos* (heads of lineage units), and chiefs were almost exclusively PPP supporters, creating a line of patronage extending from the central government down to the village level. They all served as brokers for the PPP government, assigning voter registration cards to eligible voters. People in the community who were dependent on them for resources (which they received from the central government for community development) may not have wanted to vote against the party of their choice because they feared repression. An opposition *kabilo* leader explained the patronage network favoring PPP supporters:

> If resources come through government they tend to leave it with PPP supporters and at times there is friction. Some years ago on the food for work programme the opposition was never happy because the food wasn't shared properly. The policy is one which the government come[s] and operate[s] through the *alkalo*. The PPP people are informed about food for work—they select their own labourers and go and pick up the food from the divisional capital. They would be paid before distributing it. At every juncture resources are diverted politically, right from the top. The minister gives resources to the commissioner, and when he distributes it to the district and villages it comes to the village and the PPP members benefit (Davis, Hulme, and Woodhouse, 1994: 263).

Mali

During the 1960s the Union Soudanaise Party that came to power in Mali changed Mali's policy from private sector marketing to government marketing of peanuts as well as introducing consumer's cooperatives that offered no credit to buyers (Hopkins, 1969). These statist policies reduced the status of the merchants and brought large numbers of salaried civil servants to Kita (a city in rural Mali). Political party functionaries subsequently became influential in the power structure of the community, and contending groups (including kinship leaders, merchants, civil servants) vied for these party posts. The population turned to party leaders to get children accepted into schools, find jobs and house lots, obtain redress for unfair treatment by government employees, or avoid destitution. Since this was an important aspect of maintaining popularity and winning reelection, party leaders generally responded to such requests for help. The help generally received was limited and involved pressuring a civil servant to comply with the request.

In Mali, in Africa in general, and in most developing nations a very important linkage mechanism between the poor and the political party is the bureaucratic intermediation performed by party politicians and civil servants working in the state bureaucracy. Party leaders, upon their constituents' request, intervene personally in bureaucratic procedures for their own political ends. Bureaucratic functions have become personalized as the bureaucracy has become a source of patronage in the form of jobs. The necessities of day-to-day life—documents required for admission to school or to a hospital, passports, job applications, and the like—are not easily obtained. It is often only by the personal intervention of an influential intermediary that the poor can obtain any immediate result. The poor are constrained to seek assistance from the party leader who can intervene on their behalf.

Senegal

According to Christian Coulon (1988), in the political culture of Senegal honor and integrity are linked to the politician's capacity to distribute patronage. During the 1993 legislative elections, opposition candidates in the department of Mbacka accused Bassirou Ndao, deputy of the Socialist Party (PS), of stealing large sums of money from the Senegalese lottery, LONASE, during his tenure as its director. Despite the serious charges the scandal did not hurt Ndao's popularity among his constituents, who saw themselves as beneficiaries of his largesse and reelected him to office (Beck, 1999). He was reelected by a decisive majority but was an embarrassment to the PS and was not reappointed to his ministerial post. Ultimately his lack of access to state resources eventually led his supporters in Mbacka to dismiss him as the local leader of the PS (Beck, 1999). This reaction of the Senegalese citizens will not surprise observers from other African countries or many other developing nations, as it reflects the concern of the population in developing nations with politicians' capacity to access and distribute public resources through informal patronage networks. In many developing countries, especially the most resource poor among them, it is openly recognized and accepted that rewards will be distributed according to the subject's loyalty to his or her leader. Party leaders and officials are expected to use their influence to get favors for their loyal constituency. The relationship between the elected representatives and the constituent is asymmetrical politically but reciprocal. The constituents compete among themselves for favors from the politicians, and the latter try to grant these favors so that they can be reelected. There is thus an interdependence between the politicians and their constituents.

Nigeria

Despite its formal commitment to promoting a private-enterprise economy, Nigeria, like most sub-Saharan African countries, pursued statist economic policies carried over from the colonial era. By the mid-1960s, public enterprises proliferated in Nigeria, ranging from "farm organizations to manufacturing, from municipal transport to mining, from housing to multi-purpose power, and from trading to banking and insurance" (Aboyade, 1980: 86). Under subsequent military and civilian rule, the state's economic role expanded further. The vast expansion of Nigeria's oil industry during the 1970s and its gradual nationalization led to a swollen treasury, excessive spending of national resources, and a bitter struggle for control of state power.

It was not surprising that Nigeria's brief periods of competitive party politics (1960–1966, 1979–1983) featured a political life characterized predominantly by clientelistic relations. Claude Ake acknowledged the mounting political tensions and problems in Nigeria during this period: "The crux of the problem is the overpoliticisation of social life . . . we are intoxicated with politics. The premium on political power is so high that we are prone to take the most extreme measure to win and to maintain political power" (Ake, 1981b: 1162–1163). General Murtala Muhammed (Nigerian military ruler, 1975–1976) echoed the same sentiment, commenting that during the First Republic "winning elections became a life and death struggle which justifies all means—fair or foul" (Lagos, 1976, cited in Joseph, 1983: 21).

Local communities were linked to the central government through an intricate network of patron-client ties. At the top of the patron-client pyramid were individual officeholders in the federal and state capitals. Joseph (1983: 28) cites a letter sent from businessman Haroun Adamu to the *Sunday Times* in Lagos, Nigeria, that vividly captures the clientelistic norms of Nigeria's political economy:

> A young businessman, whose contact with various groups in the state is tops, would like to know from me whether those in authority over there in Lagos are aware that they in Bauchi have no representation in the Federal Government.

> "What do you mean?" I asked.

"It is that simple," he said, "we have no one in the Supreme Military Council; we have no one in the National Council of State and we have no one in the Federal Executive Council."

"Would the state have fared any better if you had anyone in those bodies?" I countered.

"Sure. When I come to Lagos on business, I do not have anyone to go to with my problems to help me solve them. That's the difference."

During the First (1960–1966) and Second (1979–1983) Republics, clientelism provided the linkage between village and state capital in Nigeria. Nigerian party formation consisted of bitter competition to recruit people whose affiliation meant the inclusion of a community of followers (Joseph, 1983). Both Joseph (1983) and Diamond (1983) note that this was an important feature of party politics during Nigeria's Second Republic. Federal, state, and local politicians fulfilled a strategic brokering role on behalf of different ethnoregional groups. Nigerian political parties were little more than a collection of notables held together by clientelism and the promise of access to state resources. They were rarely effective at the grassroots level and lacked significant mobilizational capacity. The parties tended to be differentiated less by ideology or policy than by the narrow interests of clientelistic networks typically organized around one person. Few Nigerian political parties could gain a national as opposed to regional constituency, resulting in highly divided legislatures in which polarization was fueled by ethnic conflict (Collier, 1982). Clientelist political behavior was eventually destructive. Competition for access to resources between ethnically defined constituencies within a system of electoral politics (1960–1966 and 1979–1983) suffered the same ultimate fate in Nigeria's First and Second Republics and in many countries of sub-Saharan Africa in the first decade after independence: the collapse of civilian government and its removal by the military. The First and Second Republics' democratically elected governments in Nigeria were overthrown largely by the venality of elected officials, who used their public offices to gain access to state resources to obtain further partisan advantages and enrich themselves. The civilian governments alienated the population so completely that the latter welcomed the military coups that terminated the competitive party systems.

The Private Sector as Client of the Political Elite

During much of the colonial period, colonial authorities promoted foreign economic interests (both large multinational companies and resident non-African businesses) at the expense of indigenous African entrepreneurs. At independence, African entrepreneurship was minimal and at the lower end of the commercial hierarchy, while the higher echelons were controlled by foreign and non-African resident capital (Kennedy, 1988). Because business groups had played only a limited role in the nationalist movements for independence, business elites were poorly represented in the newly formed postindependence governments. The new state controllers were politically autonomous from African business interests, but the latter were dependent on the former for economic policies favorable to their capital accumulation. Local business called for state support (e.g., preferential access to credit, contracts, and business training programs) and demanded that foreign and non-African resident capital be restricted from certain economic sectors to protect domestic entrepreneurs from competition in areas where they were most actively involved.

In countries such as Ethiopia, Mozambique, and Tanzania, where the ideology of the political leaders was Marxist and socialist, the demands of the indigenous business met with hostility. Socialist ideology mandated state control of the economy. Private companies were severely restricted, while government-owned enterprises monopolized most economic sectors with privileged access to state-controlled credit, contracts, and licenses. In the majority of African countries, where Marxist and socialist ideology was not embraced, state-controlling elites were also reluctant to see the emergence of a strong class of local capital that could challenge the state's power. The state's preoccupation was with the creation of a large public economic sector that could distribute patronage. Therefore in most sub-Saharan African countries the opportunities for private capital accumulation were closely regulated by the state, the state itself offering support to African private enterprise. A small group of wealthy entrepreneurs did emerge in most African countries, but these were political clients loyal to and dependent on the state-controlling political elites and were unable to become an autonomous group in the political or economic arena.

In countries such as Côte d'Ivoire, Kenya, and Botswana, the government actively nurtured a capitalist class that emerged in commerce, construction, and industry. In these countries the capitalist class had some weight within the new governments at independence and was able to push for policies favorable to its interests. The state provided valuable support in the forms of credit, contracts, and concessions. Yet even among these countries there was much state economic ownership since the political elites saw a state-run economy as essential for consolidating their power. There were therefore limits placed on the extent to which business was encouraged to expand and engage in competition with the state. The African capitalist class was allowed to develop only as a dependent client of state elites. The scope for a large private sector was thereby curtailed, and the larger capitalists who emerged were foreigners and non-African residents who were close allies of the leading politicians and bureaucrats and dependent on them for sponsorship, commercial opportunities, and economic successes.

State elites have relied on patron-client ties to control the associations of indigenous business interests. Businesspeople have had to use the patronage networks of incumbent regimes, which have ensured that business supports rather than challenges the political order and accepts major economic policy decisions. Business leaders need to rely on patron-client networks because their economic weaknesses have persisted: they need funding from the state, licenses, contracts, concessions; they do not have staff, expertise, information, or resources to undertake strong lobbying with government, and they are plagued by internal divisions based on diverse economic interests. Many businesses prefer to enter into patron-client relations with individuals in the government instead of organizing business interest groups to represent the collective interests of their members. Informal channels and personal contacts in the state apparatus have been the most common and preferred route used by African entrepreneurs in pursuing their interests.

Many business leaders fear government retaliation if they should try to advance and defend their interests. The government could deny access to import licenses and foreign exchange or call in bank loans prematurely, causing great hardship, even the collapse of some firms. In Kenya during the 1980s, President Moi's administration attempted to deny many Kikuyu businessmen opposed to the KANU government the economic support they needed and worked with Asian businessmen to undercut Kikuyu economic power. In Ghana in 1993 President Rawlings demanded that the general public not buy products from some local private business interests, as they were allegedly using their profits to finance opposition political parties (Tangri, 1998).

With the introduction of neoliberal economic reforms under IMF-sponsored structural adjustment programs since the mid-1980s, international financial institutions have increased their leverage in African economies and politics. Since the IMF and the World Bank advocate a leading role for the private sector in the Africa's economic recovery, they believe it must become an important part of discussions of strategies of development. With World Bank assistance, a Private Sector Advisory Group was established in 1991 in Ghana, but it has failed to increase state-business interaction. The Jerry Rawlings regime in Ghana was not willing to deal with business groups that actively supported opposition parties in the 1992 elections (Tangri, 1998).

Despite IMF pressures to recognize domestic private sector leadership, during the decade of the 1990s many African leaders were still reluctant to do so, especially in development. The private sector has been politically and economically weak and, without state support, realistically cannot play the leading role that it has been accorded by the international lending agencies in Africa's economic transformation. Most African governments have not accepted that they must create an enabling environment for the private sector to play the leading role in national economic expansion. If they surrender this role to the private sector, they would also relinquish their control over economic resources for patronage. If a mainly market-based economy with a dominant private sector emerged, there would be no need for state economic institutions and no basis for clientelism.

The political changes leading to incipient democratization across sub-Saharan Africa since 1990 (discussed in Chapter 6) have allowed some business organizations to become more outspoken in criticizing state economic policy that directly threatens their business interests. Business organizations such as the Ghana Union Traders Association (GUTA) and the Uganda Importers, Exporters and Traders Association (UGIETA) challenged the government in their respective countries publicly over issues such as tariffs and the functioning of customs bureaucracies and have been at the forefront of political confrontations attacking the introduction of a value added tax (VAT). The governments of Ghana and Uganda have reacted to strikes and demonstrations by the business associations with repression. Leaders of strikes have been openly intimidated and threatened with loss of their trading licenses (Tangri, 1998).

At the end of the 1990s, the state still maintained the upper hand over domestic business interests in sub-Saharan Africa. Business interests (especially in manufacturing) still required protection from the state, so their dependence on state support continued. Because of this dependence, private business interests rarely speak out publicly against those in control of the state. Businesspeople did form a part of the civil society's protests against authoritarianism in the early 1990s (see Chapter 6) but rarely spoke out on explicitly and purely political matters. In Zambia, business groups were among many protesting against the incumbent Kaunda-led UNIP government but have been silent about the prevalent authoritarianism of the new Movement for Multi-Party Democracy (MMD) government. In Nigeria the Babangida military regime's annulment of the 1993 election hardly drew a response from the private sector. In Kenya in the 1990s business associations offered little backing to those organizations questioning rampant human rights abuses and violations. Business demands, when they have been made, tend to be focused on economic issues. The reasons are that authoritarian tendencies have persisted among African leaders despite incipient democratization in the 1990s and that political leaders still have ample patronage possibilities at their disposal to use as leverage on the weak and vulnerable private sector (Tangri, 1998).

State Bureaucracies as Bastions of Patronage

The Civil Service

With the end of competitive party politics by the late 1960s in most sub-Saharan African countries and the rise of repression, access to public resources became limited to a small circle of elites. Patronage practices have continued, but its political importance has been superseded by the distribution of public offices that benefit only a few highly privileged people (van de Walle, 1994b). In the absence of electoral pressures, patronage operations centered on the civil service, the army, and the police.

The African civil service has been a bastion of patronage in the postindependence period. As patronage drove political leaders to expand the ranks of the civil service, it consumed increasingly large shares of the national budget. Even military governments in countries like Ghana and Nigeria used senior civil servants to manage the state apparatus (Wunsch and Olowu, 1990). The Kenyatta regime relied on the civil service to ensure social control and limit political participation (Bienen, 1974). Zambia's Kenneth Kaunda's UNIP government relied almost exclusively on the distribution of material inducements for political survival. Kaunda neutralized his opponents and retained his supporters by finding them public sector or party jobs or other opportunities to benefit from political connections. The clientelistic basis of Kaunda's regime wasted resources, fostered corruption, and resulted in the hiring of unqualified and redundant employees into the civil service and parastatals (African state corporations). For most of his three decades in power Kaunda was able to demonstrate concretely that "it pays to belong to the UNIP." Ultimately the UNIP's patronage capacity diminished, arrested by a combination of external economic shocks and internal economic mismanagement. Neoliberal economic reforms led to the gradual withdrawal of subsidies on food and other vital commodities. Kenneth Kaunda and UNIP were subsequently defeated by Frederick Chiluba's MMD in 1992, in the country's first multiparty elections in over three decades (see Chapter 6).

A census of their civil services carried out by the Central African Republic and the Republic of Guinea in the mid-1980s discovered that 1,300 and 7,000 employees, respectively, were "phantom workers," bogus employees whose salaries were pocketed by those in on the scam (World Bank, 1988: 116, cited in Sandbrook, 1993: 43). In Cameroon the civil service roughly doubled in size within several years of Paul Biya's accession to the presidency in 1983. Biya secured and strengthened his position by finding jobs for hundreds of unemployed secondary school and university graduates from his home area of southern Cameroon. Tanzania, a country known for the honesty and integrity of its top leadership under the administration of Julius Nyerere (1961–1985), also had a pervasive patron-client system. Political patrons secured positions in the civil service and parastatals for educated middle-class clients, who owed loyalty to these patrons rather than to their hierarchical superiors (Sandbrook, 1993: 47).

The president's own clientelistic networks, rather than civil servants, generally have held most of the power. Civil servants have accommodated themselves to the realities of clientelist rule, have benefited from it, but at the same time have been frustrated by some of its features and deficiencies.

Civil servants benefit from clientelist rule in that many of them acquired their jobs as a result of political patronage. However, in many instances, economic crises led to policies which resulted in the lowering or freezing of public sector salaries. Civil servants are frustrated by these polices as their clientelistic connections can not always insulate them from the impact of reduction in public sector expenditures. Some civil servants were devastated by the economic crisis of the 1980s, which led to lower real public sector salaries. Many senior civil servants lost up to 90 percent of their purchasing power over the course of the 1970s and 1980s.

Civil servants have typically been a part of the alliance that promoted democratization in many sub-Saharan African countries in the early 1990s. Democratic transition led to less personalized rule and reinforced the power of ministerial staffs in more transparent (an open political process where elected officials are accountable to those whom they represent), cabinet-driven governments (Bratton and van de Walle, 1997). This would be to the political benefit of civil servants.

The Military

Under both civilian and military regimes, elite rule has continued despite reconstitutions of state power. Economic changes under military regimes have frequently taken the form of a redistribution of economic power among the elite, with the armed forces taking a larger share than before. In Ghana, under the Ankrah regime (1966–1969), army budget allocations increased by an annual 22 percent, the police and civil service received salary increases, but funds for social services in the rural areas were cut drastically. In Congo-Brazzaville pay increases of 20 to 40 percent for the army and civil service followed the Ngouabi military coup. In Uganda under Idi Amin there was widespread military corruption and the sacrificing of domestic needs to pay for an increased military. The regimes of Presidents Bokassa (Central African Republic) and Mobutu Sese Seko (former Zaire) have been notorious for treating national treasuries as private treasure chests (Mazrui and Tidy, 1984: 262).

In many civilian authoritarian regimes in sub-Saharan Africa the military occupied a privileged place. Those rulers who relied on coercion for regime survival had to pay a high price for military support. To keep the military content, political leaders granted to individual officers and military units generous perks, privileges, and rewards, including access to rents and commercial networks. The size of the military budget does not always reflect the full scope of the favors extended to a small number of key officers or a reliable presidential guard. In Kenneth Kaunda's Zambia in the late 1980s the army received the highest proportion of the national budget of any African country at peace, equivalent to over 3 percent of GDP. Yet the military did not play a significant part in Kaunda's system of personal rule and consistently remained outside political life (Bratton and van de Walle, 1997: 244). Giving the military generous budgetary allocations, however, may have decreased the risk of military intervention in Zambia. Weaning the military and other groups from clientelist benefits to which they had become accustomed during three decades of UNIP rule was partly responsible for Kaunda's UNIP defeat in the multiparty elections of 1992.

Presidentialism: Clientelism and Personal Rule

Presidentialism is defined as "the systematic concentration of political power in the hands of one individual, who resists delegating all but most trivial decision-making tasks" (Bratton and van de Walle, 1997: 63). In postindependence Africa personal dictators asserted total control over formal political structures (Callaghy, 1984), thus weakening them while multiplying public offices and increasing the size of governments. Power was deeply personalized, and political life structured around dyadic exchanges between "strongmen" and their followers, which together comprised clientelist pyramids.

These personalistic rulers promoted and encouraged a cult of personality. They dominated the national media, their images and pictures appeared on the national currency and public buildings and billboards in capitals, and the national printing presses periodically published collections of their speeches and writings. Some of them were presented as larger-than-life figures, "godlike," with magical qualities. Many of them preempted their own removal by declaring themselves "president for life." Noted personal rulers, like Kenneth Kaunda (Zambia), Sekou Toure (Guinea), Felix Houphouet-Boigny (Côte d'Ivoire), Jean Bokassa (Central African Republic), Hastings Banda (Malawi), and Mobutu Sese Seko (Zaire), have left a deep personal imprint on political life in all these countries. Personal rulers have remained in power for much longer periods than leaders in other regime types. Despite the frequency of coups d'etat and political instability, the average African leader from independence to 1987 still retained power considerably longer than their counterparts in postcolonial Latin America or Asia (Bratton and van de Walle, 1992).

Mobutu: An Example of Personal Rule

Postindependence Zaire provides an example of an African state plagued by continuous economic, social, and political crises affecting the majority of its citizens. Zairians have endured two wars in Zaire's Shaba province, economic decline, and oppressive state policies that have alienated most social groups and created conditions leading to mass poverty. With abundant mineral resources and high prospects for development at independence, Zaire has been an amazing disappointment. At the heart of this tragedy was its

Zairians singing praises to Mobutu.

former president, the late Mobutu Sese Seko. While his country's per-capita income hovered below $200 from 1967 to 1997, Mobutu emerged as one of the world's wealthiest leaders, with an estimated fortune of several billions, properties all over Western Europe and Africa, and capital stashed away in Swiss banks.

Mobutu's Zaire has been characterized in various ways in the literature— "kleptocracy," "predatory state," "patrimonial regime." Although these characterizations are all relevant to various aspects of state behavior in Zaire, it is my belief that clientelism is at the heart of all these phenomena and that Mobutu maintained a system of rule where presidential power was used to distribute economic resources to loyal clients who formed Mobutu's main internal support base. Mobutu's loyal clients have been called a "political aristocracy" by one scholar (Callaghy, 1988). Loyalty to Mobutu was the ultimate requirement for entry to and continued membership in this political aristocracy. This state-controlling elite consisted of three main groups: the first comprised the "presidential family" (the president's close advisers and relatives; all top administrative, political, and military officers and foreign advisers; and all council members). Within this group, power and material perquisites were enormous and almost unlimited for those closest to the president. The second group consisted of middle-level administrative and military officers in Kinshasa (the capital). The third group was made up of the remaining territorial adminis-trations and military officers in the regions (Callaghy, 1988).

Zaire's state resources became thoroughly concentrated in the hands of its president, Mobutu Sese Seko, during the last two decades of his rule. Table 4.1 reflects Mobutu's personal control of state resources over this period. As the table indicates, over a period of two decades Mobutu had allo-cated comparatively low amounts of declining state resources to social services. Twenty-five years after independence, only 15 percent of the roads inherited from Belgian rule remained passable. Moreover, Zairians faced the harsh consequences of an economy that shrank 40 percent between 1988 and 1995 and inflation that had risen 23,000 percent in 1995 (Reno, 1998: 154). While the masses of Zairians eked out a living from the informal economy that saved them from starvation (MacGaffey, 1988), Mobutu extracted re-sources from the domestic economy and received generous economic assis-tance from his foreign patrons to facilitate his patron-client network.

In 1973 Mobutu expropriated agricultural and commercial enterprises from foreign owners through a policy of "Zairianization" and converted them to political resources that he could distribute to loyal associates. Zairianization was supposed to bolster Mobutu's campaign for "authenticity" and was allegedly an effort to achieve economic independence from foreign domination. This was similar to other efforts in Africa at the time where African governments attempted to achieve greater control and ownership

TABLE 4.1   Privatization of Government Expenditures in Congo
(Former Zaire), 1972–1992 (percentages)

Year	President	Agriculture	Social Services
1972	28.0	29.3	17.5
1974	26.0	32.1	12.4
1976	29.0	30.9	13.2
1978	29.0	41.0	11.0
1980	33.0	42.0	11.0
1982	35.0	32.0	10.0
1984	39.0	30.0	9.0
1986	39.0	29.0	7.0
1988	49.0	18.0	4.0
1990	80.0	11.0	2.0
1992	95.0	4.0	0.0

Source: Banque du Zaire, 1972–1992, cited in Reno, 1998: 154.

of their natural resources. In other African countries, the state took over economic enterprises, but in Zaire these "Zairianized" enterprises were given to individuals as private property. It is estimated that between 1,500 and 2,000 enterprises were taken over by new Zairian owners, most of whom came from circles close to the president (Callaghy, 1984). Although Mobutu was able to give commercial and agricultural properties to his political clients (and thus maintain their loyalty), it was an economically destructive policy. Under Zairianization there were widespread shortages of most essential items, which led to dramatic price increases and the expansion of a parallel economy. The state subsequently nationalized some of the businesses that were previously indigenized, but only a few. Economic chaos continued under nationalization, and the state subsequently denationalized again. Some former foreign owners were invited back, and in some instances they took Zairian partners.

During the 1970s and 1980s, many politically motivated projects were developed (financed by outside sources) and used as patronage for Mobutu's loyal associates. For example, the Inga-Shaba project (estimated costs in 1983 were $1.5 billion) relied on outside sources. Construction contracts were given to foreign firms in exchange for U.S. and French support of Mobutu during revolts in the Shaba region (Shaba supplied about half of Zaire's mineral exports in 1972 and 1978 [Reno, 1998: 152]). Throughout his rule Mobutu used state power exclusively to help associates profit from clandestine trade, avoid taxation, and explore new rackets in activities that made use of state regulatory power such as passport sales, money laundering, and drug trafficking. Estimated exports of gold and diamonds from Zaire in 1992 suggest a trade worth over half a billion dollars annually. In 1986, revenues of state-run firms from copper, cobalt, zinc, and diamond exports generated $1.15 billion in the formal economy. Coffee also contributed $80 million in export revenues. All of these revenues were used to support Mobutu and his clients' accumulation needs.

Economic resources from external patrons underwrote Mobutu's patron-client network. During the Cold War, Mobutu was an extremely important anticommunist ally (in the Great Lakes region of Africa) of the United States and its NATO partners. In return for this support, in 1986 Mobutu received $448 million in aid from the United States and its allies and U.S. diplomatic support for loans from multilateral creditors (the latter in return for Mobutu's aiding U.S-backed UNITA rebels in Angola). With U.S. support, between 1976–1990 the IMF devised fourteen stabilization programs for the fiscally undisciplined nation of Zaire. The IMF returned to Zaire in 1983 after a five-year absence and disbursed $1.3 billion to Mobutu over the next five years. In addition to IMF leniency, Paris Club renegotiations led to the rescheduling of $3.5 billion of Zaire's 1985 external debt of $7.5 billion (Reno, 1998: 254).

By 1990 Mobutu faced serious challenges to his ability to rule through patronage. Not only did foreign state officials end their support of Mobutu, but many openly backed his rivals. Belgium, France, and the United States pressured Mobutu to begin political reform. France cut aid in 1991 to about $100 million, one-third the level two years earlier. The U.S. Congress voted to cut aid because of Mobutu's inability to service his debts. The World Bank broke ties with Zaire; the United States and the apartheid regime of South Africa withdrew their support for Mobutu's alliance with UNITA rebels in Angola. This further weakened Mobutu's alliance with UNITA, depriving Mobutu of a key clandestine patronage resource, since UNITA rebels controlled the diamond areas of Angola and had been selling diamonds to Zaire to fund the protracted war against the MPLA government. Mobutu lost his capacity to manage his loyal associates' clandestine diamond mining and arms transfer business with Angola (Reno, 1998: 157).

In 1991 the IMF announced that Zaire was behind on $81.7 million in payments to the organization and would receive no new loans. Three years later the IMF expelled Zaire. This action led to rapid increase in outside pressure on Mobutu, along with demands for socioeconomic reform and political change from broad sectors of the Zairian population. Mobutu responded with still more radical privatization of the state. Rather than abandon his loyal strongmen associates, after 1992 he allocated virtually no resources to social services (see Table 4.1) or physical infrastructure, using the money to replace resources lost elsewhere (Reno, 1998: 254). By 1992 it was clear that centralized power in the hands of a personalistic ruler had ended in Zaire. Mobutu's rule had become clearly unsustainable, and his regime ultimately collapsed in 1997, when he lost support of his external patrons because he failed to initiate political reform (Chapter 6).

Some Political and Economic Costs of Clientelist Rule in Africa

Ethnic Conflict

Ethnicity became a politically prominent problem in sub-Saharan Africa in the postindependence period. As mentioned in Chapter 3, under European colonial rule ethnic groups with very different political cultures, backgrounds, languages, and religions were forced to live in one political community and asked to assimilate into one nation-state. Ethnicity became politicized when the colonial authorities changed the dynamics of ethnic relations by placing particular resources in the hands of one or another of the ethnic groups within a state or dictated policy in favor of or inimical to one or another of the ethnic groups.

After the departure of the colonial powers, the fierce struggle to acquire power along with its related material benefits by both civilian and military elites fueled conflict across the African continent (e.g., in Liberia, Rwanda, Burundi, Uganda, Nigeria, Zaire, Angola, Sudan, Ethiopia). Since political dominance translates into control of political offices and better access to jobs, housing, and other valued services, competition for increased access to such scarce resources favors mobilization and collective action along ethnic lines. During the period of competitive party politics after independence, the winner-take-all practice of political competition encouraged collective action based on ethnic identity, because the practice perpetuated economic deprivation among or denied overall opportunity to losers in elections. In the political realm this meant that only members of the ethnic-based regime controlled the best access to jobs, housing, and other valued resources. This was the reason that political parties tended to be ethnic based, that particular ethnic groups would support a candidate from their own ethnic group, and that violence during elections have been frequently along ethnic lines. Competitive party politics affected ethnic groups by fomenting ethnic insecurity and increasing the potential for mobilization on a large scale spearheaded by an ethnic power elite (Conteh-Morgan, 1997).

The ruling elite throughout Africa tended to promote the interests of its own ethnic group. In some "socialist" states like Ethiopia (under Mengistu Haile Mariam) and Somalia (under Siyad Barre), the political leaders espoused antiethnic political rhetoric and operated on the idea that they would do away with ethnic differences through a focus on working-class in-terests. However, Mengistu, Emperor Haile Selassie's successor, continued to impose Amhara rule over multiethnic Ethiopia. The leader of Ethiopia and head of the ruling Ethiopian People's Revolutionary Democratic Front (EPRDF) in 2002 has attempted national reconciliation through the estab-lishment of a democratic multiethnic federation (see Chapter 7). Siyad Barre discouraged all talk of "tribes" in Somalia, where the population was over 90 percent Somali but divided among clans and subclans. However, Barre grad-ually surrounded himself with members of his own Marehan branch of the Darod clan and kept the rest of the public at a distance. Competing clan and subclan allegiances have long plagued Somalia, and for most of the decade of the 1990s Somalia has been engulfed in clan warfare between armed factions whose membership in any faction has been congruent with blood loyalties (see Chapter 7).

In Liberia, following the 1985 election, Thomas Quiwonkpa, a close as-sociate of President Samuel Doe, led an abortive coup as a protest against the Krahn domination of government and the rigging of elections. In Cameroon ethnoregional conflicts along north-south lines emerged between President Biya's predominantly Christian supporters and former President Ahidjo's largely Muslim followers. In 1984 Ahidjo's supporters in the Presidential Guard attempted to overthrow Biya, but the revolt was crushed after the death of a thousand people (Conteh-Morgan, 1997: 111). As a result, President Biya has surrounded himself with members of his own ethnic group, the Beti. In Niger a stormy relationship exists between President Ali Saibou's government and the Tuareg nomads. The government has been charged with favoritism towards members of the Zarma (or Djerma), one of the five major ethno-linguistic groups within the country. Since 1990 internecine violence has erupted between the Tuaregs and government troops resulting in the massacre of hundreds of civilians.

Market-driven economies in which certain ethnic groups are concentrated exclusively in certain economic activities can have a negative impact on interethnic relations. Some ethnic groups will continue to be privileged by market processes, and this will be reinforced by political operatives. Also, as these countries move from a traditional patron-client system to a market system, the more enterprising will be rewarded, leaving many ethnic groups behind. This certainly will lead to tensions within the political economy.

Economic Inefficiency/Economic Decay

The state's propensity to overconsume has been one major factor in Africa's contemporary economic crisis. In 1967 the average fraction of GDP consumed by the African state was less than 15 percent (Radian, 1980: 5–11). By 1982 in many countries the figure surpassed 30 percent, and in some it was considerably higher: in 1974 Zaire absorbed 59 percent of its GDP in state expenditures (Young, 1978); in Kenya public sector employment rose from 188,000 in 1965 to 390,000 in 1978, and the civil service expanded from 14,000 in 1945 to 45,000 in 1955 and 170,000 by 1980. The Senegalese government employed 10,000 people on the eve of independence, and by 1973 this number had increased to 61,000 (Abernethy, 1983). In Nigeria state expenditures increased from N (N=Naira, currency of Nigeria) 997.4 million in 1971 to N17,513.1 million in 1980 (Schatz, 1984: 19).

State consumption should not be inimical to economic development. The issues here are whether state resources have been used to support clientelist patronage and parasitic behavior, or have they been used for productive activities? A large part of state consumption in postindependence Africa went into military expenditures (discussed earlier in this chapter), monumental architecture (a $500 million presidential palace in Libreville; the coronation of "Emperor" Jean Bokassa in the Central African Republic; luxurious Organization of African Unity [OAU] conference facilities in Accra, Freetown, Monrovia, Libreville, and Kinshasa), and the parastatal sector. Public sector employment, particularly as reflected in the creation and staffing of the parastatals, has been the target of the overconsumption argument against the African state. The parastatal sector expanded in many African countries, staffed by educated middle-class supporters of the state. In most instances, they lacked the relevant managerial experience, and loyalty was the only requirement for the job.

Few parastatals reported profits, and many transferred income from peasants to bureaucrats, creating political problems for the state (Ellis, 1982). In Ghana in the early 1980s more than half of the 184 government-owned parastatals and 54 in which the government had minority shares experienced losses in the 1979–1982 period. Total losses rose from 92 million cedis (US$13 million) in 1979 to 2.9 billion cedis (US$136 million) in 1982 (*Ephson*, 1990: 2396). In Côte d'Ivoire between 1982 and 1985 100 percent government-owned public enterprises lost 85 billion CFA francs (US$175 million). A report of the Public Investment Committee of Kenya's National Assembly in 1990 documented massive losses by some of the country's 150 parastatals. It attributed this poor performance to mismanagement, inadequate budgetary control, overstaffing, and unaccountable and arrogant managers (*Weekly Review*, November 30, 1990: 36–37 cited in Sandbrook, 1993: 64).

Some of the impediments to sound performance have to do with lack of technical skills in many African countries, as well as shortage of foreign exchange and shrinkage of public revenues stemming from economic crises. As a result, many parastatals have been unable to import the necessary equipment, spare parts, and materials to run efficient operations. But the most serious political problem is parastatals' centrality to clientelistic governance in Africa. The use of friends and loyal supporters in these enterprises, who often grossly undercharge their friends and relatives who use the services, accounts for a major loss of revenue. Many unscrupulous staff members have reportedly diverted assets to their private use without being found out (Mbanefo, 1975: 289–299).

Parastatals were created all across the African continent for some very good reasons. The private sector was weak, and the civil service was not equipped to assume new technical functions; so parastatals were created to provide social services, run public utilities, and manage commercial, financial, and productive activities. Nationalizations of some foreign companies were carried out as a nationalist response to economic dependency. If parastatals had not been created, foreign companies would have continued to control many sectors of African economies. Notwithstanding these sound reasons for their creation, parastatals have traditionally been used as a way to distribute patronage both to individuals and to groups. Inexperienced or incompetent people have limited capacity to identify problems and formulate and implement policy alternatives. This obviously led to the poor performance of most parastatals and has constrained economic development in those countries.

Since parastatals have been used traditionally for political purposes, it has been exceptionally hard either to improve them or eliminate them (Herbst,

1989). The IMF and the World Bank have insisted on parastatal reform or privatization on the tenet that the indigenous private sector (provided with an enabling environment) will take advantage of new opportunities and propel their economies into broad-based growth. As a result of IMF and World Bank pressures, structural adjustment programs sponsored by these lending agencies have included privatization. The conditions now attached to loans and credits offer African governments limited options: they must either privatize public enterprises; "commercialize" them; or if public enterprises continue to lose money, liquidate them. Privatization has been attempted in some countries (e.g., Nigeria, Togo, Ghana, Kenya) with varying degrees of success. Some African countries still refuse to view it as a policy option, because it involves significant political costs. The public enterprise sector has been used frequently to meet distributional and other social objectives that would have to be sacrificed if the enterprises were transferred to private ownership.

There is a strong relationship between the limited capacity of governmental organizations and economic problems in Africa today. Interventionist states (be they state-capitalist or socialist) are not inherently harmful to economic development, as the IMF and World Bank have suggested. Interventionist states in East Asia (Taiwan and South Korea for example) have achieved unprecedented growth and development in the post–World War II period. What is required is a balanced relationship between the state and the private sector in support of development. Interventionist states cannot succeed if they support parasitic behavior rather than productive economic activities. The state-controlling elites have been interested in seeking the short-term advantages of state-assisted rent-seeking behavior rather than enforcing productive priorities upon the state apparatus. Clientelism, personalistic rule, and lack of governmental accountability constitutes hindrances to accelerated development. State elites have supported this behavior, although in the long run it stifles efficiency and growth and runs counter to the long-term interests of capital.

The State as Client of International Patrons

Since the early 1990s, conditionality has been used effectively by international financial institutions to force many African countries to undertake political reform. The reason for this apparent success in persuading reluctant and recalcitrant autocrats to announce democratic transition programs has to do with the latter's chronic dependence on external capital. External capital was a necessary part of state revenues, needed to underwrite internal patron-client networks crucial to the survival of many of the regimes.

At independence the new state was no longer limited to the functions of law and order, collecting revenues, and minimal welfare. Its responsibilities now included promoting the development and welfare of the population. As sufficient resources were never available in the domestic economy in almost all of these newly independent states, many political leaders became dependent on foreign borrowing to promote social and economic development.

There are a host of reasons for the lack of sufficient resources in the domestic economies of many African states at independence. Some have to do with the countries' natural resources, some are historical and structural, and some are related to external factors over which African leaders have had little control. Chapter 3 reviewed some of the historical and natural geographic causes, which will not be repeated here. A major problem has been the overdependence on a few primary commodity exports that are subject to the vagaries of the world market. Declining commodity prices (particularly agricultural exports) have led to declining export revenues and a subsequent loss of government subsidies to growers. Significant shortfalls in export revenues have generally led to an increase in foreign borrowing to offset declining export revenues. Mounting foreign debt has become a major problem as many governments devote more than one third of their limited export earnings to debt service. There are numerous external constraints on Africa's economic development that have roots in the bygone colonial era. African governments have limited control over many of the constraints emerging from the global capitalist economy (see Chapter 8), and the reality is that foreign borrowing has been inevitable.

Aid has played a very important part in maintaining Africa's dependence on both the Western industrialized countries and the former Soviet Union. Africa's dependence on aid increased significantly between the 1960s and 1990s. In the early 1960s, aid flows to sub-Saharan Africa constituted less than 2 percent of GNP (comparable to developing countries in other regions of the world). As a result of the economic crisis exacerbated by the 1973 and 1979 increase in oil prices, donors increased aid to the region. Between 1970 and 1985 aid levels grew by an annual average of more than 5 percent in real terms. At the end of the 1980s over 40 percent of all development aid went to Africa, compared with less than 30 percent at the beginning of the decade. In 1988 nineteen African countries received aid equal to more than 10 percent of their GNP, and for six countries (Mozambique, Chad, Tanzania, Malawi, Lesotho, and Somalia) aid amounted to more than 25 percent of their GNP (Hadjor, 1993: 26).

Foreign aid has helped to preserve the rule of many unpopular and incompetent African leaders since independence. It has been used to provide additional resources to governments, allowing them to use domestic resources for military expenditures to enhance the security of their regimes. Aid has also helped leaders consolidate their power. Aid resources have been used for patronage (indirectly, through its ability to free up domestic resources, and directly, in terms of activities it funds), which has helped many democratic as well as authoritarian governments stay in power. The state's domestic clientelist politics have made international economic transactions even more important. Reflecting the inequality in the international system, the more powerful nations controlling military, political, and economic resources (largely the United States, France, Britain, Belgium, and the former Soviet Union) act as patrons to a number of vulnerable underdeveloped client states in Africa (and in Asia, Latin America, and the Caribbean).

The postindependence period coincided with the Cold War, and the interests of many African leaders in obtaining military and economic aid to maintain power and preserve the state converged with the interests of their patrons to find allies in strategic regions of Africa as well as overseas markets for investments, loans, and grants. The convergence of both interests led many African countries into a dependent client relationship with powerful governments. Although the relationship was unequal, the important point here is that the African leaders were not just pliable puppets being exploited; they benefited from the patron-client ties with more powerful and wealthier nations.

The Cold War facilitated a strategy of clientelism, whereas the changes that have occurred with the end of the Cold War have directly challenged the viability of this strategy. With external pressures from international lenders for political reform (multiparty politics) and neoliberal economic reforms (removal of the state from the economy) as a condition for continued economic assistance, African leaders now have less leverage as clients than they had during the Cold War. With the collapse of Soviet communism and the end of the Cold War, they no longer have an alternative patron to whom they can threaten to shift their allegiance in order to extract resources from an uncooperative patron. The patrons have the upper hand now that they have numerous new clients (former Eastern European communist states) competing for foreign aid. Indeed, they have become very rigid in the criteria established for aid, and this has excluded many African nations from getting what they perceive as their fair share of foreign aid from Western countries. The colonial and postindependence formation of the African state led to its current weakened state vis-à-vis international financial actors. An African state based on the clientelist relations outlined in this chapter may not survive in that form much longer. It has to be reconfigured to adapt to the reduction of international economic support and to international challenges to the authoritarian politics anchored in clientelism.

Conclusion

The nationalist leaders who came to power at independence had strong ties with the African population, on whose support the movement for independence was built. The state apparatus which they took over represented the interests of the colonizing powers. It was organized on principles that were antithetical to the objectives of the nationalist movement. The new leaders continued to rule through the old colonial institutions, which emphasized personal authority. They were also unable to transform the state apparatus into one that was responsive to the socioeconomic needs of broad sectors of the population.

A disjuncture developed between the values of the state and the society, and in most African countries state legitimacy was very low. Many African states survived intact through clientelist rule, despite their fragility and low levels of legitimacy. Authoritarian regimes often saw clientelism as a more efficient way to win loyalty than physical repression. It preserved the interests of the state-controlling elites and inhibited the articulation of class as a source of political conflict by the lower socioeconomic groups within the population.

Since the early 1990s, political reform and economic liberalization have begun in many sub-Saharan African countries. The loss of Cold War superpower patrons and the shift away from authoritarian rule has begun to have an impact on clientelist rule. In some countries, there has been an emergence of a new form of clientelism, with a resource base in clandestine mineral export industries. As a result of the state's declining capacity (weakened by political conditionality and neoliberal economic reforms), new nonstate patrons (e.g., private entrepreneurs linked to illicit trade in minerals and narcotics) have emerged in countries such as Sierra Leone, Liberia, the former Zaire, Somalia, and Angola. This new form of clientelism will have significant consequences for the post–Cold War, externally supported projects of political and economic liberalization in sub-Saharan Africa (see Chapter 7).

For Further Reading

Lemarchand, Rene (1972). "Political Clientelism and Ethnicity in Tropical Africa," *American Political Science Review* 6, no. 1, pp. 68–90.

Flynn, P. (1974). "Class, Clientelism and Coercion: Some Mechanisms of Dependency and Control," *Journal of Commonwealth and Comparative Politics* 12, no. 2, pp. 133–156.

Clapham, C., ed. (1982). *Private Patronage and Public Power: Political Clientelism in the Modern State.* New York: St. Martin's Press.

Bratton, M., and N. van de Walle (1994). "Neopatrimonial Regimes and Political Transitions in Africa," *World Politics* 46 (July), 453–489.

Bayart, Jean-Francois (2000). "Africa in the World: A History of Extraversion," *African Affairs* 99, no. 395, pp. 217–267.

5
Political Systems of Postindependence Africa

Before the end of World War II, the emergent political elites in developing nations (influenced by the political culture of the dominant Western European metropolitan powers) saw competitive party systems as the ideal mode of state power for adoption in their nations. With the post–World War II emergence of communism in the Soviet Union and Eastern Europe (which challenged the United States and Western Europe for world leadership), the form of state power that evolved from that experience legitimized the one-party state. The one-party state, it was argued, avoided the divisions of multiparty democracy and helped hold fragmented societies together. By the late 1960s, the one-party state became as legitimate in Africa as liberal democracy, and a large number of leaders in newly independent countries saw it as an alternative to liberal-democratic development.

For the first three decades after independence, authoritarianism was the dominant state form, appearing in more than three-fourths of the countries of the region. Among the authoritarian regimes, there have been a variety of different systems of state power constantly undergoing change (monarchies, single-party systems, one-party-dominant systems, and military systems). However, regardless of the colonial heritage and the unique historical experiences of the different countries, the most common political regime types were the noncommunist single-party system and systems under direct military rule. Competitive party systems were uncommon until the 1990s, when more than three-fourths of sub-Saharan African countries reestablished multiparty electoral regimes.

What emerges here is a striking picture of seeming uniformity in political regime type during the first three decades after independence. Why did so many countries with such diverse backgrounds maintain authoritarian regimes? How did the few exceptions manage to maintain competitive party systems? Some answers to these questions may be found in an analysis of the varied ways in which the state-controlling political elites have established dominance over the state apparatus under authoritarianism as well as under competitive party systems. In particular, this chapter addresses the ways in which the political elites managed power in noncommunist single-party systems, military systems, and competitive party systems.

Divergent Regional Trends: Authoritarianism and Competitive Party Systems

Sub-Saharan African political experience since independence has evolved three main types of political regimes: single-party systems, systems of direct military rule, and competitive party systems. What distinguishes these regime types has been the varying levels of state power concentration, with military rule representing the highest level, and competitive party systems representing the lowest level. What has been most important is the consequences of these levels of state power concentration for the political economy of the various countries (Stone, 1980b).

In single-party systems, obviously only one party is allowed to contend for state power. One party monopolizes state power, and the party leader generally uses ideology to mobilize and garner broad societal support for the single party's claim to that monopoly. One common ideological justification used by African leaders has been national unity and national development. Many charismatic leaders have used populist and nationalist ideologies by, giving the single-party system excellent mobilizational capability to motivate a wide cross section of the society into service of political and national causes. In most single-party systems in sub-Saharan Africa, a monopoly base of institutional power has been built around the dominant personality of a "founder-leader" or a "maximum leader" or around a dominant institutional interest such as the military. In populist-nationalist single-party systems, no power contenders are allowed to exist outside of the single party's domain.

All groups allowed to have influence in the political arena are generally absorbed into the ranks of the party. Although this variant of the single-party system attempts to establish complete hegemonic control over state power, it often allows a wide sphere of freedom from political control at the individual and social level. In the immediate postindependence period, the populist-nationalist variant of the single-party system in Africa evolved as the predominant and most effective road by which strong authority systems developed, and it also provided a viable framework in which leaders attempted national integration of various races, cultures, and ethnic and socioeconomic groups.

The two single-party systems, communist and populist-nationalist, can be distinguished in several ways. One important difference was ideology, where the communist party used a class ideology to justify monopoly of state power on behalf of workers and peasants. The ideological framework was explicitly Marxist-Leninist, with a commitment to Marx and Lenin's theories of class struggle and a rejection of the democratic socialism embraced by the British Labour Party and other Western European socialist parties. Compared to the populist-nationalist single-party system, which accommodated a wide range of ideological tendencies, this communist variant governed under a more exclusive class ideology. This form of single-party rule often developed features, associated with communism, of regulation and extensive power concentration combined with rigid restrictions on individual freedoms. Monopoly of state power was combined with extensive and centralized planning of control of economic, social, and cultural spheres of the society at all levels. All spheres of private power were eliminated. The communist single-party system therefore represents the most extreme form of power concentration in the hands of the political elite, the lowest levels of individual freedoms and private power, and the highest level of power capability for political and administrative tasks. The communist single-party system has not been as popular a model of organizing state power in sub-Saharan Africa as the nationalist-populist form or military rule (see Table 5.1).

Military systems have been a transitional form of government. They emerged where weak civilian political institutions failed to govern effectively or collapsed into political instability by being unable to manage deep crisis or conflicts in the political system. Under military rule the security forces (military and/or police) control state power or provide the means by which an individual or faction controls the state. Lacking institutional supports, military rule rests largely on coercive power. The mass mobilization common in populist-nationalist single-party systems or in competitive party systems is largely absent or used only in crisis situations. Contenders and challengers for state power must use violence to obtain political recognition. Political freedoms are limited and are perceived by the military as a means of undermining it. Military systems discourage mass participation in politics as a threat to political stability. Military rule was prevalent in sub-Saharan

TABLE 5.1   Country Distribution of Political Regimes
in Sub-Saharan Africa, 1960s–1978

Monarchy	Competitive Party	One-Party Dominant	Military	Single Party (Non-communist)	Single Party (Communist)
Swaziland	Botswana	Senegal	Lesotho	Cameroon	Ethiopia
	The Gambia		U. Volta*	Kenya	Angola
	Mauritius		Chad	Tanzania	Mozambique
			Niger	Gabon	Benin
			Uganda	Sierra Leone	Guinea-Bissau
			Ghana	Liberia	Congo-
			Nigeria	Malawi	Brazzaville
			Burundi	Ivory Coast	
			Rwanda	Central African Empire	
				Zambia	
				Zaire	
				Congo	
				Mali	
				Togo	
				Benin	
				Sudan	
				Guinea	
				Guinea-Bissau	
				Mauritania	
				Somalia	
				Equatorial Guinea	

* Known today as Burkina Faso.

Source: modified from Stone, 1980b: 20–21.

Africa from the 1960s through the 1980s because many countries failed to
stabilize sufficiently to develop the institutional supports to sustain civilian
rule (Stone, 1980b). Most African countries shifted between military and
single-party systems during this period.

Uninterrupted competitive party systems existed for several decades after
independence in a small number of sub-Saharan African countries (notably
Botswana, The Gambia, Mauritius, Senegal, Zimbabwe). Several countries,

including Nigeria and Ghana, experienced brief periods of competitive party politics interrupted by military rule. For the first three decades after independence in the 1960s, a handful of countries held regular multiparty elections, violations of human rights were relatively few, and civil liberties were generally respected. In Botswana and The Gambia, one political party was dominant, and a peaceful transfer of power from one party to another has not yet been observed. In these competitive party systems, one saw a relatively lower level of state power concentration than in the single-party systems or military systems in the rest of the region. Those who managed the state under these systems were subjected to challenges from other organized power contenders who tried to influence the electorate. There has also been a close relationship between low concentrations of state power and high individual political freedoms. Botswana, The Gambia, Mauritius, Senegal, and Zimbabwe have all been characterized by one-party dominance. Nongoverning political parties have been allowed to exist to satisfy certain constitutional criteria for legitimacy, but these opposition parties have been in many instances fractionalized and too weak to gain state power. It is widely believed that some of these countries have had a form of government that constitutes one-party dictatorship camouflaged in constitutional trappings. At best, some of these countries are ambiguous regimes that cannot be easily placed on the democratic-authoritarian continuum, having characteristics of both state forms. Table 5.1 shows a country distribution of the main political regimes in sub-Saharan Africa by the end of the decade of the 1970s.

Noncommunist Single-Party Systems: Kenya and Tanzania (1961–1993)

Scholars have frequently compared Kenya and Tanzania in studies of post-independence African politics. They are, in many ways, very similar, having gained independence from Britain at roughly the same time (Tanzania in 1961 and Kenya in 1963) and having similar aspects of culture, history, ethnic makeup, and geography. There are notable distinctions between the two countries, such as Kenya's having to contend with internal racial and ethnic divisions emerging from land conflicts that Tanzania was not forced to address. The most emphasized difference between the two countries is that, in the immediate postindependence period, whereas Kenya became the prototype capitalist model for African nations, Tanzania chose the path of egalitarian socialism. The social and political goals of the leadership in the two countries were different in the early period following independence. However, political control was of utmost importance to the elites controlling the state in both countries.

Political control in Kenya relied on repression of the opposition, suppression of political participation, and monopolization of power through a single-party system. Similar systems of political control can be observed in a majority of African countries after they gained independence. Kenya, like many other developing countries in Africa, Asia, the Caribbean, and Latin America, is dependent upon agricultural exports. The distribution of land is a hotly contested issue that led to the "Mau Mau" rebellion of the 1950s and that has remained salient in Kenyan politics since independence in 1963. Under British colonial rule land was unevenly distributed, with the European settlers owning the largest and best lands in the so-called "White Highlands." After independence, by the mid-1970s, only 5 percent of the former White Highlands reportedly remained in the ownership of European settlers (Wasserman, 1973; Furedi, 1974). Mirroring colonial class relations, Kenya's new ruling Kikuyu political elite under President Jomo Kenyatta controlled the largest and most profitable lands in the most desirable agricultural regions, the Rift Valley and Kiambu regions.

Kenya exemplifies the negative aspects of political consolidation after independence, with Jomo Kenyatta effectively demonstrating personal domination as well as Kikuyu ethnic domination of the system. At independence, Kikuyus represented the largest ethnic group in Kenya. Under Kenyatta's rule, the African elite was almost exclusively from the Kikuyu ethnic group, although not all Kikuyus were members of the elite. The Kikuyu bourgeoisie, privileged by the British in the areas of education and business and politically strong within the broad-based multiethnic nationalist party, the Kenya African National Union (KANU), made this party the logical successor to the British in governing Kenya. The Kikuyu became dominant in the civil service sector because of their educational advantages. Kenyatta kept the public sector very large to ensure that supporters within his ethnic group, the Kikuyu, and others he personally favored could easily find employment that he disbursed through patron–client relations with them.

Kenyatta was very much a popular hero (known as Mzee, "Father of the Nation") and was an obvious beneficiary of the newly emerging state-controlling postindependence political elite. He actively participated in enriching his family and friends at the expense of the landless Kikuyu and non-Kikuyu majority. Concentration of power has been revealed in the enormous assets his family acquired. Further, every prominent Kikuyu politician in Kenyatta's government reportedly owned property in the Rift Valley and Kiambu regions. The tiny political elite commanded huge salaries and numerous perks ranging from luxury houses to chauffeur-driven cars. Kenyatta's family holdings stretched into Kenya's entire economy, from hotels to gambling to tourism. The concentration of power in the hands of a tiny elite controlled by Kenyatta led to the abuse of that power for personal benefit. The result was that the gap between the tiny wealthy elite and the rest of the population was exacerbated and class inequality became further entrenched.

Like all other former British colonies throughout the world, Kenya inherited its "Westminster model" of government. Under this system political parties exist as electoral organizations designed to increase public participation, represent multiple and competing groups in the society, and support or oppose the party in power. During the immediate postindependence period, from 1963 to 1964, Kenyatta and his party, KANU, diverted all their energies to destroying and dissolving all political opposition. Kenyatta secretly (and sometimes not secretly) removed political opponents. In the rural areas, a crackdown against all land radicals began that set an early pattern of abuse of democratic rights that soon spread to other areas of the society. The Kenya African Democratic Union (KADU), the only major opposition party, was incorporated into KANU, and the latter became defined as virtually synonymous with the state. Opposition to KANU was perceived as all but subversive (Holmquist and Ford, 1994). Kenya became a de facto single-party, authoritarian state. The Public Security Act formalized the Kenyatta regime's power by restricting rights to movement, association, and speech if the president believed that internal order was threatened. This act effectively silenced the opposition.

To further his control, Kenyatta created a patron–client system that bypassed the Westminster model of representative democracy. He used clientelism to maintain indirect political control at the lower levels as well as the higher echelons of the party. Kenyatta's power and patronage filtered down through ethnic and regional leaders, their assistants, constituency leaders, and local notables. This system eventually replaced the inherited British system, as Kenyatta assumed control of KANU and removed all the power the party possessed, concentrating it in his own hands. This became an important aspect of the single-party state in Kenya and in Africa in general: the leader wields power, the party does not. KANU was further weakened with the shift to a republican form of government in 1964.

The immediate postindependence period ended in Kenya with the death of Jomo Kenyatta in 1978, the year Daniel arap Moi became president. The repressive regime did not slacken its control. As the economic crisis intensified, the Moi regime increased intimidation and repression of the people. As a member of the minority Kalenjin ethnic group, Moi at first felt ethnically alienated in a Kikuyu-dominated political elite. He understood that the Kikuyu had gained too great an advantage from the Kenyatta government and instead desired to build a coalition of those ethnicities previously shut out so that they might get a greater share of the country's wealth. Harsh economic times prompted by high foreign debt, stagnant exports, parastatal corruption and mismanagement, and rising inflation sparked an unsuccessful coup d'etat in 1982.

After the attempted coup, Moi realized that there was little public confidence in his policies, so he increased repression to maintain political control and ensure the survival of his regime. He has come to use similar tactics that Jomo Kenyatta used to keep his opponents in check, including patron-client relations, political intimidation, restricting rights to assemble, and banning critical newspapers and detaining reporters. Like his predecessor, Moi has used his power to amass a large personal fortune. He reportedly has built a commercial empire comparable to that of the Kenyatta family (Mukonoweshoro, 1990). As Kenyatta's was, Moi's rule has been based on clientelism and coercion.

By 1990 there was widespread disillusionment in Kenya with the single-party system, and there were a desire for the rule of law, a demand for public participation and a multiparty system, and a call for more autonomy for civil society from the state (Holmquist, Weaver, and Ford, 1994). The Moi regime acceded to demands for multiparty elections almost immediately following the November 1991 Paris Group Meeting of donors, which withheld aid. Facing dramatic cuts in donor funds and escalating social and political unrest, President Moi reluctantly called for open elections in December 1992. Political parties were legalized in December 1991, and on December 29, 1992, national elections were held.

The incumbent government party controlled most of the material resources and refused its opponents any media time. National and international monitoring organizations found evidence of a lack of a "level playing field" (Holmquist, Weaver, and Ford, 1994: 222). The election results were not surprising: with four major parties competing, the incumbent received about 36 percent of the vote, and Moi was returned to office with his party, KANU, having a majority in Parliament. After the elections, authoritarianism continued, as did economic decline and opposition immobility. Regime-sponsored ethnic clashes and attacks occurred sporadically after the elections and generally inhibited cooperation among opposition groups. This ethnic violence provided a self-fulfilling prophecy for Moi's warning in 1990 that multiparty elections would breed ethnic hostilities. Despite the fact that the elections were far from free and fair and the opposition was sabotaged by the incumbent party, however, many scholars and observers agree that there has been a real democratic opening since the 1992 elections. There has been some expansion of civil liberties, press censorship has declined, political detentions have been far less frequent, and Kenyans now talk quite freely about politics. These are signs of incipient democratization, but given Kenya's legacy of single-party rule and authoritarianism, how difficult will it be for Kenya to institutionalize democracy?

In the sixties and seventies, Julius Nyerere's Tanzania, led by the Tanzania African National Union (TANU), was a self-described socialist regime and was perceived in the international community as such. In contrast, Kenya was seen by outsiders as "capitalist," despite Kenyatta's self-styled "African socialist" ideology of development. These labels are misleading in that they masked an essential similarity in the two country's political systems: the dominance of a single party. Nyerere was perhaps Africa's most ardent advocate for democratic single-party systems after independence. He believed that the only way to build a truly democratic and classless society (i.e., free of class war) was through a one-party system. Many challenged the idea of a functioning democracy in a country where there was only one party for which to vote. Nyerere's support for democracy was not easily reconciled with the one-party system he advocated. He envisioned a party and a government that represented all the people and could regulate itself through self-criticism. Nyerere's was a single-party system that ruled not by brutal force but through the support of the majority of the population. The single-party system created united political support within the country, which enabled Tanzania to resist International Monetary Fund (IMF) demands during the 1970s and 1980s and allowed the government to negotiate loans without extreme pressure from the population.

Similarities can be drawn between Nyerere's dominance of TANU and Kenyatta's dominance of KANU. Both were undisputed leaders of one-party states, and both dominated the political scene in their respective countries. But Kenyatta's (and later Moi's) rule was based on clientelism and coercion, whereas Nyerere's was based on reverence. Nyerere achieved his popularity by adhering to high principles. He refused to live in a large extravagant house as the nation's president, took pay cuts to lead by example, never tried to anoint himself "president for life," and set the presidential elections at regular five-year intervals. While many African leaders exploited their own countries and brutally repressed their own people, Nyerere remained uncorrupt and followed a high moral code. His nationalism was African, not limited to Tanzania; he was a staunch anticolonialist and anti-imperialist, opposing racial, ethnic, and class oppression wherever he saw it in the world. He believed that racial, ethnic, and class divisions were not a natural part of African societies but a result of European penetration. He looked to Africa's roots to establish an indigenous socialism, and that was the basis for his populist but economically unsuccessful *ujamaa* (socialism in villages) experiment. His goals and passion for an egalitarian society in Tanzania inspired the nation and to an extent the African continent and the African diaspora.

Political control in Tanzania was tight, but Nyerere's and TANU's monopoly of the political scene was not a result of coercion. There was a lack of political opposition there but for different reasons than in Kenya. Nyerere's socialist ideology fused the party and the state, and no opposition party developed. Further, the government controlled the economy. This led to public sector expansion and an extensive state bureaucracy that provided the largest source of employment in the country. Once the government had consolidated its power through nationalizations and popular support of its egalitarian principles, it had all the tools necessary to silence any opposition.

By the end of the 1980s, Tanzania faced many of the same economic challenges that Kenya faced. Julius Nyerere retired from politics in 1985 and was succeeded by President Ali Hassan Mwinyi. In early 1990 Nyerere, whose earlier writings had been among the most important justifications for the single-party system in Africa, publicly stated that it might be time for Africa to rethink its political options. Since then, Tanzania has liberalized both its politics and economics to meet donors' increasing demands for political pluralism and neoliberal economic reforms as conditions for continued aid. Multiparty elections were held in 1995, offering four opposition parties a chance as key contenders (Tripp, 2000). The incumbent Chama Cha Mapinduzi (CCM, Tanzania's ruling party following a merger between TANU and the Afro-Shirazi Party [ASP] of Zanzibar) won the election and still runs the government, as does KANU in Kenya. The opposition parties were too divided and weak to gain control. The tactics for competing in an environment with a one-party legacy have been similar to those used in Kenya. The ruling party has been accused of deregistering the competition, co-opting smaller organizations into government agencies, denying the opposition permission to hold meetings, and buying out opposition leadership with lucrative government jobs (Tripp, 2000). The CCM accepted political pluralism very reluctantly as the widely held view within the party was that democracy and structural adjustment programs did not go hand in hand (see Chapter 6). Since 1992 the government has allowed significantly greater freedom of the press, delinked trade unions from the ruling party, and allowed thousands of nongovernmental organizations (mainly women's and lawyers' groups) to register (Tripp, 2000).

The important difference between Kenya and Tanzania in these relatively small changes is that, whereas Kenya was forced to implement multiparty elections, Tanzania came to this decision at its own rate. After the 1996 election, which brought President Benjamin Mkapa to power, efforts toward democratization were promptly suspended. The government seemed to think that donors were interested only in elections and it had satisfied that condition. The most critical stumbling block in the way of democratization in both Kenya and Tanzania has been the absence of real opposition.

Military Systems in West Africa: The Case of Nigeria

Nigeria gained its independence from Britain in 1960. Since the end of a brief six-year period of civilian rule following independence, Nigeria has experienced six successful coups d'etat to date (2002). Military rule beginning in 1966 was interrupted by only one brief period of civilian rule under the

TABLE 5.2   Nigerian Chief Executives, 1960–1999

Dates	Name	Title	Ethnicity	Cause of Departure
1960–Jan. 1963	Tafawa Balewa	Prime minister	H-F* (north)	Coup (killed)
1963–Jan. 1966	Nnamdi Azikiwe (Appointed)	President	Igbo (east)	Coup
Jan.–July 1966	Aguiyi Ironsi	Military head of state	Igbo (east)	Coup (killed)
July 1966–1975	Yakubu Gowon	Military head of state	Middle Belt	Coup (removed)
1975–1976	Murtala Muhammed	Military head of state	H-F (north)	Coup (killed)
1976–1979	Olusegun Obasanjo	Military head of state	Yoruba	Handed over power to civilian leader
1979–1983	Shehu Shagari	President	H-F (north)	Coup (removed)
1983–1985	Muhammed Buhari	Military head of state	H-F (north)	Coup (removed)
1985–1993	Ibrahim Babangida	Military head of state	Gwari (north)	Forced out of office
Aug.–Nov. 1993	Ernest Shonekan	Interim appointed president	Yoruba (southwest)	Forced out
Nov. 1993–May 1998	Sani Abacha	Head of provisional ruling council	Kanuri (north)	Died in office
May 1998–May 1999	A. Abubakar	Head of provisional ruling council	Gwari (north)	Handed over power
May 1999–	Olusegun Obasanjo	President	Yoruba (southwest)	

* H-F: Hausa-Fulani

Source: Aborisade and Mundt, 1999: 103.

short-lived Second Republic (1979–1983). Table 5.2 indicates the number of military and civilian governments in Nigeria since independence.

How can Nigeria's pattern of political development be understood? What consequences have high levels of state power concentration under military rule had for political development and management of the economy?

There are several factors that have made it difficult for Nigeria to maintain civilian governments since its independence: a flawed federal structure, politicized ethnic conflict, the relationship between the economy and the state, corruption, and mass impoverishment vis-à-vis conspicuous elite consumption. The military regimes that replaced the civilian governments did not solve these problems, and in many instances, because of the greater degree of centralization of state power under the military, these problems were exacerbated.

There has been a widely held belief that ethnic conflict was responsible for the collapse of the First Republic in 1966 and the first military intervention. Ethnic conflict was certainly a factor, but what is far more important for our understanding of Nigeria are the ways in which both the British colonial power and the postindependence Nigerian political elites managed ethnic divisions in the society. In 1951, while Nigeria was still under British rule, Britain imposed a tripartite regional system whose boundaries coincided with the primary ethnic divisions in the country: the Hausa-Fulani were the dominant group in the north, and the south was divided into the Yoruba in the west and the Igbo in the east. Each region also had significant minorities of other ethnic groups that resented and feared domination by these larger ethnic groups. The constitution of 1954 created a federal structure that heightened ethnic divisions by making the Hausa-Fulani, Yoruba, and Igbo governmental as well as ethnic categories. The three regions were differentially incorporated into a federal structure where the north had a population majority and the south had better-educated people and more socioeconomic advancement. As Britain intended, the north's absolute population majority made it likely that its dominant class would be the dominant political force in Nigeria. The north would have political power and the south socioeconomic power. This uneasy relationship planted the seed for ethnic competition and recurrent conflict. Political parties then became organized along ethnic lines, and political conflict became a high-stakes struggle for supremacy between parties, ethnic groups, and regions. After independence, especially between 1962 and 1965, political conflict centered on a struggle between the Hausa-Fulani-dominated Northern Peoples Congress (NPC) and its southern antagonists, the Yoruba-dominated Action Group (AG) and the Igbo-dominated National Council of Nigeria and the Cameroons (NCNC).

British colonial rule left in place a state that was all-powerful relative to other forces in the society and the economy. State control was established over the greatest source of cash revenue in the country, cash crop agriculture (Ake, 1981a). Parastatals were established in the form of state corporations, and private indigenous enterprise was discouraged. By 1964 54 percent of all wage earners were employed by some level of government, and 38 percent were employed by foreign capital (Diamond, 1983: 178–179). In the north, state power became the instrument for preserving the domination of the indigenous ruling classes, in a modern alliance with new commercial and ethnic minority elites (Coleman, 1958: 353–368; Sklar, 1963: 134–152; Whitaker, 1970: 313–354). In the south, material wealth became a singular focus of the emerging new middle class, influenced by the spread of Western education, media, and consumer goods. Government power became the primary means for individuals in the south to accumulate wealth and enter the "new and rising class" (Sklar, 1979: 480–494) and for the ruling parties to recruit diverse business, professional, and traditional elites into a new dominant class. Few politicians or their clients had alternative career options that offered better material and status rewards than those of state power. State power was indispensable to material advancement for families and friends of the politicians. Because of the high premium placed on political power, the competition for state control evolved into a zero-sum struggle.

Richard Sklar's argument that "tribalism" (ethnicity) functioned as "a mask for class privilege" helps further to explain the politicization of ethnic conflict by Nigerian-dominant classes in the years preceding the collapse of the First Republic. Exploiting the structures left by Britain, the emerging new political classes used ethnicity to further their class interests. Their interests centered on controlling the state, and to do so required the electoral strategy most likely to succeed: manipulating ethnic pride and appealing to ethnic consciousness. By focusing on ethnic competition for state resources and by distributing patronage to their ethnic communities, they diverted attention from their own capitalist accumulation project and precluded effective class mobilization against it. Ethnicity became an instrument of competition within the emergent dominant class for the limited spoils of the newly independent state. To consolidate itself, the "new and rising class" depended on an expanded state. This point is central to understanding the entrenchment of corruption around the state in Nigeria during the 1960s and beyond. As clientelism became entrenched, corruption was necessary to maintain the extensive patronage networks that had been established.

Nigeria's first military coup d'etat occurred in January 1966, led by Igbo general Aguiyi Ironsi. This coup was an expression of the south's disaffection with the political domination of the north and the increasing spread of ethnic clientelism and corruption. Because the coup makers were predominantly Igbos and the lives of leading Igbo politicians like Nnamdi Azikiwe were spared, it was seen as a coup d'etat designed to impose Igbo hegemony on the country. General Ironsi replaced regional control of public services with federal control. This led many in the north to believe that the objective was southern domination. Like coup makers elsewhere, General Ironsi condemned the civilian government for its corruption, and promised to eradicate it and to restore democracy soon.

In July 1966, seven months after seizing power, General Ironsi himself was ousted and killed in a countercoup, and General Yakubu Gowon replaced him. The result of this coup d'etat was mass slaughter of Igbos in the northern region. In May 1967 General Gowon created a new twelve-state structure that effectively severed the Igbos from the economic potential of newly found oil in the Niger Delta region. This created an even greater sense of marginalization among the Igbo people. Gowon's actions led to an eastern secession movement led by Colonel Odumegu Ojukwu to create an independent state of Biafra. This resulted in the bloody Biafran Civil War. By January 1970 Gowon and the federal government defeated the Igbos, and the Biafran war was over. Gowon then began the rapid reintegration of the Igbos into Nigeria. He stayed in power for another six years to "ensure a peaceful transition to democracy." By 1975 Gowon had postponed elections and the transfer to civilian rule indefinitely. At the same time, there were high prices, chronic shortages of staple goods, growing government corruption, and a failure to address regional issues. As a result, in July 1975 General Murtala Muhammed overthrew Gowon in a bloodless coup. General Muhammed was assassinated in February 1976, and General Olusegun Obasanjo was named as his successor. Obasanjo became the first military leader to hand over power to a civilian regime within the agreed timetable. He agreed to elections in 1979; the elections were held and Shehu Shagari, from the National Party of Nigeria (NPN), was elected. This ushered in the Second Republic.

The NPN won the 1983 elections amidst accusations of fraud and intimidation. In December 1983 General Muhammed Buhari overthrew President Shagari with immense public support. Buhari condemned the economic mismanagement and the corrupt and rigged 1983 elections. However, Buhari quickly lost support when he adopted rigid austerity measures. He instituted repressive policies against any actions of "indiscipline." He declared that there would be no discussions of Nigeria's political future and detained many journalists who were critical of his regime.

In 1985 General Ibrahim Babangida easily overthrew the unpopular Buhari and rescinded many of his unpopular decrees. Babangida eagerly initiated public debate on the state of Nigeria's economy. He went to the International Monetary Fund seeking a new austerity package and tried to improve Nigeria's relations with its creditors. He was able to temporarily improve the economy. He reputedly reshuffled key officers from location to location to keep them from becoming too powerful. In 1989 a new constitution was approved in preparation for a "democratic transfer." The ban on political parties was lifted, but no new parties were allowed to form. In July 1992 the Social Democratic Party (SDP) won the legislature and, in 1993, the presidency, electing Moshood Abiola. As this was unexpected by General Babanginda, his secretary of defense, Sani Abacha stepped in and annulled the election and declared himself the new ruler. General Abacha promised to return the country to civilian rule in October 1998 but died in June 1998. General Abubukar, his successor, promised elections for 1999. Because of both domestic and external pressure, the timetable was honored. Elections were held and Olusegun Obasanjo was elected president of Nigeria's Third Republic. Recent political developments in the Third Republic and prospects for future democratic stability in Nigeria will be discussed in the next chapter.

Since gaining independence more than three decades ago, all four of the former British colonies in West Africa (Nigeria, Ghana, Sierra Leone, and The Gambia) have experienced military rule. The military intervened in these countries when the economy was at its worst, corruption was rampant, or the existing regime was not satisfying the military's expectations.

Corruption has always been the first reason given by the military for the overthrow of the civilian government. Virtually none of the coups in West Africa (or perhaps anywhere else) have been able to eradicate corruption to any significant level; in fact they have managed to increase it greatly. In Nigeria Murtala Muhammed attempted to reduce corruption by firing corrupt government officials. He was assassinated before be was able to address systemic corruption in a broad way. Generals Babanginda and Abacha were notorious for their regimes' high levels of corruption. After his death General Abacha's wife was reportedly found with almost $7.7 million in a suitcase as she tried to board an airplane for Europe. Generals Acheampong and Akufo also managed to siphon off large amounts of cash from the boom in cocoa production in Ghana. Jerry Rawlings (in Ghana) reportedly bribed countless officials to accept IMF austerity plans. Yahya Jammeh (in The Gambia) was accused (by Captain Jallow, his former cabinet minister) of stealing $3 million of state resources and placing it in a Swiss bank account.

As a result of corruption, military regimes, like civilian governments in many developing nations, have accumulated massive wealth in the face of the country's economic decline. Nigeria is the world's sixth largest producer of petroleum, yet it still has one of the poorest economies among developing nations. Per-capita income has declined continuously since 1980, and this can be attributed to gross corruption and mismanagement of revenues by military regimes that used state resources to generate personal fortunes. In Ghana economic policies carried out by General Ignaeius Acheampong contributed to decreased cocoa production, which lowered exports and led to rampant inflation. However, under Jerry Rawlings the picture has been mixed. Ghana has worked through six IMF programs, and on the basis of heavy borrowing, per-capita GDP has reportedly increased, and real wages and import/export revenues have tripled (Hutchful, 1996: Konadu-Agyeman, 1998). Both Babangida and Rawlings's structural adjustment policies led to rising inflation, unemployment, high interest rates, and slow growth.

In Sierra Leone and The Gambia, the National Provisional Ruling Council (NPRC) and the Armed Forces Provisional Ruling Council (AFPRC) began to address concerns of the common citizens almost immediately upon coming to power. In Sierra Leone, electrical and fuel supplies were improved, salaries were increased 100 percent, and roads were constructed linking the capital city, Freetown, to the rest of the country. In The Gambia, the streets of the capital city of Banjul were finally paved, twenty-nine years after independence, garbage was collected on a regular basis, and the country finally established a television station. These good deeds were minimized by the military regimes' later transgressions. The NPRC formed an alliance with the brutal and violent Revolutionary United Front (RUF), and the AFPRC squandered money on a monument, Arch 22, celebrating the military's ascent to power in The Gambia. The AFPRC was also seen to be as corrupt as the civilian regime it replaced, as its own kleptocratic behavior led to stolen state funds being siphoned off into a foreign bank. Civil, political, and human rights generally suffered immeasurably under military rule. In all cases when the military came to power, political parties were banned, politicians were detained or jailed (or killed in some cases), the old political system was dissolved, the press was shut down, journalists were suppressed, and free speech was ended. In Nigeria General Babangida came in with a commitment to civil rights, but by 1986 he had changed course. At a student protest twenty people were killed and hundreds injured. A political crackdown ensued with the banning for life of forty-seven politicians. Eight hundred others were put on trial. Continuing Babangida's trend, General Abacha used fear and public executions to remain in power. Abacha sacked Shoneken, the appointed president, and when president-elect Moshood Abiola began clamoring for his position, he was jailed. Abiola subsequently died in the military's custody. Abacha cracked down on all "dissidents," including noted journalist Ken Saro-Wiwa and the Ogoni 8 (environmentalists fighting for the cleanup of oil and reinvestment of oil revenues in Ogoniland). It was widely believed that Saro-Wiwa was framed for a political killing of four Ogoni chiefs, and he and his fellow activists were publicly hanged in 1994. Abacha had a long list of victims of torture, disappearance, intimidation, and murder. In Ghana Jerry Rawlings did not hesitate to use violence against those who opposed his IMF programs. He also curtailed political involvement, opposition parties, and the press. In 1994, when Yahya Jammeh seized power in The Gambia, his disregard for human rights and individual freedoms got The Gambia's foreign aid suspended.

In addition to the change from civilian to military rule, military governments sometimes attempted structural changes of the political system for the military ruler's benefit. In The Gambia, the thirty-year-old Jammeh rewrote the constitution, dropping the minimum age to be president from forty to thirty so that he could qualify. Strasser in Sierra Leone did the same thing. Jerry Rawlings of Ghana and Jammeh of The Gambia used a "military-turned-civilian" strategy to ensure that they would win in a democratic election. They both conveniently resigned from the military and ran as "civilian" incumbents in the "democratic elections" demanded by international donors and Western capitalist nations. Both leaders are still in power today. Murtala Mohammed of Nigeria made a structural change to the system in switching the Nigerian political system over to a U.S.-style bicameral system with an independent judiciary and a bill of rights. This may have been a positive change, but it was quickly overturned by Generals Babangida's and Abacha's hegemonic authoritarian structures.

Have there been any real differences between civilian and military rulers in Nigeria? Perhaps not. Both produced governments with leaders dedicated to self-enrichment, violence, oppression, and corruption. They have perpetuated a cycle which diminished any chance of stability and socioeconomic development. As long as capturing the state continues to be seen as the only mechanism for economic advancement, these patterns will probably continue. Since the 1990s, there has been a shift away from military authoritarian regimes to multiparty electoral systems in sub-Saharan Africa (notable exceptions are The Gambia, Niger, Côte d'Ivoire). The Organization of African Unity (OAU), along with donor agencies, stated its intention not to recognize any more military governments in the region. Western capitalist donor agencies, supported by their governments, have made the climate less enabling for military regimes to stay in power. The donors have made political as well as economic liberalization conditions for continued economic aid (see Chapter 6). This external pressure, combined with the growing strength of interest groups and associations in African civil society, may indeed prove a deterrent to frequent military interventions in the future. Several military regimes have provided just enough freedom to qualify for international aid but not enough to fear losing in elections.

Competitive Party Systems

The former colonial powers conceived decolonization of their African territories in terms of constitutional democracy. Africans were to be invested with the rights and institutions of self-government. Sovereignty was to be transferred from the colonial power to an African government formed by a nationalist party or a coalition that had gained power through national elections. The new African leadership was expected to embrace the values of the former colonial power and foster continued economic and political ties with the metropole. In accordance with this view, some form of Western liberal democracy, modeled on the constitution of the former colonial power, was officially adopted in the decolonization of almost all of Africa. The only exceptions were the Portuguese colonies of Angola, Mozambique, and Guinea-Bissau, which won their independence through wars of liberation and subsequently adopted a communist model of revolutionary single-party government.

Most African states achieved independence from colonial rule during the late 1950s and early 1960s. Independence was granted in the context of democratic constitutions, universal suffrage, and parliamentary institutions designed to allow competition. In most of sub-Saharan Africa this tradition lasted less than a decade. Electoral competition and multiparty politics were undermined almost immediately in the majority of sub-Saharan African states, as many political leaders abused the inherited constitutions, amassed personal power through manipulation of the ballot box, and subsequently monopolized the resources of the state and, as a result, impoverished the masses.

There were several factors that undermined the survival of democratic institutions during the first decade of independence. The first was the authoritarian policy-making tradition inherited from the colonial civil service system. Second was the survival from the colonial value system of the tendency to elevate political leaders as if they were mythical figures standing above the political system. These leaders were put on pedestals and were pampered with displays of royalty by followers. The effect was to give political leaders a sense of personal authority and power that is inconsistent with democratic pluralist government. Those leaders who felt the need to live out this role accorded to them changed the political system to guarantee their messianic role. Limiting competition and mass participation through one-party systems eliminated the challenge to their privileged status and limit competition for power and resources.

Third, the postindependence state was under great pressure to deliver economic and social rewards promised to the masses of the population during the nationalist struggle for independence. Unable to satisfy the rising expectations of the population and wanting to maintain power in the face of criticism and opposition, many leaders eliminated formal parliamentary opposition by adopting a one-party system. Opposition party members were sometimes co-opted into the ruling party, while in other cases their activities were proscribed or banned outright. Decision making then shifted from the legislature to the central committee of the party, which further monopolized power at the expense of any independent or representative institutions.

Fourth, political leaders appealed to the electorate in ethnic terms. Elections often politicized existing cleavages and differences. In several African countries, politicized ethnicity inserted in electoral competition led to conflict threatening the cohesion of the state. Kwame Nkrumah (Ghana), Albert Margai (Sierra Leone), and Milton Obote (Uganda) sought to dismantle the system of party competition in the name of ethnic harmony. Many African leaders, most notably Julius Nyerere of Tanzania, voted to establish one-party states, which they justified as reflecting true African democracy's encouraging the politics of consensus, whereas multiparty democracy had been divisive.

Competitive party politics occasionally resurfaced in sub-Saharan Africa following periods of authoritarianism—usually in the restoration of civilian rule after a military interlude, such as Burkina Faso, Ghana (twice), Nigeria, and Uganda. Each of these democratic experiments except Uganda was terminated by military coups. In 1980, after three years of constitutional democracy in Burkina Faso, the military intervened and regained control of the state, justifying its action by claiming that the civilians were economically incompetent and corrupt. In Ghana in 1969 liberal democracy was restored after three years of military rule, which had been preceded by Kwame Nkrumah's civilian regime. The Progress Party, led by Dr. K. A. Busia, won the elections, but in 1972 Dr. Busia was overthrown after alienating the military, trade unions, and other groups. Military rule continued until 1979. Elections were held in 1979 that restored liberal democratic institutions again, and Dr. Hilla Liman's People's National Party (PNP) was elected to office. It was subsequently overthrown in 1981 by Flight Lieutenant Jerry Rawlings. Competitive party politics was not restored until 1994. Nigeria's postindependence democratic experiment ended in 1966 with its first military coup. After four military governments the Second Republic was instituted in 1979. The Second Republic consisted of a federation of nineteen states and proved successful in controlling ethnoregional pressures. However, problems emerging from Nigeria's rapidly increasing oil exports, which were under government control and inevitably subjected to political interference, led to the overthrow of the civilian government of President Shehu Shagari in late 1983. Competitive party politics was not restored until 1999, when the Third Republic began under President Olusegun Obasanjo. In Uganda, following General Idi Amin's tyrannical rule (1971–1979), the country attempted to restore competitive party politics. Elections were held in 1985, and Milton Obote's Uganda Peoples Congress (UPC) won.

By the mid-1980s 60 percent of African countries had come under military rule (while the trend in the 1980s was away from military to civilian regimes in Latin America and Asia), and among the remaining civilian regimes, only six (Senegal, Swaziland, Botswana, The Gambia, Mauritius, and Zimbabwe) had competitive party systems. These countries managed to maintain "partial" democracies with constitutional systems, regular elections, and relatively strong human rights records. But only in a few instances

(Mauritius and Senegal) have elections ever led to the ouster of the incumbent party and the assumption of power by an opposition party. In The Gambia and Botswana the incumbent ruling party has never lost an election.

How were some African countries able to maintain decades of uninterrupted multiparty politics? The brief discussion which follows on The Gambia gives some insight into how dominant parties in some competitive political systems in sub-Saharan Africa have been able to hold successive elections and maintain hegemonic control over the state and the population.

The Gambia

For twenty-nine years The Gambia was one of sub-Saharan Africa's longest-standing multiparty electoral systems. It was perceived (along with Botswana and Mauritius) as an "exception" on an African continent where authoritarian and military regimes have been the norm. Apart from the aborted coup d'etat of 1981, The Gambia enjoyed relative peace and stability after its independence from Britain in 1965. The Gambia was said to be an "exception" once again when in 1994 a military coup d'etat removed Dawda Jawara's Peoples Progressive Party (PPP) government, bucking the post-1990 global trend away from authoritarian regimes.

Should the collapse of the PPP government have been expected? What prevented democratic consolidation in The Gambia? The Gambia's "democratic" system had serious limitations in the areas of competitive politics and development performance.

Competitive party politics was introduced by Britain through the geographical division it imposed between colony and protectorate, which coincided with ethnic demographic distribution. The colony was predominantly settled by the urban Wolloffs and the Akus, along with small groups from the rural Fula, Mandinka, Jola, and Serahuli communities. In the protectorate, the Mandinkas constituted the largest groups, followed by the Fula and the Jola. There was also a significant number of rural Wolloffs (Nyang, 1974). Initially the PPP depended on the rural areas and the Mandinkas for its base of support, whereas the United Party (UP), the other major party, drew its support from the Wolloffs in the capital city of Banjul and the Fulas outside of Banjul. The PPP subsequently adopted a new ethnic-inclusive style of politics which limited ethnic divisions and prevented regionalism from becoming an issue dividing the nation (Nyang, 1974).

The PPP emerged after independence as the dominant party, with significantly weakened opposition parties. By 1965 the UP began to decline as a viable opposition party, and in 1970 its secretary-general resigned and joined the PPP. The top leaders of other opposition parties (in the Democratic Congress Alliance) were all absorbed by the PPP and given lucrative cabinet posts or other opportunities to improve their living conditions. The National Convention

Party (NCP), founded in 1975 by Sheriff Dibba (a former member of Dawda Jawara's cabinet), soon became the major opposition party. There was little ideo-logical difference between the PPP and the NCP. The Gambia Peoples Party (GPP) and the Peoples Democratic Party (PDP) were PPP off-shoots formed in the latter half of the 1980s. They were never viable challengers to the PPP.

The most significant differences between Gambian parties emerged only in the 1980s, when the Peoples Democratic Organization for Independence and Socialism (PDOIS) emerged as an organization committed to radical socialism. There was for the first time a clear difference between the (capitalist) ruling party and the (socialist) opposition. The PPP won national elections held in 1966, 1971, 1977, 1982, 1987, and 1992, obtaining between 55 and 70 percent of the popular vote and an overwhelming majority of seats. There was no alternation between the PPP and other parties, and the state re-mained under the control of Dawda Jawara's PPP. The electoral system be-came a one-party-dominant system in which the opposition parties were fragmented and were under constant pressure of co-optation or regulation by the dominant PPP.

In principle, competitive party politics existed in Dawda Jawara's Gambia. A wide range of parties was permitted to participate in elections. However, the PPP controlled many aspects of the democratic infrastructure in order to suppress the opposition, including lack of financial assistance from business and lack of state resources for electoral campaigns, and the government con-trolled opposition media announcements. Flaws in the voter registration sys-tem gave the PPP an unfair advantage over the opposition. People who were not qualified to vote in certain areas were issued voting cards, and some people were found to be registered under the addresses of such places as the Albert Market and the Mohammedan School, clearly not residences. These voters were usually found to be government party supporters. In 1996 com-petitive party politics was restored after seventeen months of military rule. Four political parties contested the 1996 presidential election: the ruling Alliance for Patriotic Reorientation and Construction (APRC), led by retired Captain Yahya Jammeh, the United Democratic Party (UDP), the National Reconciliation Party (NRP), and the Peoples Democratic Organization for Independence and Socialism (PDOIS). PDOIS was the only party from the Jawara era that was allowed to participate; all the others were banned. The three parties other than PDOIS were hardly different in policy positions or ideology. The APRC obtained 55.8 percent of the popular vote; the UDP, 35.8 percent; NRP, 5.5 percent; and PDOIS, 2.9 percent. The National Assembly elections followed in January 1997, with the APRC winning thirty-three of the forty-five contested seats (Wiseman, 1998: 68–69). The results of these elections showed continuity in the postindependence pattern of domination by the incumbent party. These elections returned The Gambia to the electoral context of the Jawara era in regard to the level of support for the opposition. Many Gambians did not believe the APRC had won the elections fairly (Wiseman, 1998), which reflected how little the electoral process's lack of credibility had changed.

Political rights in competitive party systems are protected by the legal system and enforced by constitutional guarantees against their violation. Individual freedoms are protected under the law, and there are clear limits on the power the state is able to exercise over the individual. Under the system of one-party domination in The Gambia, these institutional protections of liberal democracy were not always present. The strength of the executive branch (the president in particular) came at the cost of an ineffectual legislature and judiciary. The legislative branch's influence was limited by the dominant PPP, which held an overwhelming majority of the seats. Posts in the judiciary branch were appointed members of the incumbent PPP government. The judiciary branch was perceived to be a tool of the PPP; hence it could not guarantee that individual rights would be protected.

Implementing neoliberal economic reforms has been difficult in sub-Saharan Africa. Its negative effects have impacted disproportionately certain politically strategic groups in the society. Within the one-party-dominant system, the PPP was able to implement economic reforms without being undermined by opposition parties. Since civil society organizations were weak or controlled by the government, the PPP was not undermined by interest groups dissatisfied with its economic policies. Structural adjustment policies introduced in 1985 led to improvement in the country's macroeconomic indicators: budgetary targets were achieved, credit policy restraint was maintained, real GDP grew by 3.3 percent between 1986 and 1993, inflation was reduced to 5 to 7 percent, and gross foreign exchange reserves of the Central Bank improved (Jabara, 1994; McPherson and Radelet, 1995). Despite these positive statistics, the living standards of the vast majority of Gambians has remained low for more than three decades.

In 1992 The Gambia was still one of the poorest countries in Africa and the world, with a forty-five-year life expectancy at birth, an infant mortality rate of 130 per 1,000 live births, a 75 percent adult illiteracy rate, 1 physician for 14,115 people, only 40 percent of the population having access to a clean water supply, over 75 percent of the population living in absolute poverty, and not one tertiary institution in the country (Economic Commission for Africa [ECA], 1993). The country had two hospitals, twenty health centers, and thirty village health posts for about 1.4 million people. At the same time, the political elites in control of the state (and their allies) enjoyed expensive and secluded homes, good schools for their children, good health care, private doctors, and overseas travel. This was the profile during the years leading up to the military coup d'etat in 1994.

In a genuinely competitive party system, the electorate would have opted for an alternative. But what we saw in The Gambia under Jawara was the failure of a stable and genuine multiparty system to take root. This failure can be linked to a combination of political and economic factors: an inappropriate electoral system of representation based on the first-past-the-post winner-take-all principle, a narrow distribution of power, suppression of the opposition, and the absence of strong civil society associations such as an independent media, autonomous interest groups, and strong unions and political parties.

Under PPP rule The Gambia had a democratic façade anchored in one-party domination. The forces that favored authoritarianism and one-party domination are as strong now as they were in the Jawara era. First, the playing field is still uneven, giving the incumbent party continuous advantage in securing the resources of the state to outcompete and co-opt the opposition. Second, the fractionalized and almost ideologically uniform opposition parties, weak civil society associations, and limited independent media, have all made it virtually impossible to mount effective dissent and accountability efforts at the national level. Third, The Gambia is still relatively weak in all the social forces that tend to stimulate demands for democratic expression—adult literacy, urbanization, a large middle class, and a large wage-earning sector are all social forces. Fourth, the military has a strong political role, supporting the Jammeh administration. Through a "soldier-turned-civilian" transfer of power, Jammeh assumed the leadership of The Gambia within an electoral framework. Pushed by pressures from international donors to restore civilian rule, Jammeh agreed to a transition program leading to democratic elections. The transfer of power to the APRC was widely recognized as undemocratic, unfree, and unfair, but Jammeh has the military behind his administration. As long as he maintains himself in power primarily through military support, a shift away from authoritarianism in The Gambia is unlikely.

Conclusion

The dominant political systems in sub-Saharan Africa from the 1960s through the 1980s were authoritarian. This form of state power converged with high levels of state management of the economies of the region. Influenced by global trends toward democratization, many sub-Saharan African governments have faced increased demands from their people for participation in political decision making. Under pressure from both domestic classes and external donors who link continued aid to democratization, authoritarian leaders in the region have thought a good deal about democracy, but many have not yet embraced it. Some have cleverly devised strategies to hold elections at regular intervals (in which victory is certain) to satisfy external donors and to maintain capital inflows; others have made genuine attempts at political reform. Neoliberal economic reforms have only led to concrete material gains for a small sector of the population, and many governments are struggling to provide basic services under severe austerity measures. It is not yet clear whether the post-1990 trend toward democratization can be sustained. This question will be pursued further in the next chapter.

For Further Reading

Stone, Carl (1980). *Understanding Third World Politics and Economics*. Brown's Town, Jamaica: Earle Publishers.

Clapham, Christopher (1985). *Third World Politics: An Introduction*. London: Croom Helm.

6

State Responses to Challenges of the 1990s: Incipient Democratization?

Africans have struggled against unpopular and repressive regimes throughout the postindependence period. Their long tradition of street demonstrations, strikes, boycotts, student riots, rural revolts, as well as covert forms of protest such as underproduction, noncompliance, and withdrawal into the parallel economy has been noted in the literature (Wiseman, 1986; Abrahamsen, 1997). In the 1980s, the most economically turbulent decade since independence, protests rooted in socioeconomic discontent occurred in many countries. The 1989–1991 period of antisystem demonstrations led to the collapse of military and single-party systems of state power and the emergence of multi-party systems in more than thirty sub-Saharan African countries. This political process has been widely heralded as a "new beginning" in Africa and as a part of Samuel Huntington's global democratic "wave" of the 1990s, which saw authoritarian regimes collapse, one after the other, in different regions and continents throughout the world. The struggles of the 1990s form part of the continuous African struggle for socioeconomic and democratic rights.

The decade of the 1990s represented a "new beginning" in postindependence sub-Saharan African politics, but it was not because a new political process had been introduced by the "domino" or "snowball" effect of global democracy movements. It was a new beginning because, for the first time since the independence period in the 1960s, domestic and external pressures converged and created an environment that no longer supported authoritarian regimes. A broad cross-section of domestic groups across the African continent revolted against the postcolonial leadership whose performance had caused them severe hardship and material deprivation. These groups generally demanded governments that would work to improve the population's standard of living. The masses of the African population demanded a democracy that embodied socioeconomic rights.

For the first time Western industrialized nations and the capitalist lending agencies were, in a surprising turn, on the same side of change as the African people. With the end of the Cold War Africa's anticommunist autocrats were of little ideological, strategic, and geopolitical value to Western industrialized nations, and the latter sought to reduce or eliminate economic and political support for them. By 1990 most capitalist lending agencies, like the World Bank, European Union (EU), and Organization for Economic Cooperation and Development (OECD), had adopted an official policy linking financial assistance to democratic governance under multiparty systems. Aid became contingent on the implementation of free market policies as well as multiparty free elections. Democracy as defined by the donor agencies and their governments was fundamentally different from how the African population perceived it. The Western industrialized countries wanted a liberal market democracy, where the state plays a minimal role in the economy and polity and **guarantees** elections and formal political rights rather than concrete socioeconomic rights. Despite the difference in viewpoints on democracy, the African population's pressures for change converged with the goals of Western capitalist agencies and governments and triggered the removal of many authoritarian regimes and secured multiparty systems. However, the neoliberal economic policies seemed unfit to address African people's socio-economic concerns and so have earned their enmity.

The authoritarian African political directorate faced a dual challenge of continuing donor-driven neoliberal economic reforms (without giving into popular demands for government spending, new protections, and new rents) while seeking simultaneously to maintain competitive party systems (without giving into popular demands for political freedom). Despite widespread apprehension (and in some cases protracted resistance), over thirty sub-Saharan African leaders held multiparty elections by the mid-nineties. It was the belief that external advocates had persuaded the population that it could enjoy the benefits of neoliberal economic reforms only under multiparty systems that ultimately convinced many of the authoritarian leaders to comply with external demands for multiparty elections. Because socioeconomic progress had been of the utmost priority for the African masses and had become linked to political reform, the political leaders realized that they would lose regime legitimacy and the ability to govern unless political changes were made.

African regimes have had diverse responses to the pressures resulting from the linkage between democratic political stability and socioeconomic progress. They range from adamant resistance to compliance and reform, with consequences for the state ranging from a reconfiguration of power in a semiauthoritarian and semidemocratic direction to fragmentation, disintegration, and collapse. This chapter will assess the transformation of the African state that occurred in the 1990s and the extent and degree of continuity with earlier periods of postindependence African politics.

Pressures for Democratization: The International Context

Following the end of the Cold War and the collapse of the discredited Soviet development model, Western industrialized countries (particularly the United States) and international donor agencies aimed to integrate as many national economies as possible into a multilateral global capitalist economy. The World Bank's 1989 report *Sub-Saharan Africa: From Crisis to Sustainable Growth* linked the failure of its policies in the region to the lack of "good governance." The bank not only encouraged African countries to develop policies favoring international market forces but also insisted that "Africa needs not just less government but better government" (1989: 5). "Bad governance" was said to have occurred as a result of the personalized nature of rule, frequent violation of human rights, lack of delegation of central authority, and the tendency of the masses to withdraw from politics (Hyden, 1992: 23–25). The bank argued that "poor governance" stood in the way of the "right" economic policies and that a "crisis of governance underlies the litany of Africa's development problems" (World Bank, 1989: 60). The benefits of economic liberalization could be attained, the bank argued, only under systems that could provide "good governance," that is, democratic systems. The international donor community quickly introduced an unequivocal policy linking assistance to "good governance" and free market reforms. The 1991 Harare Declaration of Commonwealth Heads of Government on Good Governance linked aid to good governance, as did other major donors, particularly the United States and EU.

Sub-Saharan Africa was particularly vulnerable to this shift in policy because it was the region with the most authoritarian regimes, the highest levels of poverty, the greatest political instability, and the most indebted economies. Popular demands resulting from economic discontent caused by cumulative postindependence economic policies converged with global changes favoring democratic pluralism and neoliberal economic reforms. Because most African leaders needed external donor funds to maintain national development budgets and keep their regimes in power, many found themselves in a vulnerable position where donors had significant leverage over them. This leverage allowed donors to use carrots and sticks to encourage or force many reluctant governments to initiate transition programs.

Donors and Political Conditionality

Forced compliance by way of financial pressure has been the principal external input into the democratization process in sub-Saharan Africa. Severe cases of financial pressure are found mainly in those countries whose leaders refused entirely to democratize or showed little commitment to the process once they were forced to initiate it.

In 1989 President Mathieu Kerekou in Benin faced state bankruptcy, the collapse of the country's banking system, and an inability to pay the salaries of public sector employees. Lacking other options, he approached the IMF and World Bank for assistance in paying the workers' salaries. Both lenders rejected this request, insisting that the request "lacked specific details on political and economic reforms." Because of Benin's dependence on donor aid and the government's lack of any other option among the collapsing communist regimes in the Soviet Union, Eastern Europe, China, or elsewhere, President Kerekou was forced to renounce his Marxist ideology and convene a national conference that ultimately led to elections and his losing power in Benin.

Since its independence in 1963, Kenya has been a consistent and reliable ally of Western industrialized nations, particularly the United States, as well as a favored recipient of U.S. aid in Africa. Despite its known human rights violations under both the Kenyatta and Moi regimes, failure to implement agreed economic reforms, and poor economic performance since the late 1980s, Kenya received an increase in its grants from 1 percent of its GDP in 1986 to more than 3 percent in 1990 (Sanbrook, 1992: 4). However, donors dramatically shift their policy toward Kenya in the early 1990s, linking financial assistance to political reform. In 1990, Norway, Sweden, Finland, Denmark, Iceland, and the United States condemned President Moi's repression of opposition groups in Kenya and threatened to cut off assistance estimated at slightly over 125 million pounds sterling and 25 million pounds sterling, respectively. In November 1991 the Consultative Group meeting in Paris withheld US$1 billion from the regime until it provided concrete evidence of its willingness to embark on both political liberalization and socioeconomic reforms. In December 1991 the IMF withheld loans worth US$60 million. Moi subsequently bowed to this pressure in December 1991 and scheduled multiparty elections for December 1992. Financial pressure was effective because the Kenyan government had no alternative resources (Nwokedi, 1995. 186).

In Zaire Mobutu reluctantly agreed to multipartyism in April 1990 but ordered the massacre of students involved in antigovernment protests one month later. In response to this event, Belgium suspended its US$10 million aid package to Zaire, and the U.S. Congress adopted a resolution in November 1990 cutting off all economic and military aid to Mobutu's regime. All economic aid (worth about US$40 million) for fiscal year (FY) 1991 was rechanneled through nongovernmental organizations (Nwokedi, 1995: 186).

In late 1992 the Togolese government ordered several military attacks on transitional institutions that it had reluctantly put in place. Several months later, in February 1993, talks mediated by France and Germany between Togolese president Gnassingbe Eyadema and the opposition coalition collapsed. In the aftermath of these developments, external pressure was brought to bear on Togo. France suspended its civilian cooperation with Togo, Germany stopped its development cooperation, and the United States suspended its aid, worth about US$19 million (Nwokedi, 1995: 186–187). Elections were subsequently held and won by the incumbent President Eyadema.

African leaders saw the donor nations and agencies' imposition of political conditionality as punitive and as a challenge to the sovereignty of their nations. Political conditionality had been applied first to the collapsed communist countries of Eastern Europe and then extended to sub-Saharan African regimes at a time when aid resources were scarce and keenly contested between "democratizing" Eastern European countries on one hand and "Third World" countries on the other. Many believed that without the implementation of political conditionality, many authoritarian regimes in sub-Saharan Africa would not have legalized multiparty politics nor have accepted political alternation when defeated at the polls (as happened in Benin, Congo, Mali, Niger, and Zambia), nor would political changes have occurred in countries where long serving incumbents consistently opposed multiparty elections and won questionable victories (Cameroon, Togo, and Kenya).

Technical Assistance for Transition Programs

External actors provided technical assistance and funds for organizing transition programs leading to multiparty elections. France reportedly bore a disproportionate burden in the francophone states, where it funded payment of salary arrears to public sector employees in Benin and Congo (Brazzaville) and, among other things, financed the staging of national conferences, where these were held (Nwokedi, 1995). According to published reports of the German Foreign Affairs Ministry, between 1992 and 1994 the German government gave financial support (in thousands of Deutschmarks [DM]) for the democratization process: Burkina Faso (DM70,500), Congo-Brazzaville (DM650,000), Gabon (DM100,000), Ghana (DM500,000), Kenya (DM 400,000), Niger (DM560,000), Nigeria (DM15,000), Togo (DM606,000), Zaire (DM153,457), and Zambia (DM228,000) (Nwokedi, 1995: 190).

These funds were used to cover the costs of printing election materials and preparing for elections, purchasing equipment for the electoral office, training election assistants, dispatching election observers, election monitoring, and purchasing audio equipment for national conferences. The overall figure committed by the German Foreign Affairs Ministry alone in support of democratization in sub-Saharan Africa within the 1992–1994 period was an estimated DM10 million (Nwokedi, 1995: 190). Further, the German Economic Cooperation and Development Ministry, church groups, and other nongovernmental organizations (NGOs) in Germany also played important roles in sub-Saharan Africa's democratization.

There was a surge in the growth of NGOs and human rights organizations in fostering democracy in developing nations. The governments of France, the United States, Belgium, the Netherlands, Canada, Norway, Denmark, and Sweden, as well as Western private and semiprivate foundations and government and intergovernmental agencies for cooperation and development financed the activities of human rights organizations and NGOs committed to institution building in Africa. The U.S. Agency for International Development (USAID) was reported to have given US$12 million in 1991 to several NGOs in some seven African countries, including Nigeria and South Africa. The overall sum dispersed by USAID in support of sub-Saharan African democratization was estimated to have increased from US$4.7 million in 1990 to US$83 million by fiscal year 1994 (Nwokedi, 1995: 191).

Election Monitoring and Observation

There are contending viewpoints on the role of external election monitors and observers in developing nations. The stated role of the observers and monitors has been to monitor the elections, report irregularities, and deliver a judgment on whether the elections were "free and fair." The reports issued at the end of the elections are meant to indicate the degree to which the recipient nations complied with the political conditions demanded by the donor community for the disbursement of aid. In many instances, the primacy accorded political stability often undermined the credibility of election monitoring. Deal making in the interest of peace and stability sometimes won out over the verdict of the observers on the validity of the elections. Is election monitoring simply a technical exercise to check whether the rules have been followed? Or is it meant to legitimize the government that emerges from the elections?

Between 1992 and 1994 Angola, Eritrea, Ethiopia, Liberia, Mozambique, Namibia, Sierra Leone, South Africa, Uganda, and Zambia held internationally monitored elections after years of civil conflict. The 1991 Zambian election was carefully monitored and received high praise from international observers as having "set the standard for Africa" (Nwokedi, 1995: 201). The electoral process, the observers concluded was free and fair. The incumbent, Kenneth Kaunda, president of Zambia since independence in 1964, lost the elections that he had reluctantly organized under domestic and external pressures. The Zambian election was successful in the eyes of the international community, as it was declared free and fair, and particularly as it led to regime change. However, it reportedly prompted some incumbent African leaders to strategize about how to hold democratic elections without being voted out of office (Nwokedi, 1995).

The 1992 Kenyan elections was, the international donor community believed, a significant event. Donors had suspended aid to Kenya and refused to restore it unless elections were declared free and fair. There were 150 external election observers, as well as local monitoring groups including the National Elections Monitoring Unit (NEPU); the Bureau for Education, Research and Monitoring; the National Council of Women of Kenya; and the National Committee for the Status of Women in Kenya. In contrast to the highly praised Zambian elections of 1991, international observers in Kenya (1992) and Cameroon (1992) identified serious lapses in the electoral process, especially the clampdown on opposition leaders. The United States criticized the flawed elections in Kenya and the conduct of the Cameroonian elections. It also discontinued its aid program to Cameroon. France, however, was not critical of Cameroon and, as a measure of support, rewarded the country with fresh credit. Despite the criticism of the flawed elections in Kenya, international observers unanimously agreed that the results should stand. This has been the tone for Western policy toward democratization in Kenya. Despite poor progress with democratization after multiparty elections were held, Western industrialized nations and donors exerted little influence over subsequent events. Rather than withholding aid until a credible attempt at democracy had occurred, Western countries quickly resumed aid as soon as elections were completed.

Pressures for Democratization: The Domestic Context

Protests within Civil Society

By the end of the 1980s the postcolonial model of development had been totally discredited and had alienated the African population. The struggles for independence had aimed at the termination of European rule in Africa, self-determination for African people, better jobs, better working conditions, more schools and health clinics, and basic rights and liberties. The postcolonial state, governed by military and civilian regimes, did not fulfill these goals. State resources were appropriated and allocated inefficiently mainly for the consolidation of power by autocratic regimes. Balance-of-payments difficulties, resulting from the OPEC cartel's increase in oil prices in the 1970s and misguided allocation of state funds, led to an increase in foreign borrowing that increased the debt burden of many sub-Saharan African countries. Their desperate financial condition and lack of alternative aid sources led them to accept IMF and World Bank prescriptions for adjustment of their economies: privatization, market efficiency, proper pricing policies, public sector reductions, liberalization of imports, an export orientation, and so forth. The IMF and World Bank then became actively involved in shaping and directing the response to their economic crisis. Under structural adjustment policies, a handful of countries claimed some measure of success in terms of macroeconomic stability, but this was at the expense of growth, investment, and human welfare. Depressed real incomes worsened living conditions. Gross Domestic Product (GDP) and per-capita income declined steadily or stagnated in most sub-Saharan African countries in the 1980s. In the 1960s per-capita incomes had increased at the rate of 1.4 percent annually, but this rate had declined to 0.2 percent annually in the 1970s, and -2.8 percent between 1980 and 1986. As a result, more than half of the population lived in absolute poverty. People in Nigeria, Liberia, and Niger, for instance, endured a decline in real incomes of well over 25 percent. Declines in agricultural and industrial output, rising food imports, declining terms of trade, and drastic reductions in social expenditure made everyday life very difficult for the majority of Africans. Budgetary cutbacks and declining incomes in the 1980s devastated many educational institutions, increased infant mortality rates, and worsened nutritional levels. Literacy rates, life expectancy, and employment in the formal economy remained stagnant or declined (World Bank, 1990; United Nations Development Program [UNDP], 1990; both cited in Sandbrook, 1993: 5–6).

Between 1989 and 1990 in some fifteen African countries broad sectors of the African population protested in the streets of capital cities against economic hardship and political repression and demanded changes (Bratton and van de Walle, 1992). The masses of the African poor, with support from the middle classes, joined the street protests, playing an important role in the struggle for change. Mass action played a significant part in Benin, Burkina Faso, Cameroon, Central African Republic, Côte d'Ivoire, Equatorial Guinea, Gabon, Guinea-Conakry, Guinea-Bissau, Kenya, Lesotho, Madagascar, Malawi, Mauritania, Niger, Nigeria, Sierra Leone, South Africa, Swaziland, Togo, Zaire, and Zambia. Mass protests were urban in origin, perhaps because the standard of living of urban dwellers was most immediately affected by the economic crisis and the structural adjustment policies imposed to deal with the crisis. In 1986 the Kaunda government's removal of food subsidies on maize in Zambia led to an increase of 120 percent in its price. This led to several days of violent riots in the copper belt towns of Ndola and Kitwe, which forced the government to reinstate the policy.

In November 1990 in Mali about 100,000 demonstrators marched through the streets of the capital city of Bamako in support of a general strike organized to pressure President Ali Saibou's government into accepting transition to a multiparty system. Violent suppression of mass protest did occur a year later, when security forces killed about 150 people and arrested several hundreds, but the government of Mali later reluctantly accepted political reform.

In 1991 in Madagascar President Didier Ratsiraka attempted to introduce a new constitution that reversed the previously agreed-upon political reform program and increased the incumbent president's power. Opposition groups rejected the proposed constitution and between June and September 1991 organized and held a series of mass demonstrations mainly in the capital city of Antananarivo. These attracted about one and a half million protesters. More than one hundred protesters were killed in confrontations with the security forces (Wiseman, 1996), but these protests forced the embattled President Ratsiraka to create a transitional government that included opposition figures. Multiparty elections were held in 1993, and the incumbent was defeated in the presidential election by the opposition leader, Albert Zafy (Wiseman, 1996). In other countries mass demonstrations also occurred in support of middle-class activists who had been beaten, arrested, shot, and/or killed by the government (e.g., in Kenya in 1991 and in Malawi in 1992). Mass protests did not always lead to gains for the protesters. Mass protests in Togo were met with violence from the Togolese military and yielded few gains for the people.

Trade union activists also played an important role in the struggle for political change in Zambia, Niger, Togo, Benin, South Africa, Malawi, Burkina Faso, Burundi, Cameroon, Chad, Central African Republic, Comoros, Congo, Côte d'Ivoire, Gabon, Ghana, Guinea, Kenya, Lesotho, Madagascar, Mali, Mauritania, Nigeria, Swaziland, and Zaire. In Zambia Frederick Chiluba, the longtime leader of Zambia's main trade union body, the Zambian Congress of Trade Unions (ZCTU), emerged as the leader of the Movement for Multiparty Democracy (MMD), formed in July 1990, ran as its presidential candidate, and defeated incumbent President Kenneth Kaunda in the 1991 elections. Trade unions in several countries used a general strike as pressure for political change. In Benin and Niger general strikes pressured the governments to initiate political change. The Congress of South African Trade Unions (COSATU), an affiliation of thirty-four unions, linked the trade union movement to the struggle to end the apartheid system. Its leader played an important role in the constitution-making process that led to political change in 1994 (Wiseman, 1996). The educated middle classes, through their professional associations, also provided critical support for political change. Lawyers, academics, journalists, and medical doctors were the professions most represented. These groups saw their purchasing power eroded by inflation, and currency devaluation made their much desired luxury imports unaffordable. They had become disillusioned with the existing leadership and sought an alternative.

The Nigerian Bar Association, the Committee for the Defense of Human Rights (CDHR), the Civil Liberties Organization (CLO), and the Campaign for Democracy (CD) played an active role in the struggle for political change in Nigeria, the latter two mounting the most vocal opposition to General Babangida's abandonment of the transition process in 1993. The Law Society of Kenya, Cameroonian Bar Association, Ghana Bar Association, Togolese Bar Association, and Tanzanian Legal Education Trust all contributed to movements for political change in their respective countries.

University students protested austerity measures that resulted in teaching shortages and poor study facilities, among other things. Students often faced violent attacks by the police or the army resulting in many deaths and injuries. In May 1990 the Zairian security forces killed over three hundred students after the Mobutu government had agreed to initiate a transition program leading to political reform. Embattled African governments facing student protests also closed down the universities for extended periods. Nevertheless, students continued to pressure governments for political change in Benin, Burkina Faso, Cameroon, Congo, Côte d'Ivoire, Gabon, Ghana, Guinea, Kenya, Madagascar, Mali, Malawi, Niger, Nigeria, Sierra Leone, South Africa, Tanzania, Togo, Zaire, and Zambia. Students maintained the pressure on Zimbabwean president Robert Mugabe when his government appeared ready to abandon the multiparty system (Wiseman, 1996).

Leaders from various Christian churches gave critical support to movements for political reform in many African countries. The Roman Catholic Church spoke out against Mobutu in Zaire, called for change in Benin, was a strong supporter of multiparty politics in Ghana, and spoke out against the Banda regime in Malawi. In Rwanda, the Roman Catholic newspaper pressured the corrupt Habyarimana regime to make political changes. In Kenya, the National Council of Churches of Kenya (NCCK) condemned the Moi government's decision to abolish secret ballot voting and replace it with a queuing system, and the archbishop frequently spoke out against single-party rule. From 1985 onward the Dutch Reformed Church in South Africa joined the pressure to end the apartheid system. Many church leaders also served as chairs of the national conferences held in many African countries. Both the opposition and government trusted them as neutral third parties, since they seemed not to have had a political interest in the outcome (Wiseman, 1996).

The climate of protest emboldened the opposition in many countries to call for multiparty competition. The combination of political exclusion and economic deprivation converged to set off a new and vibrant movement to end authoritarianism and restructure the state for purposes of building democracy and achieving socioeconomic progress. Political leaders in regimes such as Kenya, Cameroon, Zambia, Central African Republic, and Zimbabwe bitterly opposed political reform and argued generally that multi-party politics would incite ethnic conflict and electoral violence and that Africa was not yet ready for it. Presidents Moi of Kenya and Mugabe of Zim-babwe vociferously opposed it as an interference in the sovereign rights of African states (Bratton and van de Walle, 1992). Facing both internal and ex-ternal pressures, Moi conceded by halfheartedly launching the party reform commission in Kenya while simultaneously detaining his opponents and de-creeing a halt to public discussions of multipartyism. President Omar Bongo in Gabon banned all strikes and demonstrations but granted salary increases and benefits to striking workers. In Ghana and Malawi, where significant protests did not occur, the autocratic leaders continued to insist on the main-tenance of the status quo. Jerry Rawlings of Ghana implemented a tightly controlled program of decentralization of state structures, and Malawi's President Banda denied opportunities for dissent both within and outside the governing Malawi Congress Party (MCP).

Despite their apprehension and in some cases refusal to back down, a substantial number of African political leaders were forced to respond to popular pressures (combined with external pressures) and embark on a course of political change.

The National Conference as a Transition Strategy: The Benin Case

National conferences took place in Benin, Burkina Faso, Chad, Comoros, Congo-Brazzaville, Gabon, Mali, Niger, Togo, and Zaire. The opposition demanded but did not obtain them in Cameroon, Central African Republic, Côte d'Ivoire, Guinea, Kenya, and Nigeria. Benin was the first country in sub-Saharan Africa to use the national conference in the struggle for political change. It provided an example of one of the mechanisms many countries successfully used to involve the public in discussions of the political future. Many other countries that used the national conference strategy did not replicate the Benin model, but it did influence them. The events leading up to the crisis that produced the national conference in Benin are summarized below.

From its independence in 1960 until 1972 Benin experienced significant political instability under several civilian and military governments. In 1972 the senior officer corps appointed Mathieu Kerekou president, and stability was restored. In 1976 the Kerekou government adopted Marxism as its ideology, established and implemented a socialist command economy, and a communist party (the Party of the People's Revolution). The party retained all key policy-making authority, since power was concentrated in the president, the Central Committee, and the Council of Ministers. The state was at the center of economic development, dominating the means of production, controlling all formal sector activity, creating public enterprises, controlling export marketing through state monopolies, and regulating prices, wages, and import licenses. There was a huge social commitment to education, with an increase in secondary and university enrollments. Graduates were guaranteed jobs in the expanding public sector. The number of civil servants consequently tripled between 1960 and 1980.

The economy grew at an estimated 0.7 percent between 1972 and 1976 and saw accelerated growth of between 4 and 5 percent in real terms between 1977 and 1982. Like most of sub-Saharan Africa, by 1983 the Beninese economy entered a period of low growth and financial decline: real per-capita income declined as population growth exceeded 3 percent annually; real GDP growth between 1983 and 1987 averaged under 1 percent; the public finance gap rose to 9 percent of GDP; the balance-of-payment gap increased to 7 percent (both financed by growing internal and external arrears); agricultural production declined, and cereal imports rose from 34,000 tons in 1976 to 110,000 tons in 1981 (Westabbe, 1994: 84).

In 1989 the Benin government embraced a radical program of structural reform that received substantial IMF and World Bank support. It moved toward economic liberalization and private sector development while substantially reducing the role of the public sector. For this a US$48 million loan was approved by the World Bank in May 1989, followed by an IMF Structural Adjustment Facility Loan and significant financing from the European Economic Community (EEC), France, Switzerland, and West Germany. The Kerekou government showed a willingness to undertake structural reforms: for example, in 1986 it created the National Commission to Implement the Structural Adjustment Program (CNSAPAS), shifting power away from the Political Bureau to the president and a small group of his ministers. Creating CNSAPAS and reforming public sector management and the banking program pleased the World Bank since these reduced the patronage-granting capacity of the state as well as opportunities for rent seeking. The World Bank financed some safeguards against adverse social impacts on those affected by public sector layoffs and reduced privileges and rents (e.g., a social fund to buy medicine and school books, run retraining projects, and give deployment help to civil servants).

The success of the structural adjustment program would be based on the government's ability to achieve budgetary targets. The government failed, and the overall deficit widened when revenues fell 30 percent short of expectations. The government could not meet the conditions for disbursement of foreign budgetary aid and as a result obtained only half of its projected aid of 50 billion CFA (Communaute Financiere Africaine) francs. Domestic arrears rose to 75 billion CFA francs, higher than budgetary revenues. External arrears fell, and real GDP fell by about 2.6 percent in 1989, compared to a program target of a 2.5 percent increase (Westabbe 1994: 85). By the last few months of 1989 the economic and financial crisis made it impossible for President Kerekou to govern. Profound antigovernment dissatisfaction erupted throughout the country, as both domestic leaders and external bilateral donors voiced concern.

President Kerekou faced a crisis: he was unable to meet the state payroll or obtain credits and faced protests from all sectors of the population. He urgently asked the donors to pay the three months salary arrears for 1989 before civil servants went on strike. The donors denied the request because they felt that it lacked specific details on political and economic reform. Public pressure continued with demonstrations demanding a national conference of the "*forces vives*" (mobilized forces) of the nation.

Kerekou succumbed to pressures from civil society, called a national conference, and lost control of its direction. The national conference lasted from February 19 to February 28, 1989, and within that time the political order established by President Kerekou was swept from power in a nonviolent "revolution." The conference delegates declared themselves sovereign, contrary to the legal instruments under which the conference had been convened. The conference also made its decisions binding on the state with or without presidential ratification, disbanded the governments, and proceeded to create transitional institutions to supervise the rest of the democratic transitional process. A distraught President Kerekou was persuaded by Monsignor Isidore de Souza, the conference chair, to accept the outcome as the first genuine expression of opinion by the diverse interests in Benin's civil society.

President Kerekou subsequently agreed to abide by the resolutions of the conference: a transitional prime minister was appointed and entrusted with executive powers including the defense portfolio; a High Council of the Republic under the presidency of Monsignor de Souza was established to see the implementation of the sovereign national conference; President Kerekou was retained in office but stripped of his powers; and a Constitutional Commission was established to draw up a new political framework for a multiparty and democratic Benin. More than thirty political parties participated in the 1991 elections. President Kerekou decided to run for president at the last minute and was defeated by Nicèphore Soglo, who received 64.61 percent of the vote against Kerekou's 32.39 percent. An electoral victory for the opposition confirmed mass disenchantment with Kerekou's regime and led to the emergence of new political leadership.

The new Soglo government continued with structural adjustment re-forms, particularly state disengagement from the economy. Public finance targets for 1990 and 1991 were met, salaries were paid on time, and an ap-proximate 10 percent of civil servants were terminated by 1992. The World Bank's Second Structural Adjustment Loan led to substantial additional donor aid. By the next elections, in 1995, however, discontent over President Soglo's attempt to overreach his authority and the negative impact of the shocks from the adjustment policies led to his defeat and Kerekou's return to power. Kerekou has since maintained his commitment to structural adjust-ment policies but also promised to increase employment and to limit privati-zation of state enterprises. The economic situation in Benin remains fragile, as the government is constrained by externally imposed economic policies, rejected twice by the electorate.

The proceedings of the Benin national conference were transmitted live on radio and TV in many neighboring countries. Benin's experience rein-forced the demands made by similar democratic movements in the region for multipartyism and democracy through the national conference. The national conference phenomenon drove incumbents from power also in Niger, Congo-Brazzaville, and Madagascar but failed to achieve this goal in Gabon, Togo, and Zaire, though nevertheless changing the rules of the political game in those countries. The success of the Benin example convinced some leaders that if they contemplated democratization the national conference should be avoided. From the leaders' perspective, democratization through the national conference meant the incumbent would be ousted. It must be noted that although there was successful political change in some countries through the ballot box, this has not produced important changes such as in-creased power sharing or greater economic prosperity.

Preemptive Transition by the Incumbent

In several countries (e.g., Cape Verde, Guinea, Guinea-Bissau, Madagascar, São Tomé and Principe, Somalia, and Tanzania), political leaders announced their own self-directed political reforms in the absence of significant domes-tic protest. The diffusion effects of the democratic "wave" might have prompted initiatives toward political reform in some countries. The luso-phone (former colonies of Portugal) countries (Cape Verde, Guinea-Bissau, and São Tomé and Principe) are believed to have followed Mozambique in abandoning Marxism and allowing multiparty competition. Tanzania's econ-omy depended on foreign aid and assistance, and the political leadership per-haps anticipated that the donors' political conditionality policy would soon be extended to Tanzania, as it had been to Kenya. Tanzania initiated its own political reforms, for which it believed it would be rewarded (Tripp, 2000). In the case of Somalia, President Siyad Barre's declaration of multiparty reforms was not easily explained; many observers believed it was a cynical attempt to convince the United States to restore cuts in foreign aid (Bratton and van de Walle, 1992)

For the most part, incumbents who directed their own process of political reform remained in power. In Ethiopia the ruling Ethiopian People's Revolutionary Democratic Front (EPRDF) came to power in 1991 with the fall of the Mengistu regime. It respected U.S. demands for multiparty electoral systems and free market economic policies, formally embracing both concepts within a year after it came to power. It organized and held regional elections (1992), Constituent Assembly elections (1994), federal elections for the House of Representatives (1995), and local district elections (1996). In all these elections the EPRDF won by a very wide margin. The institutional resources of the EPRDF and its strong-arm methods, which made it difficult for the opposition to compete, led to its control of "most of the political space" in the country (Ottaway, 1999b). Party elites reportedly stated that they "cannot afford to lose the elections" (Abbink and Hesseling, 2000) and used all the tactics available to them to ensure electoral victory. There were reports of outright intimidation of the opposition in rural areas. The opposition faced certain defeat and chose to boycott the elections. The elections further solidified an autocratic dominant party and did not instill in the people very much confidence in their government (Abbink and Hesseling, 2000).

The ruling parties in Côte d'Ivoire and Gabon accepted multipartyism and went on to organize national elections. The Ivorian, Gabonese, and Zambian leadership was initially very much opposed to multipartyism and political reform and long resisted them. However, massive street demonstrations in these three countries against deteriorating economic conditions transformed quickly into political movements in favor of multiparty systems. A preemptive strategy to hold multiparty elections was the ruling parties' move well calculated to restore political order quickly and weaken the opposition's momentum.

Gabon convened a national conference that was government-initiated and directed and that led to multiparty elections in which the incumbent, Omar Bongo, was victorious, obtaining 51.48 percent of the vote against 26.51 percent for the best opposition candidate, Father Paul M'ba Abessole. Côte d'Ivoire held no national conference, but the government authorized multipartyism based on the recommendation submitted in April 1990 by the Political Bureau of the ruling Parti Democratique (PDCI). The authorization entailed the reactivation of article 7 of the 1960 Ivorian constitution which permitted multipartyism on the "condition that parties and groups respect the principles of national sovereignty and democracy and the laws of the Republic" (Nwokedi, 1995: 139). Since President Houphouet-Boigny's regime controlled the democratization procedure, his victory in the October 1990 presidential elections (he received 81.68 percent as against the Front Populaire Ivorien's (FPI) Laurent Gbagbo's 18.32 percent) and the PDCI's victory in the legislative elections in November 1990 and municipal elections in December 1990 did not come as a surprise. The PDCI remained in power after the elections but was removed in a military coup d'état in 1999. The military scheduled elections but later postponed them. Elections were eventually held in October 2000. Laurent Gbagbo was elected president, defeating the Rassemblement des Republicaine's (RDR) Alassane Ouattara, a former PDCI member.

In the cases of Malawi and Zambia, the incumbents' direction of the electoral process and huge monopoly of the state's resources could not prevent their defeat. Hastings Banda, "president for life," with a vast state machinery behind him, was removed from power in Malawi in 1994, when he was defeated by the United Democratic Front (UDF) in what may be considered the first free elections held in thirty years. Kenneth Kaunda's UNIP lost the 1991 Zambian presidential and legislative elections, which took place on October 31, 1991. Frederick Chiluba won the presidential race, receiving 75.79 percent of the vote to Kaunda's 24.21 percent (in an election international and national observers declared free and fair). The MMD believed it had received an overwhelming mandate to proceed with both political and economic reform. Economic reforms (especially privatization) have been implemented rapidly, but little has been done to reform political institutions. The public sector and civil service have remained politicized as they were under Kaunda. The president continues to wield immense power. Real economic growth has been negligible and per-capita income declined from $450 in 1990 to $370 in 1997 (World Bank, 1997). The private sector is expanding, as is civil society, but the attempted coup d'état of 1997 indicates the fragility of the transition.

Elite Pacts and Constitutional Engineering

Pact refers to a diverse set of negotiated compromises among competing elites with long-term goals of accommodating conflicts and institutionalizing the distribution of power in key aspects of state and society (Shain and Linz, 1995: 410). Pacts between elements of the outgoing regime and the incoming adversaries characterized one type of transition in the 1990s in sub-Saharan Africa. South Africa and Mozambique perhaps represented the best-known example of this phenomenon in the region. South Africa exemplifies the model of successful pact-making between black and white elites facilitating a sudden transition to a multiracial political system. Differences among the major groups, the African National Congress (ANC), National Party (NP), and Inkata Freedom Party (IFP), were ultimately resolved through a series of pacts: a political pact to share power in a Government of National

Unity (GNU) for five years, an economic pact to guarantee property rights and civil service positions and pensions, and a military pact to extend amnesty to individuals on all sides who confessed to politically motivated crimes. The international community encouraged the peace process with promises of diplomatic recognition, aid, and investment. Black and white elites ultimately forged a compromise that granted black majority rule in return for a continued place for whites in South Africa (Bratton, 2000). The new South Africa that emerged represented a reconfiguration of the apartheid state and the political and military structures of the ANC. The state abandoned its legal apartheid features and its political leadership, while the ANC abandoned its socialist ideology and independent military capacity (Joseph, 1991).

Multiparty negotiations eventually produced a transitional government, an interim constitution, and a timetable for the country's first multiracial elections. The constitution was modeled on a variety of sources—German, American, Indian, and others. It imported ideas from abroad, like proportional representation, but it was original and uniquely South African in its provision for a GNU whereby all parties also obtained seats in a coalition cabinet based on their share of the vote (Bratton, 2000). The 1994 election represented a new beginning in South Africa. For the first time, South Africa's black, white, Indian, and mixed-race people participated in elections, bringing an end to 350 years of settler colonial rule and to institutionalized racism. The Independent Electoral Commission declared the election to be "substantially free and fair." The ANC won 62.7 percent of the vote, followed by the NP's 20.4 percent and the IFP's 10.5 percent. Each party controlled one provincial legislature. These three parties formed a GNU (for five years) with Nelson Mandela as president and F. W. De Klerk as his second executive deputy. Second elections were held in 1999, and the ANC was returned to power with a similar majority.

Although the political changes made in South Africa have been dramatic and positive, the socioeconomic structures of the apartheid era have remained. At least half of the employable South Africans lacked a formal job in the mid-1990s, with unemployment being highest among Africans, women, and young people. In 1996 about 12 percent of the African population lacked access to clean water, some 25 percent had only minimal sanitation, and about 53 percent lacked electricity (Bratton, 2000: 394). The lifestyle enjoyed by white South Africans in 1996 was equivalent to that of New Zealanders, whereas the typical black South African lived under conditions similar to their counterparts in Congo-Brazzaville. Asians and coloureds fell somewhere between these extremes (United Nations Human Development Index, 1996). These severe inequalities bred high crime rates and violence. In 1997 South Africa's murder rate of 65 deaths per day led the world. Crime was much higher among black South Africans than whites. Nelson Mandela has

Voters in Greater Johannesburg turn out for the 1997 elections.

© Tomas Muscionico / Contact Press Images

urged blacks to forego rage against whites and coexist with them in a spirit of reconciliation.

South Africa's political transition remains fragile as the country faces many serious economic and political challenges. Black South Africans must begin to see a redistribution of the country's wealth in their favor, or they will not remain favorably disposed to living peacefully with whites. Black seizure of white farms in neighboring Zimbabwe to rectify unequal resource distribution might be a premonition of what the future holds for South Africa. Race remains a salient and explosive issue in the country's politics; it determined political behavior in both the 1994 and 2000 elections. With Africans holding a numerical majority of the electorate and most of them loyal to the ANC, the ANC could conceivably have a permanent built-in

Pushed out of their native lands, most black Zimbabweans make do by laboring for rich farmers, while they dwell on arid land.

© Ian Murphy / Getty Images

majority. With a dominant ANC and a fragmented opposition, the one-party-dominant system of the apartheid era could continue.

In the early 1990s a climate emerged in Mozambique that led to negotiations between warring groups to make peace and institute political reform. By the early 1980s the Mozambican economy was in a desperate condition partly because of the rebel group RENAMO's (the Resistencia Nacional Moçambicana's) protracted war against the government of the Front for the Liberation of Mozambique (FRELIMO) and partly because of misdirected economic policies (Bowen, 2000). FRELIMO adopted an IMF-approved structural adjustment program in 1987 and since then has followed policies reorienting the country's economy away from statism toward free market capitalism. Economic liberalization led to macroeconomic improvements in the economy by the early 1990s, and the government had a very supportive relationship with international lending agencies.

Liberal democratic political reform was initiated in Mozambique primarily as a result of a pact between the highest levels of leadership in FRELIMO

Protesters gather at the entrance of a white farm in Zimbabwe.

AP / Wide World Photos

and RENAMO, mediated by representatives from Western industrialized nations. Political reform was undertaken without popular agitation or support; the main objective was to end the war and institutionalize peace. The Rome peace talks lasted from June 1990 until October 1992 and involved direct dialogue among FRELIMO and RENAMO and international mediators. During the third of twelve rounds of talks, FRELIMO promulgated a new constitution that legalized political parties and accepted multiparty elections. The Rome Peace Accords of October 4, 1992, marked the end of the war and gave twelve (later twenty-four) months to prepare the country for its first multiparty elections. The population welcomed an end to the war but was less enthusiastic about multipartyism as a better way of running the political system (Harrison, 1996). This was not surprising since the masses of the population were left out of the process; the multiparty constitution was created out of the meetings in Rome and donor policy linking aid to political reform.

Domestic and external factors such as donor political conditionality, fatigue from years of inconclusive warfare, devastation of the economy, political change in South Africa, and the growing trend toward multipartyism in

Africa, all combined to force the warring factions to come to the negotiating table. The capitalist donors and the industrialized nations had a strong desire to integrate RENAMO into the polity as part of a desire to restabilize the southern African region in the wake of the end of the apartheid regime in South Africa and the release of Nelson Mandela. FRELIMO's interest in holding elections had to do with the massive international financial and logistical support given for its democratization efforts, as well as its desire to normalize conditions in the country. RENAMO accepted the elections as a way of getting access to the state after a debilitating period of war that devastated both its enemies and its supporters (Harrison, 1996). Ultimately, it was the agreements between the contending parties on the basic rules of the game that has facilitated the transition thus far. There was a widely held belief that conducting elections was a way to institutionalize peace.

Constitutional Engineering and "No Party" Elections

The Eritrean Peoples Liberation Front (EPLF), now called the Peoples Front for Democracy and Justice (PFDJ), and the Tigrean People's Liberation Front (TPLF) defeated Mengistu's military regime in 1991. Eritrea emerged from the war of independence committed to preserving the state and also to recognizing a wide array of basic human rights. In 1994 the PFDJ adopted a policy that committed the government to multiparty democracy. The PFDJ articulated and implemented a commitment to separate the ruling party from the government in organizational, financial, and personal terms. Further, the government allowed an independent forty-two-member representative Constitutional Commission to operate without governmental interference. The commission engaged public participation in the formation of the new Eritrean constitution as it developed, rather than after it was drafted. For over two years the commission toured the country, holding meetings in villages and listening to the population. The constitution produced by this process provides for civil and political rights, a unitary system with a National Assembly elected by universal suffrage and a president elected by the National Assembly from among its members, and an independent judiciary. The president is the head of state and government as well as commander of the armed forces. The constitution contains provisions that should safeguard a democratic system. But Eritrea's new state has not yet developed supportive institutions like political parties, civil society interest groups, or an independent media. Despite the lack of such institutions, there have been no reports of gross human rights violations. The government has given multiparty elections a lower priority than promoting development and equity in the society and curbing corruption (Ottaway, 1999b). Constitution formation prior to the first multiparty elections has been identified as a very important factor in sustaining democratization in Africa (Joseph, 1999).

A transition in political outlook occurred in Uganda in 1986, when the National Resistance Movement (NRM), led by Yoweri Musuveni, came to power. Uganda began to stabilize after a prolonged period of conflict following its independence from Britain in 1962. The Ugandan state collapsed in the late 1970s, during the terminal days of Idi Amin's regime, and successive regimes (1979–1986) were unable to reconstitute state authority. Musuveni inherited a country plagued by problems of economic deprivation, politicized ethnicity, regional divisions, and militarism.

Musuveni attempted a transition from military to political control in Uganda. But instead of the multiparty model proposed by international donors and Western industrialized nations, he opted for state reconstruction through the development of political institutions (other than political parties) that he believed necessary for democracy. Political parties were allowed to exist but not to hold meetings, recruit members, or campaign openly. His "no party" alternative included setting up a new form of local government through elective local councils (LCs, known as resistance councils [RCs] until 1995) and restoring the Buganda kinship. During the 1981–1986 guerrilla war, Musuveni had set up RCs in rural areas controlled by the NRM. With the NRM victory in 1986, the system was instituted throughout Uganda. Local councils, like the National Resistance Council, the Constituent Assembly, and the constitutional process, have made a political truce possible by embracing fragmented elites with different and conflicting ideologies. The NRM has been using these newly created institutions to try to solve the country's problems. It has engaged thousands of people from all levels of society in discussions. It has relied on local councils to serve as local consultative bodies at the district level, and they also have been linked to both central government ministries and to subordinate jurisdictions (Apter, 1995). There was a four-and-a-half-year consultative period in which the Constituent Assembly was established and hearings were held. This "consultative democracy," set up under the auspices of the Odoki Commission, started a national discourse on such issues as the country's history, political philosophy, constitutional principles and institutions, federalism, and unitarism. Many observers believe that this consultative process could lead to the formation of a genuine national and civil society (Khadiagala, 1995; Apter, 1995).

Musuveni realized that the status of the Buganda "ministate" had to be resolved if a stable central government was to exist. Under British colonialism Buganda had a privileged political status. It was home to most of the country's elites, was economically the most prosperous part of the country, had the most educated people, was the home of Makerere University (one of the best African universities at the time), and had the capital city, Kampala, and had its own parliament. The relationship between the Ugandan state and Buganda had been framed under a semifederal system at independence.

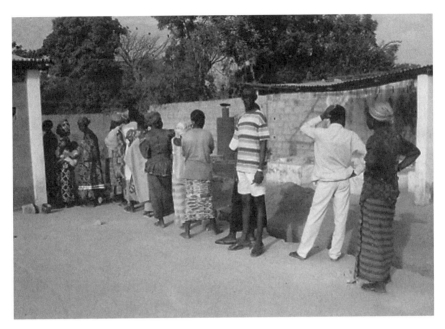

Voting in the "no party" system in Uganda.

Courtesy West Africa Magazine

Buganda maintained its privileged political status after independence, and Prime Minister Milton Obote appointed the *kabaka* of Buganda to the presidency. Obote's ideological turn to the left led to some policy changes, including abolishing the status of Buganda and other kingdom states as legal and jurisdictional entities. The economic power of the Buganda oligarchy was subsequently undermined with Obote's challenge of the *mailo* traditional land system and civil service chieftaincy. These actions undermined the *kabaka*, who was subsequently overthrown, and a civil war ensued as a single party authoritarian system developed. General Idi Amin came to power by a military coup d'etat in 1971. He further alienated the Baganda people in trying to establish his own landowning oligarchy in Buganda. Amin's overthrow in 1979 did not bring a political solution to the Buganda problem.

Musuveni fought a guerrilla war in north–central Uganda with the help of the rural Baganda and relied on this population for support for his continued legitimacy. Although the NRM had embraced a Marxist ideology opposing feudal survivals like the monarchy, it moved towards a policy of strategic accommodation with the Buganda kingdom in the early 1990s, culminating in the kingship's restoration in 1993. An important reason for this reconciliation effort has been Musuveni's use of the Baganda political and cultural elite to assist the government in channeling Ganda ethnopolitical identity toward a stable alliance with the state. Rather than seeking to resolve ethnic tensions using constitutional instruments, the NRM used a hereditary ruler to help consolidate a more productive relationship with an ethnic group long alienated from the Ugandan state. In the 1994 elections for the Constituent Assembly, the NRM won a solid majority of seats in Buganda, and a large number of Baganda people voted for Musuveni in the May 1996 presidential election. The NRM-Buganda alliance has subsequently become stormy, but Buganda remains engaged in Ugandan politics in a way that it was not in much of the postindependence period (Ottaway, 1999b).

Uganda has not made a transition from authoritarianism to multiparty politics, but the above discussion gives examples of some of the issues that the NRM government addressed in its vision of the type of society it wanted to create. The government made political changes at the same time that it launched an economic recovery program supported by the IMF, the World Bank, and bilateral donors. Positive growth rates have been achieved under the government's economic recovery program, but this recovery remains fragile and at risk. Political stability is also threatened by continuing armed opposition in parts of the country and by Uganda's intervention in internal conflicts in the neighboring Great Lakes region and in the Horn of Africa. Many believe that, within the African context, Uganda has a relatively democratic government and thus would hold multiparty elections if the United States and other international donors placed consistent pressure on Musuveni (Joseph, 1999). The fact that Uganda has successfully implemented neoliberal economic reforms and maintained a strong central authority within the country has lessened Western criticism of its leader's no-party model.

Protracted Transition: The Case of Nigeria

Intense domestic pressures for democratic transition in Nigeria precedes the decade of the 1990s. Promised since the end of the civil war in 1970, the transition perhaps began with the coup d'etat that brought General Murtala Muhammed to power. Following his assassination, General Obasanjo retained and adhered to the transitional machinery that was in place. General Obasanjo then handed over power to a civilian regime in 1979, and the Second Republic began under President Shehu Shagari. After seven years of plundering the economy and impoverishing the Nigerian people, this unpopular civilian regime was overthrown by the military, led by General Buhari.

Pressures for socioeconomic reforms and restoration of civilian rule varied in intensity between 1986 and 1999. General Ibrahim Babangida seized power from General Buhari in 1986 and announced a transition program but clearly did not want to leave office. In 1993 he organized and directed national elections that led to the election of Moshood Abiola. Dismayed by the results, Babangida annulled the elections, appointed Ernest Shonekan as interim president, and thus prolonged the transition. General Sani Abacha seized power from Shonekan, and his repressive regime (1993–1998) brought the Nigerian economy to the brink of destruction.

Domestic discontent reached the highest levels since independence in 1960 as the economy sagged, political corruption grew, and repression escalated. The independent media, interest groups, religious groups, students, workers, and the unemployed all protested against the Abacha regime. International sanctions were imposed on Nigeria, and the world perceived it as a pariah state. The Abacha regime moved against the people; many were jailed, assassinated, or driven into exile. Even the military was not spared as some officers were retired, reshuffled, or arrested. Retired General Obasanjo was jailed in 1995 in connection with an alleged coup d'etat against Abacha. Abiola demanded his right to serve and was arrested in 1994 and jailed by the Abacha regime. His wife, Kudirat, who actively campaigned on his behalf, was later gunned down by mysterious assassins who remain unknown. Abiola subsequently "died of natural causes" in the state's custody as, in the aftermath of General Abacha's sudden death, demands intensified for his release and reinstatement as duly elected president. In 1995 the Ogoni environmental activist Ken Saro-Wiwa (along with eight others) was executed after a flawed trial for Abacha's alleged murder. Political repression was accompanied by a deep deterioration of the economy. The central source of economic decay was the plunder of the economy by General Abacha and his cronies. At the time of his death his net worth was an estimated $6 billion, a sum accumulated during his brief rule.

General Abubakar, Abacha's successor, immediately responded to both internal and external pressures for democratization. With the sudden and suspicious death of Abiola in the state's custody, the situation became even more tense and urgent. Declining national stability, external isolation, dissension within the military, and strong domestic opposition to military rule convinced General Abubakar that genuine political reform was necessary. Within weeks of Abiola's death, Abubakar elaborated a new ten-month program for transition to civilian rule, set to culminate with a presidential poll on February 27, 1999, and a formal transfer of power on May 29, 1999. In contrast to his predecessor's transition programs, General Abubakar vowed to promulgate a constitution, did not restrict parties or politicians, and assured the population that the transition process would be supervised by an Independent National Electoral Commission (INEC). Evidence of Abubakar's immediate commitment to keeping his word could be seen in immediate improvements in human rights and civil liberties, his release of several prominent political prisoners within weeks of his rule (among them General Obasanjo and former finance minister Olu Falae), and his initiation of a dialogue with opposition leaders and the international community.

Olusegan Obasanjo's triumphant return to power after the 1999 election.

© Reuters / Getty Images

Local, legislative, and presidential elections were held between December 1998 and February 1999. Obasanjo's Peoples Democratic Party (PDP) won all the elections. Some opposition parties questioned the fairness of the elections, but most Nigerians and international observers (anxious to avoid any reason for the military to delay or cancel the transition) accepted the results. Many perceived the election as a referendum on military rule. Power was transferred in May 1999 from the military to a civilian government led by the retired military leader, Olusegun Obasanjo. Nigeria's Third Republic began, with Nigerians' high expectations for improvement in socioeconomic conditions under a new political dispensation.

Multiparty Elections of the 1990s: What Can We Make of Them?

Why have generally unpopular incumbents defeated the opposition at the polls? What should we make of the outcome of the elections of the 1990s? (See Table 6.1.) Is there a difference in the expectations of the international community and the African electorate? Is it the power of the incumbent that

TABLE 6.1   Multiparty Electoral Experiences in Africa
(as of December 2000)

Two Transfers of Power via Elections	Elections, No Transfer of Power	No Elections	One Transfer of Power via Election	Civilian Government Overthrown by Military
Benin	Angola	Congo (Zaire)	Cape Verde	Burundi
Madagascar	Botswana	Eritrea	Central African Republic	Côte d'Ivoire
Mauritius	Burkina Faso	Rwanda		Nigeria
São Tomé and Principe	Cameroon	Somalia	Comoros	Sierra Leone
	CIMD	Sudan	Congo- Brazzaville	
	Côte d'Ivoire	Swaziland	Ghana	
	Equatorial Guinea		Liberia	
	Ethiopia		Lesotho	
	Gabon		Malawi	
	The Gambia		Mali	
	Guinea		Nigeria	
	Guinea-Bissau		Senegal	
	Kenya		Zambia	
	Mauri Tania			
	Mozambique			
	Namibia			
	Niger			
	Seychelles			
	Tanzania			
	Togo			
	Uganda			
	Zimbabwe			

Source: Adapted from Bratton and van de Walle (1997).

determined the outcome of most of the elections of the 1990s? Or, is it both the power of incumbency and the expectations of the African electorate?

The international donor community and Western governments have had a superficial interest in democracy in Africa, equating it largely with holding elections. They want to see an end to military rule, the completion of multiparty elections, and the restoration of the formal institutions of liberal democracy. They tend not to insist that the transition program also be transparent and democratic. A few blatant examples of this problem should be mentioned here.

In 1995 the Zambian constitution was amended to read that "nonindigenous" Zambians could not contest presidential elections. A criterion for contesting the presidency is that both parents of the candidate must be native-born Zambians. Former president Kenneth Kaunda's parents were born in Malawi; hence he would not be qualified. This constitutional change was made to insure that Kaunda could not contest the elections. This tactic helped to secure Frederick Chiluba's reelection in 1996.

During the 1994–1996 transition phase in The Gambia, Yahya Jammeh manipulated the constitutional review process (which led to the lowering of the constitutionally required age for presidential candidates) so that he could be eligible to contest the elections. This was not challenged by the donor community. Once national elections are held, the international community is typically pacified, ends all pressure for political reform, and maintains its silence. Its practice has been to accept even national elections that fail to produce a transition from the incumbent party to the opposition, so long as it considers the elections to be free and fair. The donor community's judgement is what is free and fair is often influenced by its desire for political stability.

The African electorate understands that multiparty elections have been implemented in part to pacify the external donors on whose resources the political elites depend. The electorate also believes that elections have enhanced popular participation in the political process but knows that elections have not favored new actors and opposition parties. The groups supporting the opposition believe that elections serve to legitimize the incumbent, who for the most part uses incumbency power to ensure electoral victory. Realizing the complexity of the electoral process in Africa (i.e., the power of incumbency, support from external actors, electoral fraud, ethnic voting, clientelism, legal and illegal manipulation, etc.), the African electorate may have different expectations of electoral outcomes than most observers and scholars of African elections. Elections have been perceived not necessarily as an avenue for changing governments but as an instrument to use as leverage against incumbents who must deliver better government or face losing electoral support to the opposition. A general feature of African political culture that must be taken into account is that, when called upon, people tend to vote for the incumbent party or government. The legitimacy of the political opposition has not been fully accepted (Abbink and Hesseling, 2000). Understanding the power of incumbents, the African electorate has not been surprised by the trend in recent African elections that produced no transition.

In most of sub-Saharan Africa the externally-supported transition process did not provide the opening necessary for opposition parties to succeed. A relationship still existed between the state and the party in government whereby the incumbent could, and very often did, receive financial benefits through the state to stay in power. In the 1996–1997 government-initiated multiparty elections in Chad, President Idriss Deby and his party freely used state assets for their political campaigns. Ministers and government agents toured the country, frequently using state funds and administrative vehicles. In The Gambia in the 1996 election campaign, Jammeh's APRC had an advantage over the opposition in its access to army troops, who carried out many of his campaign activities. In Ghana Jerry Rawlings used his incumbency in funding party operations and using government-owned media. He also used government resources to facilitate the NDC campaigns. Incumbents used a variety of other mechanisms to remain in power. The soldier-turned-civilian strategy of maintaining power, for instance, has emerged in the region in the 1990s as a way of appeasing external demands for multiparty elections. Pushed by external pressures to restore civilian rule within competitive party systems, military leaders such as Flight Lieutenant Jerry Rawlings in Ghana, Captain Yahya Jammeh of The Gambia, and General Ibrahim Mainassara of Niger conveniently resigned from the military (several months before scheduled elections) so that they could bypass new election rules banning soldiers from office. All of these former military leaders secured electoral victories and remained in power. A slightly different twist to the model appeared in Nigeria when General Olusegun Obasanjo (long retired in 1983) became president upon the victory of his Peoples Democratic Party (PDP) in the 1999 national elections. The PDP was heavily backed by military and conservative interests. The election of Rawlings, Jammeh, Mainassara, and Obasanjo showed that the military question has not yet been resolved in sub-Saharan African politics. The soldier-turned-civilian model of leadership can bind the military to the state, thus continuing the military's agenda.

The trends that have emerged from transitional elections suggest the possibility of continued one-party hegemony. This may be the future trend if delinking of state institutions from the party in government does not take place. How can opposition parties be expected to sustain themselves and maintain followers as long as they are denied adequate financing by both government and business groups (which tend to support government in exchange for political advantages)? In the absence of state–government party delinking, there is little reason to believe that the reintroduction of multiparty systems in sub-Saharan African politics will lead to genuine democracy and "good governance." Unsuitable leaders (incumbent or opposition) could still be victorious at the polls because of the weaknesses of the multiparty system.

After Multiparty Elections, What Next?

Holding multiparty elections is only one step on the road to establishing democracy. The authorization of multipartyism and the constitutionally determined rule of law and basic human rights have not necessarily led to nonelite and mass participation, representativeness, or accountability across sub-Saharan Africa. Multiparty elections do not by themselves end social and economic inequalities or oppression. However, multipartyism does allow space for political forces to press for greater justice for the majority of the population.

The 1990s certainly witnessed greater official tolerance of free expression. The publication of newspapers, magazines, and pamphlets significantly increased. Most people may not be able to read these generally European-language newspapers, but they know someone who can read and convey the content to them. The ideas and information are then passed on in what is largely an oral culture (Wiseman, 1996). Forty new newspapers reportedly sprang up in Benin, fifteen in Mali, and several dozen in Tanzania and Uganda. The free press has long been recognized as an important pillar of a democratic society. In Uganda, Tanzania, Kenya, and Nigeria, among other countries, the independent press has grown dramatically.

A host of civil organizations with some independence from the state have emerged in countries including Guinea-Bissau, Kenya, Tanzania, Zambia, and Côte d'Ivoire: village development societies, kinship organizations, ethnic unions, trade unions, student associations, professional societies, cooperatives, religious movements, women's associations, neighborhood development associations, sports clubs, and rotating credit associations. With democratization and neoliberal economic reform, the decentralized state should create more space for citizen responsibility. NGOs have proliferated during the 1990s, assuming developmental tasks previously undertaken by the state. As the state no longer has the resources to provide services for both rural and urban populations, often local and foreign NGOs have become involved (independent of state and party structures) in developmental work, providing financial as well as technical assistance.

Opening the political system has meant that the government is forced to accept the opposition's scrutiny and that civil and individual rights, while not perfectly guaranteed, are considerably better than before. Multipartyism has allowed some actors outside the single parties to come to power in countries like Zambia, Senegal, Malawi, and Benin. For the most part, the authoritarian leaders of the past have adapted to the new climate by devising strategies to remain in power. Holding elections does represent a qualitative change in the political terrain in Africa. However, the main priority of the masses of African people is not democratization but economic and social achievement. The grassroots perception in Africa of the development agenda is world's apart from that of the donor community and Western industrialized nations. For the African population the challenge under this new dispensation is for the democratic state to mobilize and create social and economic development. How this can be done under a state with diminished resources and capacity has been the challenge. Ghana has been widely touted as a success story. Structural adjustment policies led to some improvements in the economy: food production per capita has grown, the manufacturing sector expanded, and inflation reduced. But shortcomings have also been evident: Ghana is still dependent on cocoa, whose world price has collapsed; inflation is on the increase again; foreign investors have shown no interest in the country despite its economic reforms; external debt is extremely high as loans have been used to finance about half of Ghana's imports; debt load may constrain further growth; and many Ghanaians have not benefited from economic reforms. The limited economic growth that Ghana has achieved may not be transferable to other sub-Saharan African countries because of many factors, the most important perhaps is that the international financial institutions might be unwilling to commit elsewhere the same levels of resources committed in Ghana.

The nexus of multiparty systems and neoliberal economic reforms has not produced the material changes the masses of the African population expected. Socioeconomic polarization has continued, with an increase in the wealth and income gap between the tiny affluent elite and the vast majority. Multiparty systems have done little to change access to health, educational facilities, electricity, or piped water; absolute poverty, inequalities in resource distribution and income, and high unemployment levels have all led to the general deteriorating living standards of the African population. The economic situation of the masses seems to have worsened under the new political dispensation.

Conclusion

Neoliberal economic reforms under multiparty systems have produced negligible changes in the material condition of the vast majority in sub-Saharan Africa. International donors and Western industrialized nations believed that results would improve with both political and economic reform. Many African autocrats reluctantly agreed to hold multiparty elections. But multiparty elections are meaningless if the distribution of power in the economy remains unequal. Monopolization of the economy by a tiny elite has not changed in the 1990s. The question that arises is the extent to which African leaders can make changes that can lead to social democratic reforms. The way in which sub-Saharan African states have been integrated in the international capitalist economy has perpetuated the uneven distribution of wealth. Is Africa really hemmed in as some scholars have argued? Did Africa's role in the global economy shift in the 1990s? Or has the continent remained marginalized? Can African leaders find regional solutions to the problems within their countries in this new era of globalization?

For Further Reading

Huntington, S. (1991). *The Third Wave: Democratization in the Late Twentieth Century*. Norman: University of Oklahoma Press.

Zunes, S. (1994). "Unarmed Insurrection against Authoritarian Governments in the Third World: A New Kind of Revolution." *Third World Quarterly*, 15, no. 3, 403–426.

Bratton, Michael, and Nicholas van de Walle (1997). *Democratic Experiments in Africa*. Cambridge, England: Cambridge University Press.

Joseph, Richard, ed. (1999). *State, Conflict and Democracy in Africa*. Boulder: Lynne Rienner.

7
—
State Responses to Challenges of the 1990s: Protracted Wars, Fragmentation, Disintegration, and State Collapse

In contrast to sub-Saharan Africa's dominant trend in the 1990s toward relatively peaceful transitions to multi-party systems, there were several areas where political developments were the exact opposite: violent and destructive. The Horn of Africa (Sudan, Ethiopia, Eritrea, Somalia) and the Great Lakes region (Congo, Congo-Brazzaville, Rwanda, Burundi, Uganda) saw the eruption of long-festering conflicts leading to brutal wars. In diverse cases the fall of tyrants was followed by state fragmentation (Liberia, Ethiopia) and disintegration and collapse of the state (Somalia, Chad, Congo). Noticeably absent from these conflicts were the superpowers and their allies, having retreated from African conflicts in the post–Cold War era. The geopolitical importance that some countries (Congo, Ethiopia, Somalia, Angola) had had for the superpowers was gone. During the Cold War, an adversary's advances in the Horn of Africa or in southern Africa always called for a response from the United States or the Soviet Union. The end of the Cold War led external powers to neglect these conflicts.

Some of the wars subsided, but challenges to central authority remain (Uganda, Angola, Rwanda, Sierra Leone), and other wars are still in full force (Sudan) but appear to be resolvable. Can these states develop the capacity for reconstruction? Can these states survive in their postindependence formations?

Southern Africa

The end of the Cold War and subsequent U.S.-Soviet cooperation provided the basis for resolving the wars in Angola and Ethiopia in 1991. Both governments, as well as the FRELIMO government in Mozambique, renounced Marxism-Leninism and agreed to liberalize their economies and reform their political systems in order to end internal wars and gain financial assistance from external donors.

In Angola the MPLA government put up many of its state-owned plantations for sale in 1990, and in 1991 it pledged to remove restrictions on prices and wages, privatize a range of public corporations, and encourage private investment (Sandbrook, 1997). Between 1990 and 1999 Angola made the transition from war to peace and back again twice. Portuguese-mediated talks held in Washington, D.C. (sponsored by the United States and the Soviet Union from 1990–1991) led to the Washington Concepts Paper. Under the terms of this paper there would be a cease-fire; United States, the Soviet Union, and all other countries would stop exporting lethal material to opposing factions; an amendment to the Constitution would provide for multiparty democracy; and there would be free and fair elections, the creation of a national army, and the installation of an international monitoring force. Subsequent agreement was reached through the Bicesse Accords on the national army, the date for the cease-fire, the timing of multiparty elections, and the international monitoring process. Multiparty elections were held in September 1992, with the expectation and agreement that the winner would be allowed to govern and the loser would accept the results. However, this agreement was not honored. Within a few weeks after the election, the MPLA government and the opposition UNITA plunged the country back into civil war.

UNITA returned to the negotiating table in 1994 after failing to capture the capital city and the oil-producing enclave of Cabinda. The MPLA government's purchase of new arms from abroad and hiring of a South African security firm's services also helped to put pressure on UNITA's leader, Savimbi, to negotiate. The Lusaka Protocol, signed in 1994 (but without Savimbi's participation), reaffirmed the Bicesse Accords. Implementation of the protocol was difficult, largely because Savimbi engaged in delaying tactics. In 1994 a new Government of National Unity and Reconciliation was installed. The internationally enforced peace lasted from 1994 to 1998, when

Angolan women maimed by land mines.

© Anthony Suau / Getty Images

a war erupted that has displaced over 600,000 people within the country and several thousand refugees in neighboring countries.

Angola has failed to achieve a peaceful transition to a multiparty political system. Several factors may account for both sides' inability to settle the conflict. Financial pressure placed on other African countries may not be as effective in Angola because both the government and the opposition are in control of the country's strategic natural resources—oil for the MPLA government and diamonds for the rebel force, UNITA. Both the MPLA and UNITA have evenly matched resources to purchase military hardware to maintain the conflict without a conclusive victory on either side.

There is also deep-seated mistrust on both sides, and neither side has any confidence in the peace process. Savimbi's refusal to take part in the signing of the Lusaka Protocol and in the swearing-in ceremony of the cabinet-level ministers of the Government of National Unity and Reconciliation in 1997 certainly reinforced the sense that he was not entirely committed to the 1994 peace settlement.

Both the MPLA and UNITA fought on opposing sides in the wars that broke out in Zaire and have become entangled in the broader Great Lakes conflict involving Rwanda, Burundi, and Uganda. UNITA has also been weakened by internal fractionalization. It has alienated the United States, at one time its strongest backer. The U.S. government provided more than $500 million in aid to Angola between 1994 and 1999, and American corporations invested eight times as much in the country's petroleum sector (Manning, 1999: 212). Despite the split within UNITA and the marginalization of Savimbi, UNITA remained a factor, and the war continued in Angola. In this climate the socioeconomic problems of the Angolan population have been neglected.

Horn of Africa

The Horn of Africa was perhaps the African central theater for superpower conflicts during the Cold War. The United States and the Soviet Union (and their allies) became entangled in internal conflicts in the region, sponsoring and arming governments as well as opposing factions. The history of the Horn during the 1960s through the end of the 1980s was characterized by wars, big-power intervention, droughts, famines, and widespread poverty. Did the 1990s witness dramatic political changes comparable to those found in many other regions in sub-Saharan Africa?

With the end of the Cold War and loss of support from former foreign patrons, pressures from opposition forces within Ethiopia and Somalia led to the fall of the two brutal dictatorships of Mengistu Haile Mariam (Ethiopia) and Siyad Barre (Somalia). After the fall of Mengistu's regime in Ethiopia, a political pact was formed to work out a cooperative arrangement between the various factions. The ruling EPRDF went on to hold multiparty elections and embarked on the challenging task of reconstructing the state and the economy. In the post-Barre period in Somalia, in contrast, clan warfare erupted. As a result of the pact signed among the Ethiopian factions, the province of Eritrea was granted its independence after over thirty years of war against the Ethiopian state in the capital city of Addis Ababa. The region acquired one new state, Eritrea, but the Somali state no longer exists in its pre-1990s form. The state of Sudan remained fragmented among northern, mainly Muslim and Arab elites and between the latter and southerners, mostly African and non-Muslim. With the resumption of fighting between Eritrea and Ethiopia in 1999, war has continued in every country of the region except the very small state of Djibouti. Djibouti has been the only country in the post-1960 era (at the time of this writing in 2002) in the Horn of Africa where the central government's authority has not been challenged by insurgent movements.

A dramatic difference in Horn politics in the 1990s was the absence of big-power intervention in regional conflicts. The international community did not intervene in Ethiopia and Somalia when the dictatorships fell. Outside of humanitarian intervention in Somalia for a brief period between

1992 and 1994, the international community, led by the United States, has maintained its distance from the region, leaving those countries in the post–Cold War era to sort out their conflicts by themselves. This led to unprecedented intervention by Great Lakes and Horn countries in each other's domestic conflicts during the 1990s. In some instances regional intervention may have helped to de-escalate tensions, while in other cases it fanned the flames of war.

Ethiopia

Ethiopia, Somalia, and the Sudan have all faced historic problems related to ethnoregional nationalism. The Transitional Government of Ethiopia (TGE) presided over an exclusive pact preventing previously politically dominant ethnic groups, like the Amhara, from serving in the Council of Representatives. The new Ethiopian state was transformed from a unitary state to a federation of ethnic regions, with all nationalities having the right to self-determination, even to the point of secession. Ethnic groups would be given their own states, but the party, the EPRDF, would be in power everywhere, thus keeping the country together. The EPRDF brought the ethnic parties under one umbrella that would control their respective regions.

The EPRDF has made efforts to transform Ethiopia through decentralization into a federation by building up the capacity of the different regions to carry out their function. For this purpose, the government has received considerable support from foreign donors favoring decentralization. The government has been working on strengthening its financial budgeting system and regional officers have tried to develop their own policies and systems different from those at the center. The tax base of the states remains narrow, but important states like Tigray, Arlen, and Oromo have begun to cover much higher percentages of their budgets from their own resources (Ottaway, 1999b).

The government's opponents have seen its ethnic federation as a divide-and-rule strategy designed to ensure Tigrean domination. If the economy grows and economic benefits spread across ethnicities, there is a chance that the perception of the federation as an instrument of domination may decline.

Therefore, the EPRDF has made reforming the economy a top priority. The economy inherited from the Mengistu era was war ravaged and had remnants of feudal structures from the Haile Selassie era. The TPLF has reportedly embraced economic liberalization models such as those in Taiwan and South Korea while remaining committed to keeping all lands in government hands and having the party play a central role in the economy (Ottaway, 1999b). Its commitment to economic liberalization earned the TPLF a World Bank loan of $657 million for economic recovery and reconstruction in 1992, high levels of assistance or support from bilateral donors, an IMF Enhanced Structural Adjustment Facility Loan, and debt scheduling by the Paris Club of major lending nations. The government is committed to state-driven market economies, agricultural development–led industrialization, self-sufficiency in food production, and increasing rural incomes. Public expenditure has been restructured, reducing the allocation for defense; expenditure on health and education has doubled; and expenditure on roads, especially in the rural areas, have quadrupled. Economic activity has been revived in the country since the end of the war against Mengistu. GDP growth increased more than 5 percent a year in the late 1990s. GDP growth reached a high of 12 percent in 1993, when the rains were good, but declined to 1.7 percent in 1994 because of drought (Ottaway, 1999b).

Ethiopia was the only country in the Horn in the 1990s formally to embrace multiparty elections. It gave in to donor pressures, as did many other African countries. As elsewhere, the opposition parties were weak and did not have sufficient time to organize for speedy elections. External pressure and the desire to gain credits from foreign donors perhaps motivated the Ethiopian government to hold elections, and in an electoral process that it designed and directed, it made sure that its affiliates won in every region. Reconstructing the state and the economy has been the present post-Mengistu government's main priority. Central to this goal has been the mechanism for dealing with politicized ethnicity. Ethiopia and Eritrea agreed to partition the old Ethiopia in 1993, but hostilities flared up in May 1998, and unsuccessful mediation led to renewed fighting in February 1999. There clearly has been no genuine agreement on Eritrea's right to self-determination within a separate state. The Ethiopian state remains pressured while the fight with Eritrea continues. There has been no indication of imminent collapse of the Ethiopian state; the government functions, but the transition is fragile.

Somalia

Under the Siyad Barre regime, clanism became the dominant ideology as members of three clans loyal to the president were placed in positions of power, control, and wealth. Barre manipulated clan consciousness, used divide-and-rule tactics, and encouraged clan warfare. As it was in Liberia after the fall of Samuel Doe, in Somalia after the Barre regime fell conflict erupted between warring clans seeking to fill the vacuum. The Somali National Movement (SNM), the major opposition clan formed to overthrow Barre, could not play the role of effective opposition during the transition period. It could not uphold state structures or preserve law and order. It limited its activity to the northern region, showing its inability to project its power beyond its national clan territory (Adam, 1995). The opposition movement proved to be weak, decentralized, and clan based and incapable of providing national leadership and vision.

The postindependence Somali state collapsed around 1992, and to date (2002) has not been reconstituted in its prior form. Somalia lacks an internationally recognized government, a central governing authority, a formal legal system, banking and insurance services, telephone and postal systems, public services, educational and health systems, police and public security services, and electricity and piped water systems. Chaos and violence in the capital city of Mogadishu led to a human-made famine of astronomical proportions. A U.S.-UN sponsored mission, Operation Restore Hope, intervened, intending to help feed millions of people and maintain order. The UN subsequently withdrew its operation from Mogadishu, viewing it as a failed mission. It now has a very limited operation in Somalia, operating from Nairobi, Kenya. The United States, the Soviet Union, the EEC, Italy, China, and the Arab League all contributed during the Cold War to the arms buildup in Somalia that made possible the protracted brutal clan warfare that helped to decimate the population of southern Somalia. The international community (and especially those countries that had contributed to the arms buildup) distanced itself from the crisis in Somalia, apparently viewing it as a hopeless situation.

The "state of Somalia" does not exist at this time. The old Somalia has been divided into Somaliland (which declared itself independent in 1991 but has not been internationally recognized) and Puntland (established in 1998). Somaliland and Puntland have since been fighting over the regions of Sanaag and Sool, although neither has any meaningful authority in those areas. Southern Somalia remains a war-ravaged wasteland. The Somali people will decide in the future whether they want the state to be reconstituted as it was before or as a confederation of two or more states into one.

Sudan

Sudan became formally independent in 1956, and an internal war has been going on for more than thirty of its forty-five years of independence. The fundamental reason for this protracted conflict can be linked to the formation of the present Sudanese state. British colonialism led to the consolidation of an Arab-Islamic hegemonic bloc in northern Sudan and a subordinate and underdeveloped, largely African non-Muslim south. At independence Britain handed over the state to the northern Sudanese nationalists, and since then socioeconomic development and political power have been disproportionately concentrated in the north. War broke out as the mostly Arab-dominated north and the African south clashed over the legitimacy of the state in the capital city of Khartoum and its control of state power and access to state resources.

As in many of its former colonies in Africa and elsewhere, at Sudan's independence Britain handed over a state that had structural inequality and placed political power in the hands of one favored community (the *jellaba*) in a favored region (the north). The south has been fighting a long violent battle against the central government in Khartoum that flared whenever it believed that the latter sought to appropriate its strategic resources: leadership cadres, exclusively southern military units in the armed forces, and mineral and water resources (Kok, 1995). Much of the land in northern Sudan, except for the riverine areas, is desert and semidesert lacking the capacity to support animal and human life. The central government's support of southward expansion by northerners to acquire agricultural and grazing land has generated intense conflict, including the April 1987 massacre at Daein of more than 1,500 Dinka by Rezaquat Arabs armed by the government and the massacres of more than 1,000 Shilluk by the Sabha Arabs in 1989 at Jebelan (Kok, 1995).

The southern opposition to the government in Khartoum has consisted of a number of groups united in a common cause. The Sudanese Peoples Liberation Movement (SPLM) has been the chief opposition force. Its authoritarian structure has alienated it from the population that it claimed to be liberating. Internal power struggles split and weakened it at a time when authoritarian governments in Ethiopia and Somalia were successfully challenged and removed. The Nasir Declaration of 1991 affirmed the split within the southern movement with the emergence of the Nasir faction and the Torit actions of the SPLM. The Nasir faction subsequently split into several more factions, whereas the Torit faction (under John Garang) controlled the main body of the SPLM. Intra-SPLM conflicts have led to enormous loss of life and property among the people of the south. The present National Islamic Front (NIF) government of Bashir has exploited the split in the SPLM, used divide-and-rule tactics, and offered material rewards to its members to win important military victories that have prolonged the life of the regime (Kok, 1995).

The SPLM was committed to a united socialist Sudan, not a separate Sudan. It had support from marginalized Africans in the north and professional classes sympathetic to its message. Arab Sudanese largely stood apart, threatened by the idea that the SPLM could remove the *jellaba* from the privileged position they held in Sudan. Secession of the south was less important to them than maintaining *jellaba* dominance (Kok, 1995). Support for the SPLM in the south has been mixed. Some saw the SPLM's objective of unity as a dilution of southern Sudanese nationalism and a deviation from the goal of independence for the south. SPLM's objectives appealed to all oppressed Sudanese, especially African. The SPLM's united Sudan approach made it still impossible for the *jellaba* to employ the antisecession strategy against them that they had used effectively against the southern movement in the early sixties and seventies. The *jellaba* has since shifted its strategy to using religious slogans like "jihad" designed to fan secessionist reactions in the south. War against the SPLM has now been redefined as a jihad against infidels.

The NIF government promulgated an Islamic constitution on January 1, 1999, permitting a limited range of political associations (but not political parties) to function within the context of a centralized Islamic political system. Pressured by the costs of war, which absorbed half the annual budget, on February 20, 1999, President Bashir said that the government's war with the SPLM might end with the secession of southern Sudan, because, in his words, "separation with peace is better than unity with the continuation of war." The regional and international environment is no longer negatively disposed toward secession as it used to be, as we have witnessed successful secession in Slovenia (1992), Croatia (1993), and Bosnia (1993) and in Eritrea (1993). The Washington Declaration (October 1993), National Democratic Alliance (NDA, formed by the Northern Party and the SPLM), Asmara Agreement (June 1995), and NDA's London Declaration (November 1995) have all generally accepted the right to self-determination for the people of southern Sudan and all other marginalized peoples. This opened up the prospect of a multiethnic regime, but this may not be possible without the overthrow of the narrowly based Islamic government. Can self-determination for the south be achieved? Political forces have thus far been unable to resolve fundamental problems that are destroying the country. The southern Sudanese people will ultimately make the final choice between independence, confederation, or federation.

Great Lakes Region

There could be little meaningful discussion in the 1990s of "democratic transition" in the Great Lakes region (Rwanda, Burundi, Uganda, Congo, and Congo-Brazzaville). The region was engulfed in a brutal war that made physical survival a more immediate concern than democratic transition. The present conflicts in the region have been described by some as "Africa's first world war," underscoring the multiplicity of factions and countries involved as the boundaries of the war expand continuously. Internal political conflicts in several countries have drawn in patrons from a host of different African countries: Rwanda, Burundi, Uganda, the Angolan MPLA government and UNITA rebel forces, Namibia, Sudan, the Allied Democratic Forces (ADF) from Uganda, the militant wing of Burundi's Conseil National pour la Defense de la Democracie (CNDD), and the Interahawe (the Rwandan Hutu militia). These countries and political forces have replaced the Western European, Soviet, Cuban, and U.S. patrons of the Cold War era. During the Cold War, Belgium, France, the United States, the Soviet Union, and Cuba were all involved, inserting big-power competition and the ideologies of capitalism and communism into the regional conflict. With the end of the Cold War the former patrons' lack of interest and fear of unsuccessful intervention have ensured their absence from the region. Some African leaders have intervened in conflicts on their borders or in the region to safeguard their countries from the conflicts of others. Others have intervened to fulfill personal ambitions of dominance in the region or to prevent others from achieving such dominance. Still others have intervened because they think that war can end certain conflicts in which diplomacy failed (Ottaway, 1999a).

Several factors provide a framework for understanding the very complex crisis in the Great Lakes region.

Colonial Partition

The European colonial powers' partition of Africa left ethnic and geographical maps skewed. Hutu and Tutsi can be found not only in Rwanda and Burundi but also in northern and southern Kivu (eastern Congo), southern Uganda, and western Tanzania. Invariably, ethnic strife in one country tends to have cross-border consequences.

Politicized Ethnicity

With politicized ethnicity lingering from the colonial period, when Belgium favored the minority Tutsis, there was animosity between the two groups at independence. The Hutus dominated the political economy of postindependence Rwanda following a showdown in 1959 that sent thousands of Tutsis across the border into exile in Uganda. In Burundi after independence in 1962 a constitutional monarchy evolved under a mixed Tutsi-Hutu regime. In 1965 the monarchy was overthrown by the army, and Tutsi elements captured the state. These factors can explain the deterioration of Hutu-Tutsi relations in Rwanda, Burundi, and in eastern Zaire. Ethnic strife in Rwanda has always had an impact on Burundi, and vice versa. The Hutu-led revolution in Rwanda contributed to the sharpening of ethnic cleavages in Burundi. The assassination of Burundi's first popularly elected president, Melchior Ndadaye (a Hutu), by an all-Tutsi army in 1993 was clearly linked to the 1994 Rwandan genocide (Lemarchand, 2000).

Refugee Problem

The presence of large refugee populations in all of these countries has had an impact on all aspects of the host countries' political economy and society. Exclusion-induced insurrection led to ethnic-based repression by the state, repression led to the exodus of thousands of refugees across borders, and they in turn became vehicles of further violence in both their host countries and countries of asylum. In the Great Lakes region especially, the refugee diaspora has had a strong polarizing effect on the host societies since there is a presence in all these countries of Hutu and Tutsi. Throughout the region the pattern has been one of violence leading to large numbers of refugees and refugees (as victims of repression) in turn generating more violence. Refugees have thus been an integral part of the problem of ethnic conflict in the region (Lemarchand, 2000).

What precipitated the crisis of the 1990s in Rwanda, which attracted media attention from all over the world? It was the mid-1994 genocide of at least 500,000 Tutsis and some Hutus by the Hutu-dominated government in Rwanda (Rwanda's population is 86 percent Hutu and 14 percent Tutsi). Tutsi exiles in Uganda formed the Rwanda Patriotic Front (RPF) and supported then Ugandan president Yoweri Musuveni in his fight for power in the 1980s, thereby gaining political and military support for their own cause. The RPF launched its first attacks into Rwanda in 1990. With mediation from other countries in the region, conflict was halted, and in 1993 an agreement to form a national government of reconciliation was reached in Arusha, Tanzania. Hutu "extremists" in the military as well as the Hutu militia, the Interahawe, opposed the agreement. When President Juvenal Habyarimana, a Hutu (along with the President of Burundi), was killed in a mysterious

Refugees from Rwanda stand in line for water.

© Sebastiao Salgado / Contact Press Images Photo

plane crash, Hutus launched a mass slaughter of Tutsis as well as some politically moderate Hutus. In turn, the RPF launched an all-out attack on Rwanda. After several months of fighting, an estimated 800,000 people were killed, the RPF was in power in Kigali (the capital city of Rwanda), and two million people were living in refugee camps in eastern Zaire.

The post-Ndadaye era in Burundi saw the emergence of new Hutu-dominated resistance movements (the Front for the Defense of Democracy [FDD]) and the resurrection of existing ones (e.g., the Party for the Liberation of the Hutu People [PALIPEHUTU]) (Ndikumana, 2000). This was not the first case of genocide against Tutsis or Hutus in the region. In 1972 in Burundi, following an insurgency by Hutu army elements, the government repressed thousands of Hutu civilians. In a process of "selective genocide" government security forces killed Hutu army personnel, politicians, intellectuals, and businessmen (Lemarchand, 1972). In 1993, following the assassination of President Ndadaye, bloodshed erupted, starting with Hutus killing Tutsi civilians, followed by government troops massacring Hutus. The massacres in Burundi did not receive international attention, which was focused on the genocide in Rwanda (Ndikumana, 2000).

After years of internal struggle to remove him from power, Mobutu's regime collapsed in 1997, leading to conflict, chaos, and a further weakening of the Zairian state. The crisis in Zaire became intermingled with the Rwandan ethnic crisis, thus widening the regional crisis. Several factors led to the collapse of the Mobutu regime. After decades of Western backing, Mobutu lost the support of his external patrons. He managed to stay in power for over thirty years only because he received strong support from Western external patrons (Belgium, France and the United States in particular), which valued him as a staunch anticommunist ally in the critical Central African mining region. Even as late as the mid-1990s, France had sought to sustain Mobutu's regime, regardless of his dishonesty and his inability to maintain control of the state, as the key to regional stability. The United States did not want to see Mobutu violently removed from power, as it feared revolution and the spread of violence throughout the region.

The Western powers urged South Africa's Nelson Mandela to broker a diplomatic deal between Mobutu and his main rebel opponent, Laurent Kabila, for a power-sharing government in the context of a democratic transition program. Mobutu refused to cooperate as he was unwilling to relinquish any of the power he had accumulated. As domestic and regional forces combined to topple him, neither the United States nor France intervened, embarrassed as they were by his disingenuous "democratic transition" program, violence against protesters, and continued postponement of elections.

Mobutu faced strong internal resistance after decades of policies (or non-policies) that led to the economy's plundering. Mobutu had stripped the economy of its assets (Young and Turner, 1985). It shrank more than

40 percent between 1988 and 1995; its per-capita GDP in 1995 was a mere US $117, 65 percent lower than in 1958. The Zairian currency (the new zaire [NZ]) was worthless, moving from NZ3 : US $1 in 1993 to NZ4,000 : US $1 in 1994. In 1997, 70 percent of workers in Zaire were unemployed (McNulty, 1999: 66). The informal sector saved the population from starvation (Mac-Gaffey, 1988). Transport, telecommunications, hospitals, schools, and general public services all broke down, as the state literally ceased to function. This was the condition of the economy and the society, while Mobutu remained one of the wealthiest men in the world, owning real estate in several forms, and continued to extort the country's wealth. Laurent Kabila's Alliance of Democratic Forces for the Liberation of Zaire (AFDL), formed in 1996, took advantage of Mobutu's declining regional support and lack of Western support and led an armed revolt commanded by Rwandan officers who used Musuveni's "Ugandan model" of guerrilla warfare. With little opposition at the time, Laurent Kabila's guerrilla forces, assisted by the Rwandan and Ugandan governments, seized power in Zaire in 1997 and subsequently changed the country's name to the Democratic Republic of the Congo (DRC).

The new RPF government in Rwanda, with Uganda's help, intervened in the Zairian crisis, seeking to secure its borders against counter revolutionary forces based in Zaire. Hence, Rwanda forces led the offensive against Mobutu's regime, killing refugees in Kivu province (Zaire's eastern province, where Hutu and Tutsi refugees could be found) and proclaimed that this was an inter-Rwandan affair (McNulty, 1999: 76). From the RPF government's point of view, the refugee base on Rwanda's Western border had to be broken up since the defeated FAR used it to launch attacks against the government. This belief motivated them to carry out attacks on genocide survivors within Rwanda. The stated objective was to secure Rwanda's borders. The Rwandan government sought to replace the Mobutu regime with one that would be friendlier and capable of maintaining a strong state.

Disillusioned by Kabila's inability to control eastern Congo, in 1998 Rwanda and Uganda threw their support behind a new movement dominated by Congolese Tutsis, the Congolese Union for Democracy (RCD), and a new conflict began in the Congo. The MPLA-UNITA conflict in Angola escalated again in 1998, at the time that this new conflict began in the Congo. Under Mobutu Zaire had supported UNITA, and UNITA had been involved in selling diamonds to Zaire to obtain funds for weapons. With the overthrow of Mobutu, UNITA supported the rebel RCD against Kabila. The MPLA had previously supported Kabila's insurgent movement against Mobutu, hoping that he would maintain central authority in the Congo and block support going to the UNITA rebel forces.

The conflict became even broader when the government of Zimbabwe became involved, seeking to protect mining interests in Zaire. President Robert Mugabe sent planes and troops to support Kabila. Congo-Brazzaville allowed Mobutu's former generals to launch attacks against Kabila from its territory. Zambia's capital city, Lusaka, was reportedly bombed by the Angolan government after the Zambian government denied Angola's request to use Zambian territory to fight UNITA. Zambia then stopped supplying fuel to southern Congo, hoping that this would persuade Kabila to curb UNITA activities based in Congo.

The problems in the present crisis in the Great Lakes region are extremely difficult and complex: resolving the conflict between Hutu and Tutsi; rebuilding Congo and bringing all the armed factions under control; reaching an agreement between domestic and external parties in all these conflicts; and removing other countries from the conflicts. Attempts by regional and subregional organizations have failed, largely because some of the same governments that control these organizations are involved in the fighting and are presiding over major problems of their own.

West Africa

As in the Great Lakes region and the Horn of Africa, in the early 1990s war erupted in West Africa, centered on the two small countries of Liberia and Sierra Leone. The Liberian governments of William Tubman (1944–1971), William Tolbert (1971–1980), and Samuel Doe (1980–1989) and the Sierra Leonean governments of Siaka Stevens (1968–1985) and Joseph Mommoh (1985–1992) were all vehicles of elite wealth and power accumulation through patronage and corruption. Beginning in the mid-1980s, both the Liberian and Sierra Leonean governments adopted structural adjustment policies to continue receiving high levels of aid from Western capitalist countries and donor institutions. Because these neoliberal economic policies required it, patronage networks were devastated, and weakening the state as it was no longer able to provide services to its mass and elite clients. Removal of unpopular tyrants (Doe in Liberia and Mommoh in Sierra Leone) led to the collapse of state authority and brutal wars, as competing factions outside the state sought alternative resources to fund a new pattern of patron-client politics anchored in the control of regional and international commercial networks. The end of the Cold War coincided with the transformation of patron-client politics into what has been described by William Reno (1998) as "warlord politics" in several sub-Saharan African countries, including Liberia and Sierra Leone.

Liberia

War erupted in Liberia in 1989, when the National Patriotic Front of Liberia (NPFL), headed by a former government administrator,

Charles Taylor, led an invasion force into the country's northeastern region, attempting to overthrow Samuel Doe's regime. Taylor quickly captured Doe's commercial networks, which encouraged many of Doe's supporters to desert him and seek security by cooperating with Taylor's NPFL. With multi-ethnic support, by June 1990 Taylor controlled the suburbs of Monrovia, the capital city. He was prevented from moving into the capital by ECOMOG, the peacekeeping arm of the sixteen-member Economic Community of West African States (ECOWAS).

Taylor's chief rival in the struggle for state control, Prince Johnson, led the breakaway Independent National Patriotic Front of Liberia (INPFL) and was responsible for capturing and killing Samuel Doe in September 1990. With the fall of the Doe regime, regional leaders and ECOWAS participants agreed to immediately appoint a long-time opposition candidate, Professor Amos Sawyer, as head of an Interim Government of National Unity (IGNU). Although Taylor had physical control of most of Liberia, he was denied political authority since he did not have control of the state. Lacking international recognition as head of the Liberian state, he could not use that position to bargain for resources in exchange for elections or receive large-scale foreign aid.

Taylor faced a dilemma. His goal was to control Monrovia, the seat of the Liberian state. To do this required resources to defeat the army of the very government he wanted to control as well as other opposition factions. His only option was to control local accumulation and regional markets to finance his own military operations (Reno, 1998). He quickly developed multiple alliances, establishing business ties with arms dealers and expatriate logging and mining firms. Foreign entrepreneurs supported him in their quest to keep a foothold in Liberia's natural resource markets. Large established firms like Firestone as well as a consortium of European, Japanese, and U.S. steel producers did business with Taylor, assuming that he would win the war and gain control of the state. Taylor and the NPFL's control of commercial networks yielded large amounts of revenue between 1990 to 1994 for his "warlord economy," estimated at $200 million and $250 million per year. In addition, there was trade in looted goods, stockpiled iron ore, building materials, and office equipment (Reno, 1998: 99).

Competition for these lucrative commercial networks caused the prolonged brutal war. Factional leaders and their foreign business partners profited. Few ordinary Liberian citizens benefited. More than 200,000 people were killed, and over a million and a half were displaced within Liberia itself or became refugees in neighboring countries in West Africa or the United States. ECOMOG, led by reputed regional hegemon Nigeria, failed to make the peace agreements stick and did not have the financial resources to enforce peace. Divisions within ECOWAS/ECOMOG around Nigerian foreign policy ambitions prevented unified, strong, and effective intervention.

The peace agreements left the vicious "warlord" apparatus of the 1989–1996 period intact, as factions seized every available opportunity to make commercial deals with foreign firms willing to do business with nonstate actors. ECOWAS/ECOMOG intervention was yet another example of the changing 1990s, whereby African countries tried to solve their own regional problems in the absence of military intervention of Europe or the United States. The war lasted seven years, and fourteen agreements were negotiated before the final one, the Abuja Accord II, led to the end of the war. The Abuja Accord II set out a timetable for disarmament and demobilization of forces (January 1997) and the establishment of an independent electoral commission to administer voter registration and elections. Western industrialized nations (particularly the United States) were especially pleased at the prospects for peace via elections and watched, along with hundreds of election monitors, with cautious optimism.

There were no clear programmatic differences among the parties. Johnson-Sirleaf and the Unity Party focused on reducing government bureaucracy, helping small farmers, and attracting foreign investment. Kromah and the All Liberian Coalition Party (ALCP) threatened escalation of the conflict if his party lost. Taylor and the NPP focused on his ability to enforce security, his patriotism and commitment to Liberia (as revealed by his removal of the oppressive Doe regime), and his claim that, since he participated in the war that damaged Liberia, he should be the one to repair that damage.

Charles Taylor and his National Patriotic Party (NPP) won 75 percent of the vote in the 1997 presidential election, gaining more than half of the vote in every single county of Liberia. He also gained support across different groups and different regions. Taylor had fought a long brutal war in which his faction participated in gross violations of human rights and physical destruction of the country. Yet his victory in the 1997 multiparty elections was not unexpected.

How did the NPP and Charles Taylor win the 1997 election? First, the timetable for the election was short, and the registration period chaotic. This might have helped the NPP, which had a better organizational structure than the opposition parties. Second, Taylor and the NPP had more resources to use as inducements for votes. T-shirts and bags of rice were distributed for free from NPP stocks. Taylor's radio station, KISS-FM, was used for campaigning, reaching hundred of thousands of people throughout the country. Third, the opposition parties (hurriedly assembled for multiparty elections) were weak, with either a small ethnic or urban base and no national support.

Fourth, Taylor could be viewed as the de facto incumbent in the 1997 election. Like an incumbent, he had the advantage in organization and financial resources and long-time control of a large part of the country with immense resources.

What did Taylor and Liberia achieve by holding multiparty elections in 1997? The immediate benefit was that hundreds of thousands of lives were saved. The Liberian population perhaps believed that Taylor, given his demonstrated ability to secure patronage from commercial organizations, offered the best hope for security and improvements in living standards. Taylor's government has been a commercial empire structured by patron-client relationships, with a preference for foreign patrons in exploiting the country's resources. Future governments may have problems dealing with groups with independent connections to the outside commercial world; possessing more resources than the state, these groups could destabilize or overthrow the government in power if it refuses to represent their interest. Taylor's patron-client rule reflects continuity in the political practices from the Americo-Liberians, to Samuel Doe, to Charles Taylor. Patron-client relationships will not disappear in most of the resource-scarce societies of the world, but a new system will need to be constructed in Liberia that allows the state to meet the minimum demands of broad social groups who depend on it for education, health, water, jobs, and income. Multiparty elections have been held, and the war appears to have ended. However, an election cannot guarantee stability (the Angolan example reminds us of this), because economic and political problems of the Doe era have not yet disappeared.

Sierra Leone

The political environment that created the conditions conducive to war in Liberia also existed in Sierra Leone in the early 1990s. Power was extremely centralized under the governing All Peoples Congress (APC), which ruled from 1968 to 1992. Despite much resistance from civic groups, opposition political parties, and the press across the society, the APC outlawed all opposition parties and set up a one-party state in 1978. It then systematically destroyed all forms of opposition through repression, intimidation, and co-optation (Bangura, 1997). It concentrated power in the capital of Freetown and dismantled the limited power of local governments. The APC co-opted paramount chiefs, making loyalty to the ruling party the litmus test for the government's appointments to the chieftaincies. Rural areas were neglected and had limited socioeconomic development. The state used violence to prevent dissent, squelch organized opposition, and defend the social order when it was challenged. The APC created a paramilitary force, the Internal Security Unit, staffed by marginalized elements within the society, to harass and kill party opponents and opposition groups. In the mid- to late 1980s the state's autocratic management of power coincided with its implementation of harsh economic policies to secure loans from external creditors.

It was within this context that dissident activity developed and, ultimately, the rebel force Revolutionary United Front (RUF) formed. RUF's social origin was urban disenchanted and unemployed youth. RUF rebels, supported by Charles Taylor's NPFL rebel force in Liberia, invaded Sierra Leone on March 23, 1991, and began a war for control of the state. The war in Sierra Leone thus became linked to Liberian domestic politics. Regional unity among warlords emerged as the RUF and NPFL formed a military pact. By late 1990 Taylor's NPFL had established cross-border commerce with Liberia, Sierra Leone, and Guinea that was controlled by Mandingo traders. When the fighting broke out in 1991 along Sierra Leone's eastern border, Taylor used the conflict to draft RUF to conquer the economically valuable areas of Sierra Leone and used foreign exchange earned from the country's trade to support the NPFL.

RUF leader, Foday Sankoh, early on declared his commitment to use the same force against the APC as it used against others. Sankoh violently attacked the resource base of APC/Mommoh's patronage networks. He occupied the resource-rich areas of the country; cut off the government's access to the country's diamond economy; and made deals with foreign traders and arms dealers. RUF extended its violence to the civilian population, committing appalling atrocities (public beatings, public executions of traditional authority figures, rape) that galvanized the civilian population into counterinsurgency. Thousands of civilians fled from RUF-controlled territory to urban settlements. RUF invaded refugee camps and attacked their civilian occupants. Self-defense militias, such as the Kamajoi militia, were created to protect displaced civilians from RUF attacks (Muana, 1997). Although the APC government was widely despised, the RUF would not have received popular support for its removal (Muana, 1997).

The Mommoh government had been weakened politically by structural adjustment policies. Many of its clients joined rebel leader Foday Sankoh, who had resources from the diamond trade to pay them off. Clients began to see that loyalty to President Mommoh no longer brought economic security. When Captain V. E. M. Strasser staged a coup d'etat against the Mommoh government in April 1992, it surprised not the people of Sierra Leone but external observers, who seemed disappointed at this "reversal" in the region away from the new trend toward multiparty systems. The war did not end with the Mommoh government's removal and replacement by Strasser's National Provisional Ruling Council (NPRC). Some saw an identity of interests between the RUF and the NPRC and a conspiracy between the two groups to perpetuate the armed conflict (Abraham, 1997). Both the NPRC and RUF were engaged in pillaging the resources of the country, especially diamonds, and both opposed the holding of general elections before peace was established. By the end of 1993 the NPRC appeared to be in a position to crush the RUF and end the war, but Captain Strasser did not order it. Many believed he refrained because, if the war ended, calls for restoration of civilian rule would follow and the military would be out of power and lose the opportunity to enrich themselves (Abraham, 1997). After the NPRC accommodated the RUF in 1993, the "sobel" phenomenon (soldier by day, rebel by night) came about, and both government troops and rebels turned against the civilian population. "Sobels" would attack the civilian population and loot their properties but commit atrocities similar to or worse than those of the rebels in order to shift the blame to RUF. Sobels looted civilian property to enrich themselves, since the NPRC government (pressured by international creditors to reduce public expenditures) had no money to pay them adequately.

Pressure from Western industrialized nations to restore civilian rule led to the announcement in 1995 of measures towards democratization: the ban on politics was to be lifted; the Interim National Electoral Commission (INEC), set up in December 1994, was to call a conference to discuss the electoral process; a national commission for reconciliation was to be established; elections were to be held at the end of the year and a civilian president installed in January 1996 (Davis, D. 1994–1995). The NPRC moved very slowly toward the announced transition; three months later political parties still could not function, and legislation authorizing elections was delayed for another nine months. There were announcements that the war had intensified, with RUF threatening an all-out attack on the capital. From the NPRC's perspective, no democratic reforms could be attempted in that context.

The National Consultative Conference (Bintumani I), held in August 1995, agreed to hold presidential and parliamentary elections on February 26, 1996, in the war-torn country. On January 16, 1996, a palace coup ousted Strasser for "his attempt to impede the democratic process." RUF still insisted that peace should come before elections. Bintumani II was called on February 12, 1996, and unanimously decided in favor of elections as planned for February 26, 1996. The new president, Ahmed Kabbah of the Sierra Leone People's Party (SLPP), was sworn in on March 29, 1996, and met immediately with the RUF leader, Foday Sankoh, who agreed to an "indefinite truce." In December 1996, a peace accord was signed in Abidjan, Côte d'Ivoire, between the Kabbah government and the RUF. The peace accord was intended to mark the official end of Sierra Leone's five and a half years of war. The war had killed more than 10,000 civilians, left hundreds maimed, displaced about a million and a half people, orphaned thousands of young children, led to the growth of dense urban settlements, and imposed heavy financial burdens on the population.

The Abidjan Peace Accord represented a variant of the power-sharing model. Two key characteristics were embodied in the peace accord. First, both the RUF and the Kabbah government had been hurt by the war and should rationally choose peace over war. Second, the international community should play an active role in helping the parties transition to peace and rebuild the country. The RUF was not given any post in the government, did not have any representation in Parliament, and was not in charge of any local government or province. The reason was that the 1996 elections had come off without RUF's participation brought in a new government that was not associated with the war's causes (Bangura, 1997). The RUF was asked to wait for the next elections, when it could be a contender for access to dominant political institutions.

How did the Kabbah government assure its own security against the power of rebel forces like RUF? Executive Outcomes, a South African security firm brought in to manage government security, helped protect President Kabbah from the demands of his own citizens. Monitored by international creditors, Kabbah could not use state assets to attract supporters. Like the warlords in Liberia and elsewhere, Kabbah used his privileged ties with foreigners to facilitate favored business operations. His reliance on Executive Outcomes gave him a measure of autonomy vis-à-vis local threats but involved even more foreigners in Sierra Leonean politics. Kabbah was particularly dependent on Executive Outcomes; the firm's intelligence efforts uncovered many coup plots and moved directly to diffuse them.

Executive Outcomes' contract was not renewed beyond January 1997; the company departed in February and the country's security immediately worsened. On May 25, 1997, Johnny Koroma, a junior officer, led a combined sobel force of army troops and rebels in a successful coup against the Kabbah government. International sanctions and pressures against the coup makers quickly led to the restoration of the Kabbah government in 1998. The coup makers lacked large-scale foreign connections who could help them organize profitable commercial networks outside and thus resist external sanctions (Reno, 1998).

The Kabbah government maintained control of the state and stayed on its course toward economic liberalization in the war-torn country. The Sierra Leonean people were not happy with the government; a majority of those interviewed in a public opinion poll six months after the election, in 1997, expressed disappointment with the Kabbah government's performance, citing the deteriorating economic situation, increased poverty, mass unemployment, corruption in high places, and undue exploitation of the country's minerals with no benefit to the people, among other problems (Reno, 1998: 38). RUF has continued to attack the Kabbah government, with increased violence against UN peace-keepers. Three hundred UN peacekeepers were held hostage for three months, the crisis ending in July 2000. Sporadic fighting still exists in some parts of the country, but the Kabbah government, supported by the international community, has maintained its authority to govern. It faces the challenge of reconstructing a state that respond to the collective needs of the population.

Conclusion

During the 1990s the countries covered in this chapter represented a paradox in Africa: while authoritarian and military regimes gave way to multiparty systems in much of Africa, in these countries authoritarianism gave way to anarchy, disintegration, and state collapse. The majority of the people in these countries did not identify with the states that governed them. Armed groups were in open conflict with the central government. The level of tension led to disintegration in most of these countries, total collapse in some. The debilitating effects of politicized ethnicity are obvious, leading to the state's delegitimation and collapse. Eritrea, Ethiopia, Rwanda, Burundi, Uganda, Mozambique, and Liberia appeared to have retreated from anarchy and near anarchy without big-power intervention. Somalia and Sierra Leone are still plagued by rebels with automatic weapons and warlords. South Africa removed its insidious apartheid regime, but socioeconomic disparities based on race persist despite black-majority rule. Instability still plagues most of these countries as a result of ethnic, religious, regional, and class factionalism. Big-power intervention has been withdrawn, creating the potential for escalated regional involvement. This could bring stability or continue the descent into systemic collapse and anarchy.

For Further Reading

Zartman, I. W., ed. (1995). *Collapsed States: The Disintegration and Restoration of Legitimate Authority*. Boulder: Lynne Rienner.

Strange, Susan (1996). *The Retreat of the State: Diffusion of Power in the World Economy*. Cambridge, England: Cambridge University Press.

Herbst, Jeffrey (1997). "Responding to State Failure in Africa." In Michael Brown, ed., *Nationalism and Ethnic Conflict*. Cambridge, Mass.: MIT Press. 347–398.

Human Rights Watch (1999). *None Must Live to Tell the Tale*. New York: Human Rights Watch.

8

—

Africa in the World: "Hemmed In" or New Opportunities?

For three decades following the independence of most sub-Saharan African countries, the region's international relations predictably were framed by the bipolar structure of world politics that had emerged after World War II. African leaders established ties with foreign governments and institutions capable of providing development assistance and military, economic, and political support for their regimes' survival. A secondary but important concern was terminating colonial rule in southern Africa. Key African international relations from the 1960s through the 1980s consisted of those between Africa on one hand and, on the other, the former European colonial powers, the two superpowers (the United States and Soviet Union), international organizations and financial institutions, and other developing regions, as well as intra-African relations.

By the early 1990s, dramatic changes in the world held serious implications for sub-Saharan Africa. The Cold War ended, and the post-World War II bipolar structure collapsed. Namibia won its independence in 1992. Nelson Mandela was released from prison after twenty-seven years, and black-majority rule was established in South Africa.

Nelson Mandela, Soweto, 1990.

© Peter Turnley / Corbis

Namibian and South African liberation completed the decolonization of Africa. The United States emerged as the only military superpower, exercising unlimited power and influence in many parts of the world (e.g., Somalia, Bosnia, Haiti, the Persian Gulf). With the disappearance of the communist economies of the Soviet Union and Eastern Europe, a global capitalist economy emerged (captured in the term *globalization*). Neoliberalism became the dominant paradigm in a global policy environment emphasizing trade liberalization, economic deregulation of financial markets, privatization, international production, and the retrenchment of the state. This emphasis on globalization has propelled new issues to the top of the global agenda, issues pertaining to globalization, economic integration and free trade, preservation of the environment, global climate change, drug trafficking, and democracy and good governance. In the international community, human welfare and social justice have now taken a backseat to global capital accumulation.

This chapter reviews Africa's key international relations in the postindependence period. It seeks an understanding of the varied ways different African states have managed their dependency in the global political economy. What strategies were used by these states in their external relations in their attempt to accomplish their domestic goals? What kinds of relationships developed between dependent African states and external powers and institutions? Who benefited and why? How have African states, either individually or collectively, coped with an external environment in which they were not major players? What are some of the challenges posed by the newly emerging post-Cold War international system? Have there been new opportunities in Africa's external relations since 1990 that could lead to internal development on the continent?

External Support and State Preservation

There were considerable differences among African states in the ways they pursued their external interests in the postindependence period. For the first two and a half decades after independence, the vast majority of African leaders used the state apparatus to extract resources from the international power structure to maintain the state's dominance over other domestic groups (Clapham, 1996). Because of the lack of sufficient resources in many African economies, external capital became a critical component of state revenues needed to underwrite clientelistic networks critical to many postindependence regimes' survival (see Chapter 4). The state's domestic clientelist politics made international transactions even more important. Foreign policies pursued always sought to continue the flow of transactions from the outside, providing funds necessary to preserve state power. African leaders needed assistance from external powers to preserve the territorial integrity of the state against secession, maintain an effective central government in economic, administrative, and military areas, and otherwise keep their regime in power (Clapham, 1996).

Countries in control of huge military, political, and economic resources (largely the United States, former Soviet Union, France, Britain, and Belgium) provided military and economic aid and diplomatic security in exchange for political support and military and economic penetration of Africa. This convergence of interests led many postindependence African leaders to enter into a dependent-client relationship with leaders of the superpowers and former colonizing nations. External political and economic influences have been extremely powerful in the postindependence period. Understanding the distribution of power in the international community and the inequities of the past, both conservative and radical African regimes pursued what they deemed to be pragmatic policies to ensure the survival of their regime and the state.

Relations with Former Colonial Powers

Spain, Portugal, Germany, Belgium, and Italy

Of the major Western European powers that colonized sub-Saharan Africa, France and Britain maintained the closest ties with their former colonies. Spain, Portugal, Belgium, and Italy did not manage either smooth or peaceful transitions to independence and did not develop close linkages with their former colonies in the postindependence period. Belgium and Italy expressed only minimal interest in resolving the crises in Rwanda, Burundi, and the Congo and the Horn of Africa (Ercolessi, 1994; Martin, 1995a). The Portuguese colonies fought a long and bitter war against Portugal for independence. Reestablishing relations with Portugal has been a slow and difficult process. After independence the ruling parties in the former Portuguese colonies established close ties with the Soviet Union because the latter gave ideological support and military assistance to their liberation movements, helping them in their victories against Portugal. Angola also established economic links with Western based (U.S.) companies involved in its oil industry.

Germany was a minor power in Africa and lost its holdings after its defeat in World War I. The former Tanganyika (a part of German East Africa) was at first a mandate of the League of Nations and later was handed over to Britain. The former Urundi-Ruanda was divided up into two separate countries, Burundi and Rwanda and handed over to Belgium. Germany's other colony, South West Africa (now Namibia), made an international mandate of the League of Nations, was subsequently illegally taken over by the white apartheid regime in South Africa and held until it won its independence through armed struggle in 1992. In the post-1960 period, Germany established itself as the second or third largest trading partner of the majority of African countries (Winrow, 1990).

Britain

The leading imperial power of the nineteenth century, Britain had a large number of colonies in sub-Saharan Africa (see Table 2.1): West Africa (Sierra Leone, The Gambia, Ghana, and Nigeria), Cameroon (colonized partly by Britain and partly by France); East Africa (Kenya, Tanzania, Uganda), Northeast Africa (The Sudan, part of Somalia); Central Southern Africa (Zambia); Southeast Africa (Malawi), Southern Africa (Rhodesia, Botswana, Lesotho, Swaziland), Mauritius, and Seychelles. Having Nigeria, Africa's most populous state (120 million today) and six other states with populations of over 10 million, Britain's colonies accounted for more than one-fourth of the population of sub-Saharan Africa. Free labor, agricultural products, raw materials, and mineral exports from these colonies (and others

TABLE 8.1   African Sources of UK Mineral Imports, 1977

Metal	Country	Percentages
Aluminum	Ghana	7
Asbestos	South Africa	16
	Swaziland	13
Bauxite	Ghana	72
Cadmium	South Africa	9
Chromium	South Africa	39
Cobalt	Zambia	57
	Zaire	1
Copper	Zambia	29
	Zaire	2
Iron Ore	Liberia	3
	Mauritania	9
Manganese	South Africa	31
	Gabon	18
Platinum Group	South Africa	41
Silver	South Africa	3
Tin	Nigeria	15.5
	South Africa	5
Tungsten	Rwanda	5
Uranium	N/A	
Vanadium	South Africa	55

Source: Cornell, 1981.

in the Caribbean and Asia) contributed to industrial development in Britain and facilitated its rise as an imperial power (Rodney, 1972). (See Table 8.1.)

Economically weakened by World War II and faced with rising national-ist movements for independence throughout its colonies, Britain was forced to decolonize most of its holdings in Asia, the Caribbean, and Africa. It managed peaceful and successful transitions to independence in Africa and transferred power to African political elites who were committed to the maintenance of British representative institutions and capitalist forms of eco-nomic organization. Africa was not considered to be a significant part of its empire by then, having been surpassed by India and the white dominions of New Zealand and Australia. In the postcolonial period, Britain was primarily concerned with its economic interests in East and southern Africa, buying out white farms from British settlers in Kenya and Rhodesia, compensating Zambia for some of the economic damages caused by Rhodesia's Unilateral

Declaration of Independence (UDI) in 1965, and providing technical aid programs to Malawi and Lesotho (Clapham, 1996).

Except in southern Africa, Britain has avoided a political role in African politics since granting independence to its colonies. Supporting the unpopular white settler regimes in Rhodesia and South Africa put it on a collision course with many of the independent African states and drew it into the conflict between those settler regimes and "black" Africa. Because of its own political and economic interests and its changed circumstances in the world, Britain opted to grant political independence to its colonies and use the Commonwealth's organizational framework to manage its postcolonial relations with all of them. Rather than dealing with separate African countries or Africa as a region, it dealt with all its former colonies through the Commonwealth.

The British Commonwealth is an association solely for Britain and its former colonies. All the members are English-speaking countries, but it is not an "anglophone community" seeking to cement cultural ties between Britain and its members. Personal relationships between British prime ministers and the prime ministers and presidents of member states might have existed from time to time, but neither Britain nor the member states have been interested in seeking as significant and deep a relationship as France has had with its francophone African community. The relationship with Britain was sometimes strained while Britain supported the white settler regimes in southern Africa. Annual Commonwealth meetings have been attended by members from the entire Commonwealth. African states have formed the largest group, but meetings have not been devoted only to African issues. It served as an important lobby group in the 1970s for the developing regions of the world to present Third World economic issues. Newly independent countries joining the Commonwealth maintained the British monarch as the titular head of state of their country. Many sub-Saharan African states changed their constitutions within a decade after independence, replacing the inherited system of constitutional monarchy with a republican form of government. The British monarch was then replaced by an African president.

Britain did not have the economic clout nor direct control through the Commonwealth to maintain dominance of the political economies of its former colonies. Britain's former colonies have moved away from dependence on the pound sterling and have diversified their financial relationships. During the decolonization period, Britain's African colonies had secured an independent central bank as one of the essential supports of sovereign statehood (Bangura, 1983). Yet Britain remained an important trading partner for Nigeria, Kenya, Zambia, and Zimbabwe and the principal source of foreign investment in most of its colonies across the region.

By the early 1960s Britain's decline as a world power led it to turn its attention inward to rebuilding its war-ravaged economy. It was not interested in offering protection to former members of its empire. The leaders of its former African colonies (e.g., Kwame Nkrumah, Julius Nyerere, Jomo Kenyatta, Kenneth Kaunda) were very nationalistic and not predisposed to entering into patron-client relationships with British leaders for protection and support. Britain, in turn, was focused on rebuilding its economy and therefore was preoccupied with establishing a special relationship with the United States, one of the emerging superpowers and leader of the Western alliance. Britain's involvement with its African colonies was limited to forming alliances with the United States in its bid to prevent the spread of communism in the Congo, protecting British commercial interests in the white settler regimes in southern Africa, protecting trade and investments, and providing aid to African governments to help keep them within the liberal market order and to buttress British exports.

In 1960 Britain joined the United States in undermining the Patrice Lumumba government of the Congo and encouraging the Katanga secession. It aligned with the federal military government of Nigeria against Biafran secession in 1968. Large quantities of British arms were sent to Lagos (then the capital of Nigeria) to protect British commercial interests there. Between 1965 and 1980 Britain was involved in the Rhodesian conflict, in which it was unwilling to bring back under its control the white minority government of Ian Smith, which had unilaterally declared itself independent. After more than a decade and a half of war with no side having a clear victory, Britain negotiated the Lancaster Accords that paved the way for black majority rule in an independent Zimbabwe. British commercial interests (in agriculture, manufacturing, mining, livestock) in Rhodesia and South Africa brought it into conflict with African pressures for sanctions against those two white settler regimes. British investors and exporters were intent on maintaining a strong presence in those countries. The white minority governments lasted as long as they did because of Western (largely British and American) support.

Britain's aid record in sub-Saharan Africa between 1960 and 1990 was a modest one; since 1990 its aid transfers have been integrated into aid from the European Union. In 1977 southern and East Africa received the lion's share of British aid transfers, with southern Africa receiving 38.5 million pounds, East Africa 23.4 million pounds, and West Africa 13.5 million pounds (Bangura, 1983). By the beginning of the 1980s Britain was the fifth largest donor overall, after France, the United States, West Germany, and Japan. About one-third of Britain's bilateral financial disbursements (1,326 million pounds in 1980) have traditionally gone to Africa. British aid to Africa in 1987 was US$325 million, less than 35 percent of Italian aid and 16 percent of the $2,046 million provided by France. In 1987 Africa received no more than 3.2 percent of Britain's exports and provided only 1.9 percent of its imports (Ravenhill, 1991: 182–183).

Britain's limited activities in sub-Saharan Africa have further diminished since 1990. Britain was a part of the Western alliance that imposed political conditionality on authoritarian African regimes in the early 1990s. It has disengaged from African conflicts and problems since black majority rule was established in Zimbabwe (1980) and more recently in South Africa (1994). A relatively smooth transfer of power there has thus far allowed for the security and safety of its commercial interests. Both the Mugabe government in Zimbabwe and the Mandela and Mbeki governments in South Africa established cordial relations with Britain but quickly diversified their economic relations after independence. Britain's interactions with Africa continued in the post-Cold War period through the Commonwealth, the European Union, private groups, and European NGOs concerned with humanitarian issues. Unlike France, Britain refrained from projecting its military power into its former African colonies after independence. In the 1990s Britain served as a part of UN peacekeeping forces in Sierra Leone and the Great Lakes region. British aid to Africa, concentrated in the 1990s mainly in Nigeria and South Africa, has also declined overall since 1993, dropping from US$662 million in 1994 to US$619 million in 1996 (Lancaster, 2000: 211). Although bilateral economic relations continued, economic transactions with former British colonies in Africa are now increasingly carried out by the EU. Multilateral relations have now become the norm in the post-Cold War period.

France

France had colonies in eighteen continental sub-Saharan African countries, containing just over one-fourth of the region's people. Of all the major powers in sub-Saharan Africa, France has had the longest commitment to an active presence. France consistently pursued a strategy of maintaining its own political and economic interests in Africa, which have often been different from those of other Western powers. France maintained cultural, economic, military, and political ties with all of its former colonies in West Africa (except Guinea) after granting their independence in 1960.

French policy makers believed it necessary to sustain cultural influence in order to achieve their foreign policy goals. In keeping with its "civilizing mission" ideology from the colonial period, France promoted cultural assimilation and conformity to French traditions in francophone Africa. The French language, intellectual traditions, and way of life were all promoted. Those who successfully imbibed this culture would be accepted as equal to the French people. Sub-Saharan Africa has the largest number of French-speaking people of any region in the world. From the period of President Charles de Gaulle until today under President Chirac, the community of francophone Africa has been very special to France. French presidents over the past five decades have reportedly perceived Francophone Africa as "constituting a natural French preserve off limits to other foreign powers" (Martin, 1995a: 168), regardless of whether these foreign powers were allies (e.g., the United States) or adversaries (such as the former Soviet Union).

France preserved a very close relationship with its former colonies, maintaining influence in these countries through financial and technical aid (and military agreements in some instances) combined with close personal relations with leaders. Regularly scheduled (biannual) Franco-African summits, attended by the presidents of France and all francophone Africa, were designed to cement personal ties between the patron leaders of France and their clients in Africa. Very close ties developed between French presidents, from Charles De Gaulle to the present Jacques Chirac, and African presidents Houphouet-Boigny of Ivory Coast, Leopold Senghor of Senegal, and many others. France benefited from close ties with notorious dictator Jean-Bedel Bokassa, raking in huge sums when he purchased hugely expensive goods in France for his coronation as "emperor" (modeled after Napoleon) of the Central African Republic.

Chad, the Central African Republic, Gabon, Côte d'Ivoire, Mauritania, Niger, Togo, Djibouti, all relied on the close relationship they had with France for technology, education, communications, internal security, and administrative personnel. These newly independent countries depended on France for their technical advisers and the civil servants required to staff state bureaucracies and provide basic services. There was an infusion of French technocrats into many African countries in the first two decades after independence; by 1977 there were 4,000 French "assistant techniques" in Côte d'Ivoire alone. This was the situation in key ministries of most francophone African countries. In 1995 more than 10,000 French technical assistants were still in Africa. With this kind of support the French hoped to create a welcoming environment for French capital investment.

France supported the creation of a common currency—the Communaute Financiere Africaine (CFA franc)—for all its former West African colonies (and eventually included the former Belgian colonies and Equatorial Guinea), assuring tight financial links among all of them and a measure of monetary stability throughout the francophone community. The CFA franc's creation was a particularly important part of Franco-African relations. Some observers viewed it as a part of France's neocolonial strategy to keep its former colonies under its control. Others viewed it as benefiting politically influential urban African elites as well as French exporters, who thereby gain a protected market (Clapham, 1996). In 1948 the CFA franc was tied to the French franc and guaranteed by the French treasury at the exchange rate of 1 franc to 0.5 CFA francs. In 1968 the parity was adjusted to FF1 to CFA50. In return, members of the CFA franc zone were required to hold 65 percent of their foreign exchange reserves in French francs with the French treasury (Ndikumana, 2001). The CFA franc has been used for international transactions, while foreign exchange earned by exports was kept by the French treasury. This gave France fiscal and economic control over its former colonies.

The CFA franc was maintained from 1968 until its 50 percent devaluation in January 1994 at a fixed rate against the French franc, with which it was fully convertible. It enabled African urban political elites who adopted French lifestyles to have ready access to convertible currency to purchase Western imports. Heads of state, such as the late president of Côte d'Ivoire Houphouet-Boigny, reportedly transferred substantial sums in convertible currency (as much as one-sixth of Ivorian cocoa revenues) to foreign banks, and President Ahidjo of Cameroon transferred up to 70 percent of Cameroonian oil revenues (van de Walle, 1991: 383–405). French entrepreneurs have had almost unlimited privileges. They have been able to move capital freely and repatriate all profits from their African investments, while the African countries have had little power to ensure that such investments were compatible with their national interests.

Sub-Saharan Africa has been an important source of strategic raw materials for France as well as a market for its manufactured goods. In the 1980s France was 100 percent dependent on Niger and Gabon for uranium, 90 percent dependent on Guinea for bauxite, 76 percent dependent on Gabon and South Africa for manganese, 59 percent dependent on Zaire and Zambia for cobalt, 57 percent dependent on Zaire and Zambia for copper, 56 percent dependent on Madagascar and South Africa for chromium, 55 percent dependent on Morocco and Togo for phosphate, and 31 percent dependent on Liberia and Mauritania for iron ore (Martin, 1995b: 171). Defense agreements worked out between France and several African countries after independence gave France exclusive access to such strategic materials as oil, uranium, lithium, and helium. These raw materials had to be sold to France on a priority basis as required by the defense agreements. These materials have been necessary to maintain France's high-tech industries and have contributed to the continuing prosperity of the French economy.

French economic assistance to sub-Saharan Africa relative to other European countries in the postindependence period is shown in Table 8.2. France has clearly been the largest single source of aid to Africa for several decades. Even in 1991, when political conditionality led to drastic reductions in aid from Western donors to African authoritarian regimes, French aid to Africa was US $2,973 million, more than 60 percent above the second largest donor, the International Development Association (a soft-loan arm of the World Bank) with US $1,839 million (Ravenhill, 1995: 100). French financial assistance reportedly went to support development projects as well as patronage payments for African leaders.

In addition to financial assistance, trade relations also reflects a powerful French presence in the former French colonies. France alone accounts for

TABLE 8.2   Net Disbursements of Overseas Development Assistance to Sub-Saharan Africa, by Donor (in US$millions at 1995 prices and exchange rates)

	1980	1986	1993	1994	1995	1996
DAC Bilateral						
Australia	30	40	59	69	60	55
Austria	21	25	85	81	76	97
Belgium	501	496	263	240	196	207
Canada	294	376	287	263	275	266
Denmark	237	369	414	411	367	458
Finland	66	165	109	104	79	82
France	1,686	2,678	3,555	3,550	2,700	2,448
Germany	1,257	1,488	1,568	1,366	1,268	1,268
Ireland	11	20	30	42	62	75
Italy	97	1,434	582	407	359	292
Japan	692	879	1,154	1,258	1,352	1,253
Luxembourg	—	—	17	20	—	31
Netherlands	628	782	612	605	695	709
New Zealand	2	1	2	5	4	4
Norway	194	419	360	411	380	386
Portugal	—	—	211	242	155	147
Spain	—	—	82	120	79	209
Sweden	426	608	604	491	388	433
Switzerland	126	319	232	227	219	201
United Kingdom	659	500	530	662	601	619
United States	1,024	1,161	1,503	1,490	1,050	623
Total DAC	7,952	11,762	12,259	12,062	10,366	9,865

Source: Development Assistance Committee, OECD, 1997, cited in Lancaster, 2000: 211.

about 60 percent of the external trade of the francophone countries. Further, although the latter's association with the EEC/EU provides them with access to a larger market, France is still the major purchaser of their products (Martin, 1995a). The colonial structure of production remained in place, as sub-Saharan Africa continued to provide primary commodities and raw materials to France and France retained control over the production and export of manufactured goods. France's main trading partners included Côte d'Ivoire, Cameroon, Congo-Brazzaville, Gabon, Niger, and Senegal. In 1992 these six countries accounted for 22 percent of France's imports from

Africa and for 26 percent of its exports to the African continent. France has always maintained a positive trade balance with sub-Saharan Africa, even while maintaining chronic deficits with the rest of the world. Franco-African trade has declined since the mid-1980s, but in 1992 French exports to Africa amounted to F72 billion, ranking Africa as France's third main export market behind Europe and North America (Martin, 1995b: 173).

France has maintained military bases, trained the military and police, and supplied arms to its former colonies. In the postindependence period, France was the leading arms merchant on the African continent, selling weapons to francophone as well as nonfrancophone countries such as Libya, Nigeria, Somalia, Kenya, and South Africa (Chazan, Mortimer, Ravenhill, and Rothchild, 1988: 354). France intervened militarily in several African states—Chad (1961), Gabon (1961), Cameroon (1960, 1961), Congo-Zaire (1977, 1978), and Niger (1963)—and assisted in preserving weak conservative regimes. In 1979, 1,000 French troops flew into Bangui with David Dacko to overthrow Jean-Bedel Bokassa of the Central African Republic (Gavshon, 1981: 168–169). The French troops' role was to assure internal security, not to protect the regimes against external threats. In 1961 French troops reversed a coup d'etat against Leon M'Ba's government in Gabon. The French government subsequently stood by M'Ba's successor, Omar Bongo, despite his reputation for violations of democratic rights. France intervened at various times in Chad during its more than twenty years of civil war, dispatching troops on several occasions. During the 1977 and 1978 Shaba invasions in Zaire, France sent in the Foreign Legion to help shore up Mobutu's government. Senegal, Côte d'Ivoire, the Central African Republic, Comoros, Gabon, and Djibouti had French troops stationed on their territory as a result of defense treaties with France. Even left-leaning governments in Benin, Madagascar, and Congo maintained military technical cooperation agreements with France, though these did not include direct French military involvement. Agreements of this sort existed in seventeen African countries, including Burkina Faso (1961), Algeria (1967), Tunisia and Morocco (1973), Burundi (1969), Madagascar (1973), Congo-Brazzaville and Congo-Zaire (1974), Benin and Rwanda (1975), Chad and Mauritania (1976), Mali and Niger (1978), Libya (1978), and Seychelles and Mauritius (1979) (Martin, 1995b).

The global changes that have occurred in the world economy since the end of the Cold War have affected French foreign policy toward Africa. Although still of economic importance to France, francophone Africa has been repositioned in its foreign policy agenda. By the early 1990s, there was strong domestic pressure from groups within French civil society demanding a transparent African policy, condemning military and economic support for unstable authoritarian regimes, and demanding an end to military intervention in Africa. The pressures at home, pressures from thousands of protesters in a host of African countries, the demands of European integration, the recession in France, all combined to force some changes in Franco-African relations.

In June 1990 at the Franco-African summit in La Baule, France, President Mitterand announced that France would from that point onward favor those African countries that were either democratic or promoting democratic change. The new La Baule Doctrine sent a message to African leaders to initiate a process of democratization if they expected to maintain their privileged ties with France (Boulaga, 1993). Two years later, at the seventeenth Franco-African summit in Gabon in October, France qualified its policy by stating that democratization movements accompanied by instability would be unacceptable. The French prime minister, Pierre Bere Savoy, stated that the expectation was that African countries would prioritize their objectives in the following order: (1) security, (2) development, and (3) democratization (Glaser and Smith, 1994: 102). Continuity and stability were of such importance to France that it rewarded the incumbent president Houphouet-Boigny with over $1.6 billion dollars in aid from 1990 to 1992 (an increase from $549 million received during the preceding three-year period) for managing a successful transition that led to his election in Côte d'Ivoire's multiparty elections of October 1990 (Schraeder, 1996: 149). After massive street demonstrations and public protests that made France uneasy, Houphouet-Boigny reluctantly held multiparty elections, and a stable order was quickly restored.

Though espousing the rhetoric of democratization and political conditionality like its Western allies, France sent military aid to its embattled allies resisting democratization. Military aid to resist pressures for democratization was estimated at FF6,000 million in 1990–1991. Seven hundred officers of the French Gendarmerie were deployed to Benin, Togo, the Central African Republic, Chad, Comoros, Congo-Brazzaville, Madagascar, and Niger. In addition, technical help and material support were provided for their police forces, riot control units, secret services, elite guards, and intelligence agencies. In 1993 FF200.7 million was allocated for an ongoing program designed to benefit the twenty-four francophone African counties linked to France by defense and/or military agreements (Martin, 1995b: 17).

The devaluation of the CFA in 1994 represented a major change in Franco-African policy. The IMF had recommended devaluation much earlier, repeatedly arguing that the CFA was overvalued. Under pressure from its African clients, like Houphouet-Boigny of Côte d'Ivoire, France resisted. Devaluation was ultimately motivated by the recession in France, financial crises in francophone Africa, and the realization that France had urgent priorities within its own economy and within the EU and therefore could not afford to carry Africa's debt burden. Following the 1994 devaluation, countries in the CFA zone experienced significant improvement in economic performance. The average growth rate in per-capita GDP for the group was

2.3 percent per annum in 1995–1998, compared to –2.8 percent in 1990–1994. Exports were also higher in 1995–1998 for all the countries in the CFA zone, with the export-to-GDP ratio averaging 36 percent in 1995–1998 compared to 28 percent in 1990–1994 (*World Development Indicators 2000*, cited in Ndikumana, 2001: 24). Although macroeconomic indicators improved in the CFA franc zone, devaluation reduced the purchasing power of the majority of the African population and caused great dissatisfaction throughout the CFA zone countries. Devaluation also raised fears among African leaders about the future of French monetary guarantees. This fear led francophone countries to set up their own integration mechanisms: the UEMOA (Union Economique et Monetaire Ouest Africaine) and the UDEAC–CEMAC (Union Douaniere et Economique de l'Afrique Central–Communaute Economique at Monetaire de l'Afrique Centrale). The results of these efforts have not yet been assessed.

Economic competition among Western industrialized countries (particularly France and the United States) increased in the post-Cold War period and provided the opportunity for some African leaders to lessen their country's dependence on France. President Diouf of Senegal withstood French pressure and signed contracts with South African and U.S. companies in 1995 to exploit oilfields discovered off the southwest coast of Senegal (Schraeder, 1996). Facing a desperate economic situation left by his predecessor, in 1992 the newly elected president Lissouba of Congo-Brazzaville sought funds from Elf-Aquitaine (the French oil company in control of 80 percent of the country's oil production) to pay the salaries and pensions of civil servants before the May 2 legislative elections. On two occasions, the request for funds was denied. A deal was made between the government and an American oil company to deliver 75 million barrels of Elf-Congo's projected share of the three new offshore oil deposits in exchange for a cash payment of US$150 million. The money reached the government the day before the legislative elections, in time to pay the 80,000 civil servants before the first round of legislative elections. President Lissouba's presidential majority obtained 62 of the 125 seats in the National Assembly (Martin, 1995a: 16). Both Senegal and Congo-Brazzaville played the "American card" to get a better deal for their countries. The post-Cold War period gave these countries more room to maneuver within the international system to acquire the best possible deal.

French economic aid to sub-Saharan Africa has been in a downward trend in the 1990s, falling from US$3,555 million in 1993 to US$2,448 in 1996 (Development Assistance Committee, Organization for Economic Cooperation and Development [OECD], 1997). However, France is still the largest donor to Africa and its leading Western partner. In contrast, Britain and Germany preferred to hand over their diminishing African commitments to NGOs, the EU, and private groups. The Franco-African summits have continued, providing a forum for African leaders to air their difficulties, but they do not receive any commitments from France to help resolve their problems. France has shifted the economic burden of maintaining its impoverished client states to international financial institutions like the IMF and World Bank. Loans from France are now always contingent on a previous agreement with the IMF. But at the same time France has expanded its relations with African states in the nonfrancophone zone (e.g., the former Portuguese territories of Angola and Mozambique and the former Belgian colonies of Congo, Rwanda, and Burundi), actively pursuing economic relations with those countries that it believes would enhance its commercial interests. There has been continuity and stability in French policy toward those countries that are central to France's economic interests (e.g., Côte d'Ivoire, Cameroon, Gabon, Togo).

Relations with the Superpowers

The direct involvement of the post-World War II superpowers (the Soviet Union and the United States) in sub-Saharan Africa began in the early 1960s and increased in intensity from the mid-1970s through the mid-1980s. Both superpowers were relative newcomers to Africa, a continent viewed as within Western European powers' sphere of interest. Following the independence of the majority of sub-Saharan African countries, most of their leaders embraced ideologies of nationalism emphasizing anticolonialism and anti-imperialism. They continued economic relationships with their former colonizing powers and sought new economic relationships with other European countries, the United States, Soviet Union, China, and other regions of the world. Bound by the charter of the Organization of African Unity (OAU), to which they all belonged, they professed neutrality (nonalignment) in the East-West conflict between the Soviet Union and the United States. Inevitably, however, they all became linked to one or the other superpower as they tried to use ideology as leverage to obtain much-needed resources for military, political, and economic needs. Both superpowers sought opportunities to spread their ideologies and influence and to pursue political and economic interests in Africa and other developing regions. The United States wanted to export Western-style liberal democracy and capitalism and halt the spread of communism, whereas the Soviet Union wanted to encourage the emergence of communism worldwide.

The United States and the Soviet Union played a limited but important role in Africa during the Cold War, maintaining embattled regimes in power and transferring the global ideological conflict to the African continent. In 1960 fearing the spread of communism in the Congo, the United States (and other Western powers) intervened in the crisis there, undermining the radical nationalist government of Patrice Lumumba and encouraging the

Katanga secession (and the ultimate demise of the Lumumba government). Exploiting Western countries' fear of the spread of communism in the Great Lakes region of Africa, in the 1970s Mobutu shrewdly used France, Belgium, and the United States in promoting his interests (Chapter four).

Before the Cold War, Ethiopia had long been a U.S. ally. The United States built up and equipped Emperor Haile Selassie's armed forces and strengthened the power of the Amharic-dominated state at the expense of other nationalities in Ethiopia. Between 1953 and 1977 the United States extended $279 million in military aid to Ethiopia and trained more than 3,500 Ethiopian military personnel in the United States (Selassie, 1980: 63, 170). The Soviet Union had a strategic interest in the Horn of Africa and sought a presence in the region because of its location on the Red Sea route from the Mediterranean to the Indian Ocean. As early as the 1960s it sought to improve relations with U.S. ally Emperor Haile Selassie of Ethiopia, supported Jafaar Nimeiri of the Sudan and Siyad Barre of Somalia when they came to power. Somalia was the major Soviet client state in Africa until 1974, receiving some $180 million in arms deliveries and having major Soviet naval installations at Berbera (Chazan et al., 1988).

The 1974 coup d'etat that removed Haile Selassie from power changed the alliances in the Horn of Africa. The Derg that replaced the Selassie regime espoused leftist rhetoric and made overtures to the Soviet Union. Failing to reconcile Ethiopia and Somalia and make them both Soviet clients, the Soviet Union chose Ethiopia. In response, the United States backed Somalia, dropping its former ally Ethiopia. In exchange for nearly US$2 billion worth of arms to the Derg by 1980, which helped to turn the tide for the Ethiopian government in the Ogaden and Eritrea, Ethiopia permitted the Soviet Union to establish a major servicing facility off the coast of Eritrea (thus enhancing Soviet capabilities in the Indian Ocean). Soviet military support, backed by Cuban soldiers, helped to preserve the Ethiopian state and regime; Western (largely U.S.) military support preserved the regime of Siyad Barre. The state was preserved in both countries, and the conflict continued for another decade and a half until both regimes were overthrown in the early 1990s, following the withdrawal of superpower support.

Cold War conflict became entangled in domestic conflicts in Angola and Mozambique and in the white minority regimes of Rhodesia/Zimbabwe and South Africa. The Soviet-backed liberation movements in Angola (MPLA) and Mozambique (FRELIMO) won their independence from Portugal in 1974–1975. The United States believed that, if the MPLA was allowed to control Angola, a domino effect could be expected throughout southern Africa. In Angola three major factions fought for power: the MPLA, the National Front for the Liberation of Angola (FNLA), and UNITA. The MPLA was supported by the Soviet Union, and from 1975 to the 1980s Cuba maintained tens of thousands of troops in Angola, which proved decisive in the party's hold on power. The FNLA and UNITA were supported by the United States against the MPLA government. Portugal was also supported by the United States in its war against the liberation movements fighting for independence. The United States supported dissidents in Angola and Mozambique, backed the Ian Smith regime in Rhodesia, and extended support to the apartheid regime in South Africa. Its support for the status quo in the white minority regimes in southern Africa and its opposition to the MPLA and FRELIMO were largely motivated by its desire to halt the spread of communism in the region. The liberation movements in Angola, Mozambique, Rhodesia, and South Africa were heavily supported by the Soviet Union (and to some extent China), and the United States perceived the possibility of their eventually seizing the state as jeopardizing Western economic interests.

Most of the strategic raw materials required by Western industrialized nations were imported from southern Africa. The Soviet Union was the other major source of these strategic minerals. If anticapitalist regimes came to power in Africa, Westerners believed, they could, allied with the Soviet Union, gain enormous control over many Western industrialized economies. This perhaps explains, in part, the U.S. government's consistent support for South Africa in the face of domestic public opinion against apartheid. It consistently opposed sanctions and other forms of isolating the apartheid regime, arguing always for dialogue and coaxing the regime into accepting civilized values. It gave aid to the apartheid regime and billions of dollars of U.S. investments were there until the late 1970s, when, forced by massive boycotts, many American companies were forced into divestment. U.S. support for the white minority regimes in southern Africa antagonized many African states, and the United States was viewed, along with Britain, as an obstacle to the complete decolonization of Africa.

After the collapse of the Soviet Union, Russia emerged as the strongest and largest in the Commonwealth of Independent States. Establishing ties with Western industrialized nations (especially the United States), Japan, and other Pacific Rim countries, became one of its most important foreign policy priorities. Russia perceived these countries to be most capable of contributing to its economic development. No longer in competition with the West for influence in Africa, Russia was interested in certain areas of the continent where it could pursue mutually advantageous economic cooperation.

In 1992 a decision was made to close the Russian military mission in Luanda (Angola). Since 1989 there had been no Russian military advisers there, only seventy to seventy-five military experts. Of that number, forty-five were reportedly doctors (Polsky, 1996). Trade with Africa had declined from 3.4 billion rubles in 1984 to 2 billion rubles in 1990. Africa's share in the Soviet Union's trade was less than 3 percent even in the best of times. By 1991 the Soviet Union maintained significant ties with six African nations, only two in sub-Saharan Africa, Guinea and Ethiopia. The trade volume with each of these countries formed almost 85 percent of its trade with Africa. But trade with Russia only constituted about 3.3 percent of these countries' entire foreign trade (Polsky, 1996).

Although the U.S. government has steadily withdrawn from Africa since the end of the Cold War, U.S. involvement has continued through the activities of American NGOs (especially human rights NGOs), missionaries, educational institutions, and private citizens and groups, especially African Americans. In the 1970s and 1980s the African American groups were influential (via the Congressional Black Caucus [CBC] and Transafrica Forum) in pushing the U.S. government to accept no less than black-majority rule in South Africa. Many members of the CBC have developed close friendships with members of the African political elite, and the CBC was an advocate for President Clinton's economic initiatives in Africa in the late 1990s. The current secretary of state, Colin Powell, and the national security adviser, Condoleeza Rice, are both African Americans. For the first time African Americans are at the center of U.S. foreign policy making. It is not yet clear that their presence will increase the very modest influence that African Americans have historically had on U.S. foreign policy toward Africa.

The U.S. government's retreat from Africa is clearly demonstrated in the decline in trade and investments. Trade and investments have been limited to a handful of countries in East Africa, Nigeria, and southern Africa. Foreign aid has dwindled (see Table 8.2), but military assistance is still provided (though not arms) to Uganda, Eritrea, and Ethiopia. Involvement by U.S. government personnel and high-ranking members of the American political elite has been limited to mediation and logistical and financial support for peacekeeping operations. In the post-Cold War era, the United States tried to mediate in some internal wars and conflicts. In 1992 Cyrus Vance (a former secretary of state) engaged in some mediation between the ANC secretary general and the minister of constitutional development of South Africa. In 1997 former secretary of state James Baker, acting under the auspices of the UN, mediated on the Western Sahara issue between representatives of Morocco and the People's Front for the Liberation of Saquiet el-Hamra and Rio de Oro (POLISARIO). This meeting led to an agreement on the size of the electoral college to be used in the referendum on the territory's self-determination (Rothchild, 2000: 170). In 1991 Assistant Secretary of State Herman Cohen convened a meeting of EPRDF forces, EPLF, and the Oromo Liberation Front to try to work out a transition program for a new government in Ethiopia. The interim government was ultimately taken over by the EPRDF forces, which Secretary Cohen sanctioned. Secretary Cohen also mediated an agreement in Zaire between Mobutu, the president of the High Council of the Republic, and the prime minister for a power-sharing government during the 1992–1994 transition period. Mobutu accepted the agreement but subsequently refused to abide by its terms. U.S. Assistant Secretary for African Affairs Chester Crocker played a central role in mediating conflict between international actors involved in the conflict in Namibia. An effective and enduring peace agreement materialized that led to Namibian independence in 1992. In Angola the United States also played a mediating role in 1987–1988, but the peace agreement was highly ineffective as rebel leader Jonas Savimbi did not honor the Bicesse Accords (see Chapter 5).

Peacekeeping was another form of U.S. involvement in Africa in the immediate post-Cold War period. After the collapse of the Siyad Barre regime, clan rivalry led to chaos, lawlessness, the collapse of the state, and mass starvation in Somalia (see Chapter 7). The UN Security Council dispatched a peacekeeping force (United Nations Operation in Somalia, or UNOSOM I) to Mogadishu. Unable to engage in effective military and humanitarian operations, UNOSOM I was unable to restore peace. Mass starvation occurred as the world watched dreadful images of emaciated Somalis on television. Under the auspices of the UN Security Council, 25,000 U.S. troops led a UN Interim Task Force (UNITAF) under the code name Operation Restore Hope to mount a massive humanitarian operation to save the population from starvation and restore order in Somalia. UNITAF was successful in reducing starvation and handed over the country to UNOSOM II before the clan conflict was resolved.

UNOSOM II was given the responsibility for "the consolidation, expansion and maintenance of a secure environment throughout Somalia." (Rothchild, 2000: 178). In June 1993 Somali National Alliance militiamen attacked a UNOSOM II inspection team and killed twenty-four Pakistanis and three Americans. After that attack UNOSOM II launched a series of raids to try to find General Aidid, the clan leader deemed responsible for the casualties. The raids culminated in an October 3 battle that left eighteen Americans dead and hundreds of Somalis dead or injured. This incident influenced American public opinion and triggered widespread demands for a withdrawal of American troops. The United States withdrew its troops by March 1994, followed by the general withdrawal of UN troops by March 1995 (Rothchild, 2000: 179).

The debacle in Somalia influenced the U.S. response to the genocidal killings in Rwanda in 1994 (Chapter 7). The United States was unwilling to intervene again, so soon, in what appeared to be another hopeless African conflict. Neither the United States, its allies, nor Russia intervened to try to stop the carnage, avoiding their obligation under the Genocide Convention. The United States was no longer willing to involve its own troops in peacekeeping exercises and influenced the UN Security Council to vote to withdraw the majority of UN peacekeepers from Rwanda, leaving only about 264 men.

The U.S./UN failure in Somalia led to a shift in the United States' view of international peacekeeping. President Clinton signed Presidential Directive

25 in May 1994, which, though recognizing that UN peacekeeping operations would at times be the best way to prevent or resolve conflicts, also emphasized that other factors, such as American interests, a significant threat to international peace and security, the specific objectives of the intervention, and the means to carry out the mission, should all be considered before the United States would support such an undertaking. After Somalia the United States watched from a distance while intrastate conflicts killed thousands of Africans in Rwanda, Congo (Zaire), Burundi, Liberia, and Sierra Leone. In 1996 President Clinton proposed the idea of an African Crisis Response Force, later named the African Crisis Response Initiative (ACRI), which sought to develop the capacity of African peacekeepers to respond rapidly and effectively to respond to eruptions of violence. The United States would train African military units for peacekeeping but otherwise remain uncommitted and on the sidelines of the conflicts that have erupted.

At this time (2002), the U.S. government remains relatively disengaged from Africa. There are no signs that President George W. Bush is likely to become reengaged with Africa immediately. At the end of the Clinton administration, aid levels to Africa decreased, with the fiscal year 1999 foreign appropriations bill granting Africa less than previously (Rothchild, 2000: 181). Yet there has been an interest in South Africa because of its perceived potential as an engine of growth in southern African and sub-Saharan Africa in general. U.S. policy toward South Africa has always been in favor of engagement with that country. The Bush administration may want to continue U.S. involvement in southern Africa so as not to lose that regional market to its EU competitor. Part of the U.S. government's historical interest in southern African stability has been its strategy of building bridges to new markets to further worldwide economic expansion. While the African American population remains sensitive to the plight of those suffering in Africa and has enormous empathy for the struggles of the African people, it seems unlikely that the African American lobby (strengthened by the presence of Colin Powell and Condoleeza Rice) can force positive U.S. government reengagement in Africa in the next several years.

Relations with the European Economic Community/European Union

In addition to bilateral relationships between individual African and European countries, in the postindependence period EEC/EU-African relations have been strong. The Treaty of Rome established the EEC in 1957. The founding members were France, Belgium, Italy, Luxembourg, the Netherlands, and West Germany. Upon France's insistence, the EEC preserved special treatment through trade preferences and aid for its colonies in Africa. With the independence of most of France's colonies in 1960, the arrangements were renegotiated, and the Yaounde Convention signed in 1963 with eighteen African states and Madagascar. Nigeria (1966) and Kenya, Tanzania, and Uganda (1968) acceded to the convention by special trade agreement. Britain joined the EEC in 1973, causing anxiety among its Commonwealth members who feared the loss of traditional preferences in Britain. A compromise arrangement that would unify francophone and anglophone countries in Africa was reached with the signing of the first Lome convention in 1975. The Lome Convention unified aid and trade arrangements between the then nine members of the EEC and forty-six African, Caribbean, and Pacific (ACP) countries in a single treaty. At the end of the Cold War, in 1992, the twelve-member EEC formed the European Union (EU).

Five Lome conventions have been signed (1975, 1979, 1984, 1989, 1995), helping to keep the former colonial power as the largest trading partner of most sub-Saharan African countries. Europe remained a vital trading area for sub-Saharan Africa, with the EEC/EU accounting for more than 50 percent of its trade and more than 80 percent of its foreign aid (Khadiagala, 2000). The Lome conventions covered a wide range of trade and cooperation issues. All ACP manufactured goods and 96 percent of the ACP countries' agricultural exports were allowed to enter the EEC/EU free of import tariffs or quotas. This arrangement required no similar reciprocal action on the part of the ACP. The Export Earnings Stabilization (Stabex) Scheme provided the ACP countries with protection against price and production fluctuations of bananas, coconuts, cocoa, coffee, hides and skins, iron ore, palm nuts, tea, timber products, and raw sisal. An Export Stabilization Fund provided some compensation for large earnings losses from export price drops, though such compensation was never enough to substantially cover shortfalls in ACP countries' export earnings. The EEC/EU also provided financing for development projects in the form of grants and loans. Other commitments by the EEC/EU involved promoting private investment, transferring technology, providing industrial and managerial training programs and trade and market information, and helping ACP countries to market ACP products and obtain various infrastructural requirements of trade.

Through Lome, duty free access to European Community markets was critical for many of Africa's commodities. Although Lome protected many of Africa's traditional exports, it did little to stimulate African countries' export expansion. Export diversification, either by sector or by product, remained marginal. Despite the apparent trade benefits of Lome, imports from ACP countries declined as a share of EEC/EU trade and even more as a share of world trade. However, protection of traditional staples was an important gain for the African countries, as Lome guaranteed them reasonable market access for their primary exports and an assured flow of export earnings. The Lome Convention maintained the rhetoric of a partnership between equals, but it was the European Community alone that had the ultimate responsibility for interpreting the treaty, determining aid levels and use of aid, and directing future changes in the convention. For these reasons, critics viewed the Lome conventions as a neocolonial device that maintained European influence in Africa.

The changing international environment of the 1990s had important implications for Euro-African relations. The new General Agreement on Tariffs and Trade (GATT), finalized in the Uruguay Round, ushered in a new climate of liberalization spearheaded by the World Trade Organization (WTO). Europe supported a transition to a postpreference, WTO-like world trading system based on reciprocity and equal national treatment. The expectation was that these principles would be established in the renegotiated Lome Convention to be put in effect after 2000.

What changes have occurred in the relationship between the EU and the African states since 1992? Have those changes helped the African states find solutions to their problems? The combined impact of the fall of communism in the early 1990s and the European integration of 1992 generated momentum in Europe for disengagement from Africa and decreasing colonial ties there. European integration led to collective decision making and a focus on economic integration, monetary union, and harmonization of foreign policy. Western Europe shifted its focus to cooperation with other developed countries, eastern and central Europe, East Asia, and Latin America and to new functional considerations such as illegal immigration and drug trafficking. Rescuing Africa from economic malaise was not a priority.

Amidst globalization Europe indicated that what it now wanted was a "partnership" with Africa, not a special relationship. What was implied here was that Europe wanted shared responsibilities and mutual obligation (if not equality) between the regions. To suggest that there could be a partnership between Africa and Europe baffled many observers. Many asked the question, how could there be a partnership among unequals? How could there be a partnership between Africa and Europe when the GDP of the entire sub-Saharan African region was less than the GDP of the tiny country of Belgium? Khadiagala (2000) has argued that a real partnership between Africa and Europe that transcends postcolonial political and economic relations hinges on meaningful institutional and leadership changes in Africa. Multiparty politics and neoliberal economic reforms have not brought the hoped-for African renewal. Faced with the possibility of having to build alternative economic arrangements, many African leaders viewed European disengagement as marginalization and abandonment. The economic devastation of the 1980s and the mismanagement of African economies by authoritarian dictators reduced any leverage that the African nations might have had to try to negotiate with Europe in 1992.

The EU joined the United States and international financial institutions in their demand for good governance and democracy as a condition for continued aid and trade. Starting with Lome III in 1985, Europe made aid conditional on the recipient country's observance of human rights. The EU applied pressure on recalcitrant African dictators like Togo's Eyadema, Zaire's Mobutu, Kenya's Moi, and Malawi's Banda. The EU suspended cooperation with The Gambia, Liberia, Sudan, and Somalia for violating either human rights or standards of good governance. It imposed sanctions against Eyadema and condemned his regime as "one of the most brutal dictatorships in Africa." Sanctions were also imposed on Nigeria when General Sani Abacha annulled the 1993 presidential elections. Influenced by civil society groups in its member countries, the EU has been pressured to stop selling arms to African dictators. In 1995 an alliance of eight hundred European NGOs called for the establishment of an "enforceable" European "code of conduct" to put arms sales under EU legislation. This advocacy culminated in the passage of the European code of conduct on arms control in June 1998 (Khadiagala, 2000: 101).

Post-1992 Europe began to focus on integrating African countries in the global economy; relating economic development cooperation to poverty elimination (especially among women); and including conflict prevention and peace building as areas of cooperation between Europe and Africa. Most important, Europe wants a greater degree of reciprocity and a stronger regional dimension in ACP-EU relations. The EU believes that Africa can become incorporated into the world economy through successful regional integration. Offering the EU as a model, it believes that Africa can build on the existing experiments of the Southern African Development Community (SADC), UEMOA (West Africa), UDEAC (Central Africa), and the East African Community (EAC). SADC appears very attractive to the EU because South Africa has the potential to be southern Africa's economic and political center. These groups are said to be slated to form the foundation for future regional economic partnerships agreements with Europe, which would replace the old trade preferences. A number of reservations have been expressed in response to these proposed regional agreements. First, SADC, UEMOA, UDEAC, and EAC do not comprehensively cover all of sub-Saharan Africa but exclude nineteen countries (seventeen of which are among the least developed countries). Second, of the forty-eight African ACP countries, thirty-three are classified as least developed and as such have had their nonreciprocal Lome parity extended. They would be obliged to provide free access for EU imports if they joined a regional free trade agreement. They would need to choose between reciprocal preferences and the offer they had to continue nonreciprocal Lome parity. Third, wide economic differences within these regional groupings limit the potential for mutually beneficial trade integration (McQueen, 1998).

Europe wants to multilateralize its African relations largely through the WTO. The WTO's free and competitive trade regulations undermine the Lome Convention's multiple privileges and preferences, which allow Africa access to European markets. Trade liberalization threaten Africa's less than 3 percent of world trade, as most of its primary producers would lose about $173 million per annum of revenue, or 0.7 percent of their total sales to the EU. ACP's overall share of the EU market fell from 4.7 percent in 1990 to 2.8 percent in 1995. Liberalization would neither ameliorate Africa's severe dependence on the export of a few primary commodities nor make these goods any more competitive.

The EU would like to eliminate the Stabex and Sysmin commodity compensatory schemes in Lome as a way of streamlining aid. These programs are unpopular in Europe because they are very costly and have neither stabilized commodity earnings nor contributed to economic diversification. Although Africa wants them to be retained, it is unlikely that they will survive in a global climate that shuns economic subsidies.

The EU is still the world's largest aid donor. Although Africa still accounts for the largest share of EU aid disbursements, that share declined sharply, from over 70 percent at the beginning of the 1970s to under 40 percent by the mid-1990s. In addition to the decline in the quantity of aid, disbursements have been slow. For example, disbursements under the 1975 Lome I Convention were not completed until 1990, and of those funds agreed to under the 1984 Lome III Convention only 64 percent had been disbursed by the end of 1992 (Khadiagala, 2000: 89). To meet the substantial drop in development assistance, Europe proposed greater differentiation among aid recipients on the basis of relative wealth, geography, past use of aid, and commitment to effective reforms. These criteria strengthened the mechanism for aid accountability and conditionality but put many African countries at a disadvantage vis-à-vis other recipient countries.

The EU has proposed new cooperation agreements with the ACP. Mutual obligation remains at the center of those proposals. They include political development (human rights, conflict prevention, peace building), poverty-focused aid for the empowerment of women, development of the private sector, aid based on merit and need, and aid based on regional differentiation. Regional trade cooperation is emphasized as a factor in development. Sub-Saharan Africa is having a difficult time redefining its relationship with Europe. Since independence the region has had to respond to fluctuations in the international economy such as oil shocks in the early and late 1970s, recession in industrialized Western countries, and most recently, globalization. The postcolonial era of "special relationships" has been called off by those who established them, and assistance is now based on an assessment of the country's "real needs." This has been a challenge for most African countries. The EU will remain an important trading partner for Africa for some time in the future. Africa's objective should be to find new markets in the global economy and lessen its dependence on the EU.

Intra-African Relations

Pan-Africanism

Pan-Africanism is an ideology based on the view that African unity is the only practical foundation for the liberation and development of the African continent. During the 1920s, Jamaican activist Marcus Garvey launched a militant nationalist movement, the Universal Negro Improvement Association (UNIA), in the United States. The UNIA promoted Africa as the home of all black people and mobilized Jamaicans and African Americans to look upon African unity as an important weapon in their fight against oppression. Pan-Africanism as a political force first appeared in the African diaspora. Under the influence of African American scholar W. E. B. Du Bois, a series of Pan African conferences were held in 1900, 1919, 1921, 1923, 1927, and 1945, bringing together representatives from all parts of Africa and its diaspora. Future leaders of the nationalist movement for independence (such as Jomo Kenyatta of Kenya, Nnamdi Azikiwe of Nigeria, and Kwame Nkrumah of Ghana) attended the 1945 conference in Britain.

Following the 1945 Pan African conference, Ghana became the center of Pan-Africanism as Kwame Nkrumah and his Convention Peoples Party (CPP) explicitly committed to that ideology. Nkrumah called for a "Union Government" of Africa and received widespread popular support as well as the support of some African leaders. Those who favored political unity argued that a divided Africa would be unviable economically and too fragmented to resist external political pressure and economic domination. Julius Nyerere of Tanzania in his book *Africa's Freedom* wrote that "only with unity can we ensure that Africa really governs itself. Only with unity can we be sure that African resources will be used for the benefit of Africans." Nigerian historian Adekunle Ajala wrote in *Pan-Africanism* (1974) that "Africa has many untapped resources and is majestically situated between East and West. With a population of 350 million [at that time] it exceeds those of the United States and the USSR. There is therefore nothing to prevent a united, stable, economically strong and highly industrialized Africa from competing with them in world politics."

In 1958 the formation of the Guinea-Ghana union represented the first step toward African unification between two independent African countries. Prior to independence, in the French colonies of West Africa there were efforts by the RDA to form two big independent federations, one for West Africa and one for Equatorial Guinea. These efforts failed in large part because France was opposed to them, as well as some leaders, such as Felix Houphouet-Boigny of Côte d'Ivoire and Hamani Diori of Niger. New national assemblies in Senegal, Soudan (present-day Mali), Dahomey (Benin), and Upper Volta (Burkina Faso) voted in favor of federal unity after independence. Dahomey and Upper Volta subsequently pulled out of the plan under French pressure. Left alone, Senegal and Soudan voted to form a federal state together (under the name *Mali*). This federation fell apart in 1960. Mali then joined the union with Guinea and Ghana in 1961 (Davidson, 1989).

By 1961 it was clear that most of the anticolonial leaders still gave rhetorical support to the ideas of Pan-Africanism but were more concerned with winning political power within the colonial boundaries and were not prepared to unite. That majority sentiment led to the formation of the Organization of African Unity (OAU), established to promote continental unity but within the boundaries of postcolonial institutions. Members favored economic cooperation rather than political unity. Pan-Africanism as a worldview among Africans is still relevant despite many setbacks over the past three decades. A new generation of Africans has given the subject attention recently, as the search for alternative development strategies in Africa has entered a new phase (Bakut, 2000).

The Organization of African Unity (OAU)

In 1963 thirty-one of the thirty-two independent African states agreed to form the Organization of African Unity. Organizationally the OAU had several components. There were an Assembly of Heads of State and Government, a Council of Ministers appointed by the Assembly, a General Secretariat based in Addis Ababa, and a Commission to settle disputes. All major decisions and resolutions have been adopted by the Annual Assembly of Heads of State and Government after biannual meetings of the Council of Ministers. All member states are equal, unlike the UN, where the five big-power permanent members of the Security Council (the United States, Britain, France, Russia, and China) dominate. Funds to run the OAU were to come from member states. Each was asked to contribute on the same scale as its contribution to membership of the UN.

The OAU's very ambitious objectives included working for unity and solidarity among African nations, planning and acting together for a better life for African peoples, defending the sovereignty and territorial integrity and independence of Africa, removing all forms of colonialism in Africa, and working for common action with nations outside Africa. The OAU charter also affirmed the principles of equality of all member states, noninterference in the internal affairs of member states, respect for the existing frontiers of member states, and peaceful settlement of all disputes between member states. The charter also declared the loyalty of member states to the policy of nonalignment, as well as the need to work for the liberation of African peoples still under colonial rule in southern Africa. The OAU did not embrace the idea of a continental government, but it was the only continental organization in the postindependence period of which all African states (except colonial territories and those under white rule) were members. Its aim was to focus on African states' shared interests and be an advocate for Africa in international affairs.

Was the OAU effective in the international arena? The consensus is that it has not, because it has either failed to live up to its guiding principles or has been prevented from taking serious political action because it was constrained by those principles. On one hand, the OAU's adherence to the principle of respect for colonial boundaries might have prevented a host of intrastate and interethnic disputes all across the continent. Given the arbitrary divisions in the colonial period of so many ethnic groups across several states, there could have been many more interethnic and intrastate conflicts in the postindependence period. Generally, ethnic groups have managed to live relatively peacefully together in these artificial nation-states. On the other hand, the unwavering support of the OAU for postcolonial state formations resulted in blanket support of all central governments in the capital city, legitimate or not. Secessionist movements in Biafra, Eritrea, and Sudan never got OAU support. It refused to sanction aid to Biafra and voted resolutions in support of the federal government of Nigeria. It did not recognize northern Somalia's independence nor encourage the southern Sudanese to secede. Rigid adherence to the principle of territorial integrity prevented the OAU from serving as an effective mediator in these disputes. Many observers were surprised that the OAU recognized the independence of Eritrea from Ethiopia in 1993. The OAU's position was that in this case there was no violation of colonial boundaries. When Italy left Eritrea it was not part of Ethiopia; Ethiopia subsequently annexed Eritrea. Thousands of Africans have been killed in war, fighting against the state imposed on them by colonialism. Many people believe that the artificial boundaries will continue to create political problems and, moreover, that they stand as an obstacle to economic development in Africa.

Member states were not penalized for failing to adhere to the principle of nonalignment in the OAU charter. The member states were not prevented from pursuing independent foreign policies that served their domestic interests. The francophone countries had a close relationship with France and in most instances were also pro-United States. They did not believe that this compromised the principle of nonalignment. Nor were Ethiopia, Angola, Mozambique, and other countries penalized for being pro-Soviet Union. Few countries were truly nonaligned; Tanzania was a good example. It maintained relations with the United States, European countries, the Soviet Union, China, the Middle East, and developing countries. The reality was that in practice it was very difficult for countries with poor, dependent economies to adhere to the principle of nonalignment.

Noninterference in the internal affairs of member states has probably been the most vexing of all the OAU's principles. The OAU was unable to prevent Libya from intervening in Chad, and Angola, Sudan, and Ethiopia from getting support from neighboring states. At the same time, in the 1970s the infamous regimes of Idi Amin (Uganda), Jean-Bedel Bokassa (Central African Republic), and Macias Nguema (Equatorial Guinea) were not condemned, nor were there any OAU interventions to try to help the citizens of those countries escape from those oppressive regimes. In the case of Amin in Uganda, President Nyerere of Tanzania was the only African president who condemned him and supported exiled forces in the overthrow of his regime in 1979. The Abacha regime in Nigeria in the 1990s was another example of the OAU's looking the other way. Ken Saro-Wiwa and others were executed, yet there was no OAU condemnation or isolation of the regime. Noninterference in the affairs of these brutal regimes led to external criticism that damaged Africa's advocacy for support on the issue of white South Africa's human rights violations.

There has been a noticeable shift in the OAU's position on noninterference in the affairs of member states in the post-Cold War period. An ECOWAS-led force (ECOMOG) intervened in the conflicts in Liberia and Sierra Leone with OAU support. The OAU acted in part because the external powers retreated from African conflicts and Africa had to find its own solution or allow those conflicts to spread across West Africa. The OAU itself did not have a military force capable of peacekeeping in Liberia and Sierra Leone.

The OAU has been unswerving in its opposition to colonialism and white minority rule in Africa. In the 1960s the OAU was principally concerned with the white minority regimes in Rhodesia, Namibia, South Africa, and the Portuguese-controlled territories of Angola, Mozambique, Cape Verde, Guinea-Bissau, and São Tomè and Principe. Although the OAU kept the issue of African liberation on the agenda in international affairs, the organization was not able to liberate those countries from colonial rule. Although there was consensus among both conservative and radical African regimes on the question of terminating colonial rule in Africa, the OAU was unable to get its members to break ties with Britain over its failure to bring Rhodesia back under its control after its Unilateral Declaration of Independence in 1965. Further, the OAU did not have the financial resources to provide military aid to liberation movements fighting colonial rule. It established a Liberation Committee in Dar es Salaam, Tanzania, to aid liberation movements in finding economic and military assistance. Neighboring countries were able to offer only their territories as bases for training, bases from which to launch attacks against the enemy, and bases for refugees.

On the issue of settling disputes between member states, the OAU's record of success has not been very good. It helped to settle the frontier dispute between Algeria and Morocco in 1963-1964. Acting as mediator, it proved valuable in bringing about an agreement in 1964 and again in 1970

(Davidson, 1989). It was not involved in the Angolan war of 1975 nor in settlements in Zimbabwe, Namibia, or South Africa. Adherence to the principles of territorial integrity and noninterference in the affairs of member states impeded the OAU's ability to mediate and resolve these conflicts. The OAU did not have the capacity to set the parameters for conflict resolution in Somalia, Liberia, or Sierra Leone when those states collapsed. The ECO-MOG intervention (instead of an OAU intervention) in Liberia and Sierra Leone pushed the OAU to adopt a resolution to create a Mechanism for Conflict Prevention, Management and Resolution (Zartman, 1995b). This mechanism has not yet been tested in any African conflict.

On a few occasions the OAU passed resolutions that had political significance in global politics. Expressing solidarity with Egypt, an OAU member, the OAU passed a resolution in 1973 condemning Israel's occupation of the Sinai during the 1967 Arab-Israeli war. The resolution recommended that African states break ties with Israel. It was passed at the 1973 summit and supported by a huge majority of members, demonstrating OAU solidarity with the Arab states. As a result of OAU support for the Arabs against Israel, wealthy oil-producing states rewarded some African countries with grants and loans and other forms of economic assistance. This resolution led many African countries to break diplomatic ties with Israel for more than a decade. Although important, resolutions such as those condemning the dumping of toxic waste in Africa by Western companies and those calling for measures to alleviate Africa's debt burden have been viewed by many as inconsequential.

The OAU held its thirty-seventh annual meeting in Zambia in July 2001. This meeting was dubbed "the burial of the OAU." It was said to be its last one, since OAU members signed a treaty that calls for creating the African Union (AU), modeled after the EU and other successful regional organizations. There seems to be growing optimism for the AU as Africa attempts to make a "new beginning" (by abandoning the OAU) and seeking an organization in the AU that can aggressively intervene in world affairs during this era of globalization.

Regional Integration

The first postindependence governments sought to copy the European Economic Community and create regional entities capable of promoting regional integration and cooperation. In 1981 the Lagos Plan of Action for the Economic Development of Africa, 1980-2000, proposed the "eventual establishment of an African Common Market (ACM) as the first step towards the creation of an African Economic Community (AEC) by 2000" (Martin, 1992).

The fundamental premise for the idea of regional integration in Africa is the promotion of economic development through industrialization and trade

Lusaka, Zambia: The old Organization of African Unity gives way to the new African Union.

New African, London

arrangements. The benefits often alluded to included the creation of economies of scale that enabled countries to embark on large infrastructural and industrial projects and to undertake profitable product differentiation; the transfer of technology through the exchange of goods, services, and factors of production; increased investment opportunities; creation of opportunities to master production skills; expansion and strengthening of the regional industrial base; diversification of economic activities; the possibility for national economies to shift where they can begin to strategically complement each other in world trade; and support for competition between countries especially in the areas of liberalization leading to general policy improvement. Regional integration is also expected to help break dependence on former colonial powers, increasing regional self-reliance and the region's bargaining power in the global market. Integration is also seen as a mechanism to provide functional collaboration in several areas: development of regional ports to help African countries utilize modern shipping technologies and realize economies of scale in transport; construction of regional road and rail systems to facilitate the transfer of goods and people across national frontiers; and cooperation on monetary and financial matters to encourage domestic and foreign investment.

Regional groupings are abundant in sub-Saharan Africa; together with Latin America, sub-Saharan Africa has the highest number of regional groupings in developing regions. Some groups have limited objectives, whereas others have been committed to full-fledged economic integration. Some groups originated in the colonial period (e.g., the South African Customs Union [SACU],West African Customs Union [WACU], and the East African Customs Union [EACU]), but the vast majority of integration schemes were adopted after independence during the late 1960s and 1970s. In most instances, the grouping comprised countries sharing colonial ties to the same foreign power or countries with geographic proximity.

By the end of the 1980s there were 160 economic organizations in Africa, 32 were in West Africa alone. Some of the most widely known and most active sub-Saharan regional groupings include the Economic Community of West African States (ECOWAS), Communaute Financiere Africaine (CFA), Communaute Economique de l'Afrique de l'Ouest (CEAO), Central African Customs and Economic Union (CACEU), Communaute Economique et Monetaire d'Afrique Centrale (CEMAC), Economic Community of Countries in the Great Lakes (EPGL), Preferential Trade Area for Eastern and Southern African States (PTA)/Common Market for Eastern and Southern Africa (COMESA), Intergovernmental Authority on Drought and Development (IGAD), East African Community (EAC), Southern African Development Community (SADC), and Southern Africa Customs Union.

Most of the African regional groupings have had mixed to poor records; there have been few instances of outright success. Many factors are responsible for the lack of success. The lack of resources and institutions within the regional bodies prevented them from maintaining member discipline and member commitment. The homogeneity of sub-Saharan African economies (dependence on primary products) was a serious constraint on intraregional trade. Bilateral relations and trade continued with former colonial powers; hence intra-African trade remained poor. Sub-Saharan African countries have little to trade with each other; Africa's nonoil exports are highly concentrated in a few products and none are important in regional imports. Many African countries have a common comparative advantage in the same items (e.g., sugar preparations, refined petroleum products). Intra-African trade is also highly concentrated within sub-regional geographic groups. There is very little trade occurring between East and West Africa, for example. Transport and other logistical problems may account for this. Political problems also factor in, where we see that some independent governments have been reluctant to cede power to regional bodies, and many leaders have also been unable to incorporate regionally adopted policies into national programs (Kimuyu, 1999).

A new form of regional cooperation in functionally specific areas (e.g., transportation, energy, and telecommunications infrastructure; hydroelectric projects on common rivers) has been proposed for sub-Saharan Africa. This form of regionalism does not require political leaders to give up national control of foreign trade and investment to the regional organizations, a previous source of conflict. SADC represents this new form of regionalism and has been touted as a new and excellent model for economic cooperation in Africa. SADC has attempted cooperation in a variety of functional realms, most notably transportation. There has been much optimism around SADC for various reasons. First, SADC includes South Africa, the most industrialized country in Africa. The hope is that South Africa will provide SADC with an engine of growth that will reinvigorate southern Africa and ultimately the entire continent. There is optimism that SADC can reduce southern Africa's dependence on foreign economic interests and create the basis for self-sustaining autonomous development in the post-Cold War era. Second, except for Angola and Mozambique, the other countries are English speaking. There would thus be only one language of communication. This would eliminate a potential source of conflict. Third, since the early 1990s there has been a decline in ideological differences among the members of SADC. Angola and Mozambique are no longer pursuing Marxist policies, South Africa's apartheid regime has lost power, and Tanzania and Zambia are no longer implementing statist policies. There is consensus among SADC members that effective regional cooperation should be based on a shared commitment to a liberal capitalist model of development. Fourth, SADC is committed to conflict resolution. Except in Angola, the wars in the region have ended. In 1995 SADC considered institutionalizing cooperation in the new functional area of "political cooperation, democracy, peace and security." Regional integration has had severe limitations, but the consensus across the African region seems to be that the regional integration movement needs to be widened to be more in line with the current integration realities in the global economy. Many believe that if the regional integration and cooperation process can be strengthened, this could create an enhanced economic space for sub-Saharan Africa in the world economy.

Lobbying in the International Arena

By the end of the 1960s Africa was a part of a Third World coalition that changed United Nations policy and issues to focus on economic matters. The United States showed its great dissatisfaction with the Third World's use of the UN by frequent vetoes in the Security Council and suspension of its share of payments for certain UN activities. At the end of the 1960s Africa had the largest number of states of any region in the UN. Along with other developing regions, it held more than a two-thirds majority in all UN bodies except the Security Council, where the veto power of Britain, the United States, the Soviet Union, France, and China blocked majority rule. Reflecting the organization of the Third World majority, a UN Conference on Trade and Development (UNCTAD I) was organized in 1964. For the first time an international debate took place on the economic problems that impeded development in Latin America, the Caribbean, Africa, and Asia. The economic conflict between the North (Western industrialized countries) and the South (underdeveloped countries of Asia, Africa, Latin America, and the Caribbean) was placed permanently on the UN agenda, shifting UN activities and the debate away from East-West, Cold War tensions to the economic gap between the rich North and the poor South. The United States has consistently opposed UNCTAD, underscoring its displeasure with the UN generally during the 1970s, 1980s, and 1990s. UNCTAD provided the foundation for the evolution of the Group of 77 (G-77, those seventy-seven countries that participated in UNCTAD I) and the Non-Aligned Movement (NAM). G-77 and the NAM signaled unity among the developing countries, and this was evident at nearly all international fora concerned with development.

Following article 4 of the charter of the Organization of African Unity (OAU), all its members were committed to the principle of nonalignment in the then existing bipolar international system. Viewing the Cold War as an East-West problem that had serious ramifications for Africa, the OAU joined Asian, Caribbean, Latin American, and Mediterranean countries in the Non-Aligned Movement, professing their neutrality in the conflict. In 1961 twenty-five countries joined the NAM; eleven were African. In 1964 nineteen more African governments participated. Nonalignment meant that they should be free to trade and do business with both capitalist and communist countries without allegiance to one bloc or the other.

Although all members of the OAU claimed to be nonaligned, few were really neutral and many were closely linked to one side or the other either by choice or through economic dependency. Most African countries had been unable to diversify trading partners and have continued to be dependent on trade with the former colonial powers. Notwithstanding the reality of this dependence, African leaders like Julius Nyerere, Kenneth Kaunda (Zambia), and Kwame Nkrumah (Ghana) emerged at the forefront of the Non-Aligned Movement and advanced economic issues that were a clear priority for Africa (and other developing regions) and sought an independent Third World presence in world affairs.

The Non-Aligned Movement was politically important because it was the organizational symbol of the concept of a Third World with very different priorities than the First and Second Worlds. The members of the NAM, especially those from Africa and the Caribbean, formed the core of the Group of 77 in the mid-1970s demanding in the UN General Assembly a program of action for the establishment of a "new international economic order" (NIEO). As an objective, the NIEO demanded a complete restructuring of the world economy in favor of the South. The South, led by Africans like Julius Nyerere, believed that the world capitalist economy discriminated against the world's poorer countries.

The principal proposals put through various resolutions in the NIEO included, but were not limited to, the following: lowering of tariffs and non-tariff barriers on manufactured exports from the South; linking aid to the creation of special drawing rights at the IMF, which should become the world's reserve currency in place of the dollar; attaining UN global development aid targets (0.7 percent of the GNP of the donor countries); compensation for damage done to natural and other resources during colonialism; the right of countries to sovereignty over their natural resources; eliminating restrictive practices in international trade that restrict the market share of Third World countries; reforming the procedures and structures of the IMF, the World Bank, and the International Development Association to facilitate financial transfers to the Third World; renegotiating and reducing Third World debts; requiring multinational corporations (MNCs) to contribute to Third World development; and restructuring the UN to meet development needs of the Third World (Hadjor, 1993: 227).

A new international economic order did emerge, but it was a far cry from what was envisaged by the Third World during the 1970s. There are more debt, less support for primary products, and less aid and the markets of the North remain closed to most products from the South. The North ignored the call for a NIEO. A fundamental change did not take place in the relationship between the industrialized countries and the Third World. The distribution of the world's wealth and economic equality are still relevant issues today.

African Security in the Post-Cold War Period

Foreign Solutions to African Conflicts: Private Security Forces

Violent intrastate conflicts in Africa at the end of the Cold War led to the loss of thousands of lives, state disintegration, and state collapse in some instances (see Chapter 7). Beleaguered governments under siege by insurgent movements (often with a military lacking the capacity to protect them) sought external assistance to protect their regimes. As the big powers have been reluctant to intervene militarily in African domestic politics in the post-Cold War period and the UN does not always have the capacity to carry out effective peacekeeping, a market for mercenary or private military companies has emerged. These mercenaries have offered their services to collapsing mineral-rich states, for example Angola and Sierra Leone. They were not

President Bill Clinton visiting Africa, August 2000.

AP / Wide World Photos

always paid in cash but sometimes were granted oil and diamond concessions. Private military companies such as Sandline International, Executive
Outcomes (EO), Military Professional Resources Incorporated (MPRI) are
huge multimillion-pound businesses, not only providing security but also
holding huge commercial interests.

Executive Outcomes is the world's largest mercenary group. It is a private
army manned with former South African Defense Force (SADF) combat
veterans, who came largely from South Africa's former 32nd Battalion,
the Renaissance Commandos, the Parachute Brigade, and the paramilitary
"Crowbar." These groups were at the center of apartheid South Africa's military destabilization forces in Angola and throughout southern Africa in the
1980s. The 32nd Battalion became South Africa's most highly decorated unit
since World War II. After the signing of the Brazzaville Accords in 1988,
which led to the withdrawal of Soviet, Cuban, and South African military involvement in Angola and Namibia, South Africa ended its regional destabilization policy.

Many combat soldiers subsequently left the SADF. By 1992 the Renaissance Commandos and the Parachute Brigade were at half their 1989
strength, and both the 32nd Battalion and Crowbar were effectively disbanded (Howe, 1998). There was some fear that these unemployed soldiers,
who were committed to the apartheid order, might derail political reforms

and a transition to majority rule. A potentially disruptive force within South Africa, EO became a stabilizing force outside South Africa, in Angola and Sierra Leone.

Mercenary interventions have been supported by Western governments and institutions, such as the IMF and World Bank. Those who support the use of private armies in Africa note that they do stabilize conflicts and often force a negotiated settlement. In Angola, EO military assistance to the MPLA government forced UNITA to sign the Lusaka Peace Accords (see Chapter 7). Executive Outcomes was introduced to a desperate MPLA government in late 1992-early 1993 by the CEO of Heritage Oil and Gas. The 1991 Lusaka Peace Accords between the MPLA and UNITA had resulted in the September 1992 elections, which the MPLA appeared to have won. UNITA's Savimbi had rejected the incomplete returns and returned to the countryside to resume fighting. Savimbi soon controlled 80 percent of the countryside. Because of the previous agreement signed, Cuba and the Soviet Union could not provide assistance. EO's services were desperately needed, and the MPLA government signed a one-year contract with it for US$40 million in 1999. EO provided specialized skills to enhance the effectiveness of the MPLA's forces. It fielded about 550 soldiers and trained thirty pilots and about 5,000 government troops in skills such as artillery, motorized infantry, engineering, and medical support as well as sabotage and reconnaissance. EO personnel fought on some occasions and were important in the recapture of the diamond areas of Cajungo in mid-July 1994 and the oil installations at Soyo by November 1994. EO has been credited with assisting the MPLA to turn back the resurgent UNITA. Savimbi subsequently signed the Lusaka Protocol in mid-1994, which ended the fighting and prepared the ground for another round of elections. The Lusaka Protocol also called for the repatriation of all mercenaries in Angola, but the MPLA requested that EO remain for another thirteen months. The first group of EO left for South Africa in June 1996, but up to half of EO personnel remained in Angola often taking jobs in security companies (Howe, 1998).

In May 1995 the government of Sierra Leone contracted with EO to help it in its four-year fight against the RUF. The same CEO of Heritage Oil and Gas who introduced EO to the MPLA in Angola introduced it to the government of Sierra Leone. By May 1995 RUF had advanced to within twenty miles of the capital city of Freetown. The country was devastated by war, with approximately one and a half million refugees and hundreds of thousands killed over the three years of war. The economy was in shambles because RUF had closed down the bauxite and diamond sectors while it ran clandestine diamond export operations. The government army was corrupt, had been hastily built up, lacked proper training, and lacked military discipline. EO went in, trained 150 government soldiers, and provided technical services and combat forces. Its immediate tasks were to push RUF away from

Freetown, open the roads to the capital for food and fuel transport, and protect the Kono diamond district. By January 1996 government forces, backed by EO, had retaken the bauxite mines and the southern coastal rutile mines. EO tipped the military balance in favor of the government and forced RUF to the negotiating table and the Abidjan Accords in 1996. In February 1996 elections were scheduled, and the new Kabbah government signed a peace settlement with RUF that continued into early 1997. EO departed Sierra Leone on completion of its contract in January 1997. The Kabbah government was overthrown four months later by soldiers supportive of the RUF (see Chapter 7).

Were EO's services beneficial to these states? How lasting have the settlements been that were forcibly obtained by mercenaries? There were concerns about the highly advantageous concessions granted to Heritage Oil and Gas, which mortgaged the countries' future to this company. Highly favorable concessions obviously lessened future government revenues. The Kabbah government was overthrown four months after EO's departure because a political solution was still not found. EO's role had been only to obtain a military settlement. There was also fear that companies like EO that depend on strife for profit may understandably work to start or prolong conflict. There is also a fear that any government that finds itself in a difficult position can hire mercenaries to stay in power. There is fear that EO's training and combat skills may only increase the militarization and destabilization of a desperately poor continent. EO's record in Africa is mixed and its future is uncertain.

African Solutions to African Conflicts: ECOMOG

The Economic Community of West African States (ECOWAS) has been committed to the promotion of economic development of West Africa. Regional integration, its major objective, was expected to help break dependence on former colonial powers, increasing self-reliance and the region's bargaining power in the global market. ECOWAS has been an economic integration organization for over two decades, but in the 1990s it took on a regional security responsibility with the formation of the ECOWAS Monitoring Group (ECOMOG), a peacekeeping force, to help resolve the two major conflicts in West Africa, in Liberia and Sierra Leone. At the initiative of Nigeria, a peacekeeping force was established with troops from Nigeria, Ghana, Sierra Leone, The Gambia, and Guinea. The transformation of ECOWAS into ECOMOG came as a result of the interplay between economic development, democratization, and regional security. In both countries, the state collapsed and the economy was devastated. In Sierra Leone the constitutional government had been removed, thousands of people were brutally killed or maimed, and a state of anarchy existed.

ECOWAS intervened in Liberia and Sierra Leone, disregarding the OAU principle of nonintervention in the domestic affairs of member states. Facing state collapse, a refugee crisis, rampant crime and vicious murders, and a situation that could spread rapidly across borders in the region, ECOWAS decided to take action as the UN and the United States ignored calls for assistance to the region. After ECOWAS's action the UN and the United States endorsed ECOMOG's operations. The UN was willing to endorse ECOMOG and involve itself in the operations in a marginal way, operating as a partner rather than as the leader. The UN gave its moral authority to the operations and gave international legitimacy to ECOWAS's efforts. The UN gave the appearance of fulfilling its primary responsibility of maintaining international peace and security while at the same time avoiding direct responsibility for costly and protracted internal conflicts. The United States contributed $106 million to cover the costs of non-West African peacekeepers from Tanzania, Uganda, and South Africa (brought in to try to "de-Nigerianize" ECOMOG) and for military assistance to individual countries involved in ECOMOG. The Netherlands contributed $4 million, Britain $3.4 million, and Germany an undisclosed amount (Jaye, 2000: 170). The OAU fully supported ECOMOG interventions, which subsequently influenced the former to produce a resolution for conflict prevention, management, and resolution. At the 1995 OAU summit, a decision was reached to create a continental peacekeeping force to be deployed in African conflict situations. In 1998 ECOWAS foreign ministers meeting in Abuja, Nigeria, agreed to a draft treaty setting up ECOMOG as a permanent regional conflict resolution mechanism with a military dimension.

ECOMOG became a "surrogate" state authority, using its force to preserve law and order. It succeeded in helping to reconstitute the Liberian state and restoring constitutional rule in Sierra Leone. Many may question its reason for restoring an illegitimate postcolonial state not supported by the majority of the population. In this regard, critics have seen ECOMOG as an organization serving to maintain colonial artificial boundaries and state formations operating in the Westphalian international system (Clapham, 1996). However, ECOMOG must be given credit (by even its critics) for halting death and destruction.

Both scholars of conflict management (Haas, 1994; Francis, 2000: Jaye, 2000) and the UN Secretary General Kofi Annan (1998) agree that ECOMOG's handling of peace and security in West Africa serve as an important model providing lessons for conflict resolutions in Africa and other areas of the world. ECOMOG also set a precedent for collective action by a regional organization intervening in intrastate conflicts without sanctions from the UN. ECOMOG was a homegrown African strategy that Africans devised to help resolve their own conflicts when no external assistance was forthcoming. It was the first intra-African force to manage successfully and settle two

African conflicts. ECOMOG, as a regional multinational force, was more likely to be acceptable to the warring factions than peacekeepers from Europe or the United States.

Those with objections to the role ECOMOG played in resolving the conflicts did so on several grounds. Samuel Huntington (1993) and Robert Kaplan (1994) warned that ECOMOG could lead to "generalized chaos" for the future of Africa as a result of the complex combination of domestic and international political, socioeconomic, cultural, and environmental factors. There were also concerns about many problems that could have derailed the operations: Nigeria's domestic and foreign policy ambitions, regional political divisions between anglophone and francophone countries, fierce opposition to an ECOMOG peacekeeping force by the NPFL (the chief warring faction in Liberia), lack of consensus among ECOWAS at the time of intervention (those fearing Nigerian domination in the region opposed the intervention as a Nigerian was the force commander), lack of centralized control authority for operation in the ECOWAS Secretariat, and ECOMOG's compromised neutrality in Liberia.

These are all legitimate concerns. African and foreign interests became involved in the ECOMOG operations for their own reasons. Participation in ECOMOG and its successful resolution of the conflicts did boost the international image of Nigerian dictator Sani Abacha in the aftermath of his regime's execution of environmental activist Ken Saro-Wiwa and eight other people. Nigeria lacked the moral authority to lead a force to "restore democracy" in Sierra Leone, in light of the fact that the Abacha regime derailed Nigerian democracy and prolonged the "transition process." However, as the most populous nation in West Africa, and in Africa, and possessor of the most highly trained military in the region, with much international peacekeeping experience, Nigeria inevitably emerged as somewhat of a military power in the region. With the retreat of the big powers from African conflicts, it was not surprising that Nigeria would try to provide regional security in the security vacuum left by the UN, western European governments, and the former superpowers.

Sandline International assisted ECOMOG by shipping thirty-five tons of Bulgarian arms. Sandline was reportedly interested in exploiting the diamonds in Sierra Leone through mining concessions granted by the restored president Kabbah. Britain also sought to protect its commercial interests in Sierra Leone by cooperating with the Nigerian military government and Sandline in reinstating the ousted Kabbah government.

ECOMOG could not implement postconflict reconciliation and reconstruction in Liberia and Sierra Leone because ECOWAS lacked the quantity of resources required. By itself, ECOMOG cannot establish sustainable security. The brunt of peacekeeping in Africa falls on the shoulders of the OAU, or any new organization that represents the continent. The

ECOMOG interventions pushed the OAU into considering working out permanent collective security arrangements. In the post-Cold War period, Africans have come to the realization that they must settle their disputes internally. There may be continued calls for external assistance, since with its pressing developmental problems, resources may not be available to carry out conflict management operations successfully. In the case of the ECO-MOG operations in Liberia and Sierra Leone, external assistance was granted, but the African countries set the parameters for resolving the conflict. This should be the wave of the future.

Conclusion

The above discussion has shown that in the interaction between the major powers and African states, both have tried to advance their own interests. When a particular African country or region was considered to be important and strategic, the African leader(s) in those areas would gain a bit more leverage in international relations. Also, when African states acted collectively or in solidarity with other developing regions, they got the world's attention and were able to reshape North-South relations. The economic crisis of the 1980s and the collapse of the Soviet Union and the subsequent emergence of a capitalist world order have weakened Africa's present global position. Western industrialized nations, with whom Africa is most closely linked economically at this time, seem to have all the leverage for pressure on African governments.

Africa's place in post-1960 international politics has been largely influenced by its legacy of imperialism. Today, African nations remain heavily dependent on one or a few traditional export commodities for which world prices fluctuate and are not likely to remain high. Africa remains at the bottom of the international stratification system, having the largest number of impoverished countries in the world. Among Africa's former colonizers, France has remained very influential in African affairs, although its involvement has decreased since 1992 as its foreign policy has been consolidated through the European Union. The other European powers and the two former superpowers, the United States and the former Soviet Union, have all disengaged from the African continent. This is reflected in the decline in foreign aid, the linking of development assistance to "good governance," reassessment of special trade preferences by the European Union, the retreat from political conflicts, and the unwillingness to intervene militarily in those conflicts. This has forced Africa to become self-reliant in finding solutions for its security problems. External private armies have been used to force peace agreements in Angola and Sierra Leone, and the ECOWAS Monitoring Group, ECOMOG, was used to end the wars in Liberia and Sierra Leone. Regionalism was reassessed in the late 1990s as Africa grappled with development and peace and security issues as it entered the twenty-first century.

For Further Reading

Willetts, P. (1978). *The Non-Aligned Movement: The Origins of the Third World Alliance*. London: F. Pintor and New York: Nichols Publishing Company.

Adedeji, A., ed. (1993). *Africa within the World: Beyond Dispossession and Dependence*. London: Zed Books.

Clapham, C. (1996). *Africa and the International System*. Cambridge, England: Cambridge University Press.

Oyebade, A., and A. Alao, eds. (1998). *Africa after the Cold War: The Changing Perspectives on Security*. Trenton and Asmara: Africa World Press.

Bakut, T. B., and S. Dutt, eds. (2000). *Africa at the Millennium: An Agenda for Mature Development*. Houndsmill, England: Palgrave.

9
—

Conclusion: Africa's Prospects for a New Beginning in the Post–Cold War Era

I have argued in this book that the African state established under European colonial rule, clientelistic forms of governance by African political elites, and the external vulnerability of the region all combined to create the failure of the postcolonial state in sub-Saharan Africa. The legacy of the colonial state and its impact on political development and economic policies was discussed. I noted that political conflict in sub-Saharan Africa emerged from poverty and resource scarcity, and ethnicity and regionalism emerged as the main cleavages of conflict across the region.

The modern African state that evolved after independence was controlled by political leaders who pursued their own narrow class and ethnic interests. In this context a specific type of domination was imposed on the society over which the new African political elites ruled. Practices of clientelism and patronage, coupled with charismatic as well as authoritarian modes of exercising power, prevailed across both democratic and authoritarian regimes. Entrenched political systems developed in which clientelistic allocation of resources became predominant over the formal institutions of democracy. Pressures from elites as well as the masses of the population to obtain benefits from the state often led to chaos, violence, and political instability.

The region's external dependence stemmed from the colonial past, when African economies were integrated into European economies as suppliers of raw materials. Although power relations between the rulers and those they ruled have been linked to Africa's development problems, one of the themes of this book is that the region's external dependence and marginalization in the international economy determined the parameters within which domestic politics evolved.

During the 1980s (the "lost decade" for most developing nations), Africa's development problems reached crisis proportions. International lenders recommended IMF-sponsored economic reforms that entailed policies promoting exports, deregulation of the state, devaluation of local currencies, liberalization of imports, and reduction in public sector expenditures. There was little evidence that these reforms brought socioeconomic advancement to the African population. Austerity measures exacted high social costs, which led to increased political pressure on corrupt authoritarian governments to provide socioeconomic benefits for the population. Internal pressures from broad sectors of the population and external pressures from Western governments and international financial institutions combined to force political change across the region.

Since 1990 more than three-fourths of the countries of sub-Saharan Africa have shifted from single-party authoritarian and military systems to multiparty systems. The intended objective was greater political democratization. Yet troubling trends apparent since 1990 include the continued financial and organizational advantages of the ruling parties, elections that did not provide real opportunities for competition, clientelistic parties functioning merely as electoral machines, little programmatic differences between the competing parties, and weak legislative bodies.

Economically the region has acquiesced to neoliberal economic reforms mandated by international lenders such as the World Bank, IMF, and EU in order to avoid sanctions or withdrawal of aid. Neoliberal reforms have not had a uniform impact on sub-Saharan Africa. In those countries identified as successful reformers, fiscal deficits have been trimmed, privatization of state enterprises have occurred, and trade regimes have been liberalized. Even among the successful reformers (e.g., Ghana, Uganda, Tanzania), direct foreign investment has not been significant in the 1990s. The bulk of foreign investment has been concentrated in the mining sector and in large economies such as Nigeria and South Africa. Foreign investors still perceive sub-Saharan Africa to be a high risk area because of its economic weaknesses and political instability.

At the beginning of the twenty-first century the African state is at a crossroads in its postindependence history. Can it restructure itself and develop a capacity to address the collective needs of the African population? Can the new international environment provide opportunities for the transformation of state-society relations in Africa? Or will the new global order, dominated by the neoliberal model of development, foreclose opportunities for a reconstituted state? The discussions throughout the book indicate that the prospects for a new beginning are mixed but only modestly encouraging. The transition in the African political economy remains uncertain because of several challenges: (1) the region's economic vulnerability, (2) the shift from authoritarian clientelism to new forms of clientelism as vulnerable poor people continue to seek access to state and nonstate resources, and (3) unresolved social justice issues remained.

Economic Vulnerability of the Region

Africa's economic situation has reached unacceptable, crisis proportions. The suffering, impoverishment, disease, and conflict that tragically affect the vast majority of African people must be addressed. What are the prospects that Africa's economic vulnerability can be reduced in the post–Cold War period? Can Africa become less "hemmed in"? At the beginning of the 1990s, with the end of the Cold War an external environment emerged that assisted the African people in removing long-serving, corrupt authoritarian governments. There needs also to be an external environment that can enable African economic development. Unfortunately, the vision for African economic development that prevailed in Western industrialized countries over the past two decades has centered on neoliberal economic polices. Successful attempts at economic stabilization and structural adjustment have been limited, with negligible impact on the overall economic problems facing Africa. Western nations and their international financial institutions remain committed to policies that have not been able to provide quick solutions to Africa's economic problems. Their conclusion is that Africa's problems are intractable. This viewpoint has resulted in a lukewarm commitment to economic change and development in Africa. Their policy is now based on unloading burdensome economic arrangements with African countries on institutions like the IMF, which is now responsible for collecting debts on their behalf. Their attention has now been focused on eastern Europe, where they seem more committed to building democracy and helping capitalism to flourish.

The European colonial powers had a huge role in Africa's current economic crisis. I believe that they should play an important role in assisting Africa in solving its economic problems. However, morals do not dictate foreign policy, and it is clear that the former colonial powers of Europe are mainly interested in their own economic prosperity. To the extent that

Africa can contribute to their prosperity without being a burden, they are willing to pursue economic relations with selected African countries and selected trading blocs within Africa.

The European Union decreased its aid to sub-Saharan Africa in the 1990s, although it remained Africa's largest donor. It obviously should no longer grant aid to finance unpopular corrupt African governments, nor to build palaces, cathedrals, or monuments like Arch 22. The commodities from Sub-Saharan Africa continue to enter the principal European markets duty free (the exceptions are certain items that Western nations produce, e.g., sugar, beef, tomatoes, and cut flowers) despite anticipated changes in preferential agreements. However, Africa's share of European imports has declined, whereas Europe continues to be Africa's primary market. Africa is hemmed in by a colonial legacy that created an economic relationship with Europe that has become impossible to break.

Africa needs assistance from Western industrialized nations in resolving its debt problems. Africa's debt to Western creditors is comparatively low. In 1990 Africa's total share of Third World debt was only 11 percent. In that year 83 percent of its debt was to public sources such as the governments of OECD countries and the multilateral agencies such as the World Bank and IMF (World Bank, 1991). As Susan George argues, the US$136 billion owed to Western creditors in 1990 was peanuts to them but represented a crushing load for the African region (George, 1993). Africa did not have the capacity to pay and service those debts, but it was bled dry through structural adjustment programs with the IMF to reimburse those Western industrialized nations.

If the debt burden continues, Africa will remain hemmed in. The reasons for this pessimistic prognosis are several. Africa's debts provide its creditors with all sorts of leverage. Raw materials can be bought on the cheapest terms. Debt-for-equity swaps can occur where assets and infrastructure can be taken over. Debt can prevent political mobilization against the North (Western industrialized nations) by the South, (developing nations) as in the 1970s, as the African countries may be too timid to confront creditors. Debt continues to weaken the power of the state, as it is forced to accept IMF prescriptions, accompanying the loans that takes power from the state and places it in the hands of external actors. IMF officials fix macroeconomic policy, and the state is left to work out minor details. IMF officials also have control over the currencies of debtor nations and can recommend devaluation as it sees fit. The indebted state is practically deprived of its authority over economic decisions and left only with the responsibility for judicial functions and the maintenance of political order.

Some Western creditors have been willing to reschedule some of Africa's debts but less eager to cancel them outright. Some scholars have argued against debt cancellation as they believe doing so would take Africa out of the global economy. Canceling debts should perhaps be attached to an agreement that no future loans would be given for a specific period until the country regains its creditworthiness. Many believe that another condition for debt cancellation should be a commitment by the debtor country for greater popular participation in political and economic decisions.

Uniting under a single debt-negotiating banner (along with Latin America) to negotiate debt repayment might be helpful. This unity might give debtor nations a louder voice and force Western countries to listen to alternative proposals for repayment. Innovative solutions for repayment, such as paying debt service in local currency over a long period, ought to be considered. Hard currency export earnings would then be free for more useful purposes than debt service. This would reduce immediate pressures to export, thus gradually allowing commodity prices to rise. The hard currency would be used to purchase imports from Western countries so that the latter would receive the same income as before. In this way, however, Africa would participate in the global trading system as a regular partner and not as a mendicant (George, 1993).

Africa will need to find its own solutions to its economic problems. Given its political and economic marginalization in world politics and the world economy, it must look for solutions within Africa and perhaps within the South (other developing regions).

Reduction in Defense Spending

Although the Cold War has ended and this has led to the termination of many conflicts fueled by superpower support, many African governments continue to spend huge sums on the defense sector. In the case of South Africa, defense spending has increased for several reasons: to prevent the military from derailing the new democratic order, to put the military in a position to maintain the social order to facilitate the necessary climate for foreign investment, and to maximize foreign exchange earnings from selling arms. It is widely believed that the ANC government has plans to reduce defense expenditures in the long term. In countries where there is peace after long periods of strife, there has been reduction in defense spending (e.g., Mozambique, Ethiopia). Zimbabwe, Uganda, and Tanzania have also promised to cut defense spending. This is an area that African governments can control, and they ought to reduce defense expenditures and reallocate those funds to social services, infrastructure, and education.

South-South Cooperation

South-South cooperation has been pursued in the past and remains on the agenda today. In the 1970s the NAM and G-77 encouraged the theory of

South-South cooperation. Today the need to reduce dependence on old metropolitan links is urgent. Regional economic integration as a counterdependency strategy has been attempted in Africa over many decades with modest results. Understanding that they run the risk of seeing their economic preferences seriously eroded by the EU, sub-Saharan African countries are now making great efforts to strengthen many of their regional associations (e.g. ECOWAS, EAC, SADC, UMEOA, UDEAC). In addition, recognizing the low level of intra-African trade, a group of African countries set up an African Export/Import Bank (Afreximbank) to promote Africa's exports and intra-African commerce. The regional organizations have been plagued by

AFRICA FOR SALE!

GOING FOR THE JUGULAR ...

How long will Africa remain hemmed in?

Tayo Fatunla

financial hardships, have been operating by trial and error, and have made mistakes. They are still committed to correcting those mistakes and moving closer toward development cooperation.

Africa's political leaders (from North Africa, except Morocco, and Sub-Saharan Africa) met in July 2001 in Lusaka, Zambia, at the thirty-seventh and final summit of the OAU. There they resolved concrete measures for establishing the newly proposed AU. This demonstrated contemporary African leaders' desire to make a fresh start and a determined effort at intra-African development cooperation. The AU promises to take Africa to a much higher level of political and economic unity than the defunct OAU. The proposed AU hopes to adopt a structure that is modeled on that of the EU and other successful supranational organizations in Asia and the Western Hemisphere. The organizational structure will consist of a Secretariat; a Pan-African Parliament; a Pan-African Court of Justice; an Economic, Social and Cultural Council; a Mechanism for Conflict Prevention, Management and Resolution; and Specialized Technical Committees. In addition, a Millennium Partnership for the African Recovery Programme (MAP) was adopted to address the continent's economic stagnation. It has as its objectives ending poverty and underdevelopment, deepening democracy, and defining a new relationship with Western industrialized countries. There was consensus at the summit that the AU and MAP could not be successful unless ordinary Africans from across the continent participated in the implementation of its objectives.

Since the summit, there have been legitimate reservations raised. Will Parliament be effective or just become a talking shop? Will the Court have binding authority over certain legal areas in all member countries? Will member states cede jurisdiction to this court? How difficult will it be to establish a single currency in a central bank? If establishing the Euro caused such a headache in the industrialized West, will it not be even more difficult in underdeveloped Africa? The African people are understandably skeptical. Given the OAU's track record, why should they not be pessimistic? With the differences in the capacity of various countries, many see this as another effort doomed to failure. One cannot be too cautious about ideas that are great on paper but have not yet been implemented. However, Africa has a wealth of experience based on practices tried and failed, and it does have some committed and competent new leadership. One has to wait and see whether the AU is just the OAU with a new name or can bring about real political change and economic recovery. It took almost half a century for the EU to come to the point where there is a single market and it can now think about political integration. It will take some time for the African people to establish a fully functioning AU. The necessary first steps taken should be encouraged.

Another level of South-South cooperation that ought to be examined again is interregional cooperation. In the 1970s the NAM, G-77, and Lome conventions demonstrated the efforts by developing countries to alter their situation in the international community. Despite the fact that these efforts have not changed the structural inequality between the North and the South, these were important examples of collective bargaining power over the terms of some important aspects of the North-South relationship. This style of articulating the interests of poorer countries ought to be attempted again in the post–Cold War period. It perhaps can only be done within the context of a revitalized UN.

Interregional cooperation ought to be increased in as many areas as possible. First, markets for some of Africa's minerals could possibly be found in Mexico, Brazil, and Cuba and other newly industrializing countries. This possibility should be vigorously explored. Second, development strategies tried and found to be successful in other developing regions could be examined to see whether or not they could work in Africa. For example, the Grameen Bank, an indigenous organization established in Bangladesh to address poverty reduction and human development, has been a huge success. The government provided seed money, and the bank provided small loans averaging $100 to poor people (but many loans were as small as $10–$20), especially women, who could not qualify for regular bank loans. The bank provided loans to more than 1.6 million borrowers in 34,000 villages, lending about $30 per month. Over 47 percent of these borrowers have risen above the poverty line, and among Grameen families it is reported that "the nutrition level is better than in non-Grameen families, child mortality is lower and adoption of family practices is higher, and all signs confirm the visible empowerment of women" (Grameen Bank, 1997). In 1997, there were 2,131,107 members with 1,084 branches of the Bank serving 36,935 villages with a cumulative disbursement of US$1,993 million (Grameen Bank, 1997).

Replication of the Grameen Bank model was attempted with varying degrees of success in Malawi, Tanzania, Ethiopia, Guinea Lesotho, Nigeria, Kenya, Uganda, Burkina Faso, Mauritania, and Zimbabwe as a part of efforts by grassroots associations to help the weakened African state with economic development efforts. The Malawi Mudzi (village) Fund (MMF) was the first attempt by an international donor to replicate the Grameen Bank model in another environment. Like the Grameen Bank, the MMF was targeted at the poorest of the poor, the majority of whom were women and those who were excluded from the smallholder's credit scheme. Initially the MMF enjoyed great success as loan repayments were high, but within six months new loans were stopped because only 54 percent of all loans had been repaid. Owing to high operating costs the MMF was forced to suspend operations and merge with another rural financial institution (Pal, 1999: 146). In Burkina Faso the Credit with Education (CE) project, modeled after the Grameen Bank, was established with funding from USAID (United States Agency for

International Development), UNICEF (United Nation's Children's Fund), and (IFAD) and designed by the American NGO Freedom from Hunger and the local Reseau de Caisses Populaires de Burkina Faso. The CE was intended to build on the existing credit union movement, which was successful but did not reach the poorest people, especially women. The CE approach combined village banking with basic health education. In 1997 CE had 18,000 members, was operating in both the central and central plateau regions of Burkina Faso. It covered all its expenses with income from loan repayments and the interest on members' savings, thus becoming a sustainable institution. Outstanding loans in 1997 totaled US$791,138 and the average loan was US$65. The CE introduced group lending, made savings compulsory, and addressed social development.

State-Society Relations

The structural constraints of an international economy dominated by neoliberal ideology have reduced the African state's capacity for intervention in the economy. Neoliberalism rejects state capitalist planning and internal market-oriented policies that postindependence African governments emphasized. Government policies of subsidizing price or increasing wages for workers to create an internal market would be dismissed by the IMF or the World Bank.

Has there been a restructuring of state-market relations as neoliberal reforms intended? Or has the state continued to dominate economic actors? The results are mixed. The state has withdrawn from the economy through privatization of government-owned assets and deregulation of finance and trade. However, it has simultaneously increased its intervention in other macroeconomic processes—for example, fixing exchange and interests rates, setting conditions for privatization, and directing public foreign indebtedness toward specific goals.

The African state is smaller than it was two decades ago. The retreat of the state has exposed the majority of citizens to a market that is biased in favor of large capital owners and multinational corporations. The state is now unable to deliver levels of welfare and social services similar to those in the 1960s and 1970s. Yet pressures on the state to provide economic support and deliver social services have persisted. Some former poor clients have found other mechanisms for social participation and economic benefits. With the decline of the state's economic capabilities and the increasing demands on the family, the informal economy has expanded. White-collar workers and professionals of various occupations have set up private businesses to try to survive. Before 1990 women dominated the informal economy, but in the past decade large numbers of men have also become participants, with their activities centered on urban transportation, tourism, mineral smuggling, and narcotics trafficking.

On balance, a decade of participatory politics and state reduction have not eliminated clientelism in sub-Saharan Africa. The "welfare state" political culture among large sectors of the population has continued as they seek to have their demands met within the new democratic pluralist framework. Clientelism has again become an integral part of the political strategies of political parties in the 1990s. This reflects continuity from the earlier period of party politics in the 1960s (see Chapter 4). It is not surprising that clientelism would continue to be used as an organizing tool in party politics. The newly formed party systems were often weak, and the myriad of parties (especially opposition parties) that emerged lacked serious programs. Many of them were formed quickly to participate in the transition elections that were funded by international donors. It was clear to many party leaders that alternatives to neoliberalism would be unacceptable (despite populist demands for policies that would require state intervention); therefore there was little debate on ideas and policies in many election campaigns. In the absence of programs, parties resorted to the old familiar pattern of clientelism, and thus ethnicity and relations of kinship are still important in gaining access to state resources.

How do poor, vulnerable people get access to the resources of the state without becoming subordinate clients? How can clientelism be broken down in sub-Saharan Africa? Should clientelism disappear when regimes make the transition from authoritarianism to multiparty electoral systems? It has been suggested that clientelism can be broken down gradually in developing countries after extended periods of democratic elections, associational autonomy, urbanization, increased education, structural economic shifts or through political action.

The transition from authoritarianism to competitive electoral systems is a very recent phenomenon in Africa. There would need to be a much longer period of electoral competition before autocrats could be weakened (assuming they can be). Autonomous associations (largely women's groups, farmers, professionals, and NGOs) have proliferated since 1990 and have received support from external donors assisting with democratization efforts. As the political culture becomes more democratic, interest groups will demand broader access to the state while maintaining their autonomy and the ability to articulate their own interests. Urbanization and expansion of education are social changes that will take place gradually. However, with the reduction in state resources, educational advancements have been hampered. Extending social welfare outside the party or state institutions without attaching political conditions (such as with food stamps in the United States) would broaden the political terms of access. This would represent deliberate political action to try to undermine clientelism.

African political systems are in transition between authoritarianism and democracy. It has been argued that in developing nations involved in regime transitions, the authoritarian clientelism of the past could slowly give way to "semiclientelism" (defined as unenforceable buying of political support) before it can be replaced by resource allocation not conditioned on political subordination (Fox, 1997).

Poverty allocation programs administered with World Bank and UN support through foreign and domestic NGOs have appeared throughout sub-Saharan Africa since 1990. International donors have supported these programs because they have reduced the likelihood of mass mobilization against austerity and market reforms. Further, international donors are more comfortable handing over funds to NGOs than to governments that may be corrupt. The state's welfare role has been somewhat restructured as the inclusion of NGOs in poverty alleviation programs altered state-civil society relations.

Unresolved Social Justice Issues

Popular protests in the early 1990s called for democratic governance and socioeconomic reforms across sub-Saharan Africa. For the first time since independence in the 1960s, Western industrialized countries withdrew their support from authoritarian regimes facing popular uprisings demanding their removal. The external environment was no longer enabling for African authoritarian rulers (or authoritarians in general); hence, the most significant factor that previously accounted for the persistence of these authoritarian governments was removed. Without external support from powerful patrons, long-serving leaders were swept from power under domestic pressure. The withdrawal of support for dictators in Africa indicated a shift in the foreign policies of Western European countries and the former superpowers. As Chapter 8 indicates, those countries embarked on a "new beginning" in their foreign policies toward Africa.

Incipient political liberalization has occurred across the region, although not uniformly. Elections have been held in the vast majority of countries, party systems have been introduced, federalism and decentralization have been placed on the agenda for discussion, civil service and legal system reforms have occurred, autonomous media and other institutions of civil society have emerged, and legislative bodies have been given some legitimacy. I believe that these are encouraging signs, although a more pluralistic polity has not yet translated into an environment in which the benefits of neoliberal reforms have been realized.

Political liberalization should result in a more open policy-making environment, but as Nicholas van de Walle (1994a) points out, it has not yet altered the structural characteristics of policy making in Africa. The agenda-setting process is still controlled by the tiny political elite in conjunction with international donors. Policies adopted by many leaders often had little to do with democratic procedures. Public debate and discussions by legislative bodies hardly affected decisions made by the state on issues such as privatization of state enterprises or devaluation of national currencies. Policies have been implemented following external directions.

Political liberalization has not yet been able to break the cycle of economic despair. Indeed, many have argued that socioeconomic polarization has deepened as a result of structural adjustment policies mandated by international donors. The severity and mix of specific adjustment programs vary by country. Some African countries have been able to extract better terms from the IMF than others. Ghana has been touted as a success story. It had a good working relationship with and support from the IMF. Structural adjustment policies implemented since the mid-1980s led to improvements in the Ghanaian economy: food production per capita increased, the manufacturing sector expanded, and inflation decreased. Ghana is however still dependent on cocoa, and the world price for cocoa has collapsed. Ghana's external debt is also extremely high as loans have been used to finance imports. There was popular resentment toward the government and their external sponsors as a result of deteriorating living standards and increased poverty among the majority of the population. Elections were held (three since 1990), and each was said to be more democratic than the previous one. The last election (held in 2000) even led to the victory of one of the opposition parties. The World Bank has viewed Ghana as an excellent case study for political and economic liberalization in Africa. Despite this approval from one of the premier international lending institutions, foreign investors have shown little interest in the country.

Economic growth has occurred in Ghana, Uganda, Tanzania, and several other countries in the region that had extremely devastated economies in the 1980s. However, when one looks at the African region, the nexus of multi-party systems and neoliberal economic reforms has not yet produced the material changes expected by the vast majority of the African population. The international media continue to point to the impoverished African continent, where the population has little access to health and educational facilities, electricity, or piped water. Inequalities in resource distribution and income and high unemployment levels have led to the general deteriorating standards of the population. Although economic growth has occurred in several countries, the economic situation of the majority of the population in Africa has worsened under the new political dispensation.

During the 1980s and the first half of the 1990s, per-capita income in sub-Saharan Africa fell by 1.3 percent per year. In the mid-1990s close to slightly more than 50 percent of Africa's population lived in absolute

Africa's future: mixed signals as seen in different faces of Zambia

© Jeremy Homer / Corbis, © Tom Owen Edmunds / Getty Images, © Ian Murphy / Getty Images

President Wade of Senegal after his victory in multiparty elections in 2000.

Courtesy West Africa Magazine

Ghanaians in election mood in 2000. Do people participate in government only at election time?

Courtesy West Africa Magazine

Eritrean women participating in civic education.

© Jenny Matthews / Network Photographers Ltd.

poverty. World Bank economists estimated that by the year 2000, at least 75 percent of the African population will live in absolute poverty (NG and Yeats, 2000). At the end of the 1990s (see Table 2.6), sub-Saharan Africa still lagged behind other developing regions in areas such as life expectancy, infant mortality, malnutrition, education, and income levels, with the region appearing in the bottom half of 175 countries covered in the UN Human Development Index. More than 75 percent of the countries with a score at the bottom half of that index are African. These figures underscore the region's continuing widespread poverty and low human resource development.

How meaningful has it been to democratize the state if neoliberal reforms have destroyed its capacity to represent popular interests? Democracy will lose credibility among the population because it will become irrelevant

With health sector reforms, hospitals and clinics charge fees, and many Africans suffer more.

Courtesy West Africa Magazine

to those whose utmost priority is socioeconomic achievement. To date the evidence indicates that elected governments have not been able to do much better than their authoritarian counterparts in making the system equitable. With their numerical strength, the African electorate is expected to vote governments out of power if they do not deliver, and this process should give it the leverage to force social and economic reforms. Experience in other developing countries provides useful lessons for the new multiparty systems of Africa. Jamaica has had multiparty elections for over five decades, and there have been four different governments in power since independence in 1962. Yet profound social and economic inequalities continue to exist between the elite and the majority of the population (Edie, 1991). The record is similar in Haiti (Dupuy, 1997), El Salvador, Ecuador and Nicaragua (Peeler, 1985), Senegal (Coulon, 1988), Botswana (Holm, 1988), and The Gambia (Edie, 2002). Elections have brought political change, but in most developing nations they have not led to the reallocation of economic resources to reduce the gap between the rich and the poor. The African electorate may have large numbers on its side, but it does not have the clout to pressure the state to implement policies in its favor in the post–Cold War era of neoliberal ascendancy. Given its dependence on external capital, the state has been forced into compliance with the liberal-capitalist ideology of the post–Cold War global order. The weakened state has shown little capacity to develop alternative solutions to neoliberal economic reforms.

For Further Reading

Kayizzi-Mugerwa, S., ed. (1999). *The African Economy: Policy, Institutions and Future*. London and New York: Routledge.

Glossary

apartheid: word (meaning "separateness") derived from Afrikaans, the language spoken by the Afrikaners (also known as Boers), descendants of Dutch settlers in South Africa. The apartheid system was introduced by the Afrikaner-led National Party, which held power in South Africa from 1948 to 1990. Apartheid laws included the Pass Laws, which restricted the black population's freedom of movement (a pass was required for blacks to enter certain areas); the Population Registration Act, which registered all individuals by racial group—e.g., African, White, Coloured (Mixed Race), Asian; the Mixed Amenities Act, which segregated public facilities by race; the Group Areas Act, which separated urban suburbs; the establishment of Bantustans (homelands for blacks only); and the Immorality Act, which made sexual relations and marriage between Africans and Whites illegal. Under the apartheid system, nonwhites could not vote and their freedom of expression and movement were restricted. Africans had to seek government permission to live and work in urban areas. All of South Africa's rural areas were racially segregated, with Whites in control of 83 percent of South Africa's farmland. The apartheid system gave rise to numerous resistance movements from the African population—e.g., the African National Congress (ANC), Black Consciousness Movement (BCM), Azanian Peoples Organization (AZAPO), Pan African Congress (PAC), and United Democratic Front (UDF). ANC member Nelson Mandela was imprisoned for twenty-seven years for fighting against the apartheid regime. He was released in 1992 and was elected president of South Africa in 1994.

Arch 22: monument built at the entrance of the capital city of Banjul to commemorate military rule in The Gambia. It also symbolizes the squandering of resources in developing nations by authoritarian regimes. An estimated US$5 million was spent on Arch 22.

authoritarian: describes a political system with highly restricted opportunities for political mobilization. Power is exercised by a leader or a small group of leaders who are not formally accountable to an electorate. There are no effective constitutional limits to the exercise of power.

civil society: refers to a social milieu characterized by pluralistic discourse, tolerance, and moderation; the public space between individuals and the state.

coup d'etat: forced removal of a government. In Africa, coups d'etat have been carried out largely by the military; some have been violent, others bloodless.

democracy: refers to a specific type of political system marked by competition, participation, and legal protection of civil liberties. Economic democracy provides for the individual's right to own property, to apply his/her capital to improve his/her quality of life, to work in an activity of his/her choice, to enjoy a decent basic living standard, and to count on social amenities like health and educational facilities, clean water, and decent housing.

democratization: the process of moving toward conditions favorable to democracy.

dependency theory: a diverse body of literature that emerged in the late 1960s in Latin America and the Caribbean in response to discussions on the causes of the lack of development in the Third World. Modernization theory was the main orthodoxy in the post–World War II period and advanced the view that lack of development in the Third World was due to internal obstacles, such as the absence of entrepreneurial spirit, lack of pluralistic political institutions, the persistence of "backward" traditional social and cultural institutions. In order to develop, the Third World was encouraged to adopt Western political, economic, and social institutions, embrace Western values, and attract foreign capital. In response to this perspective, dependency scholars (e.g., Andre Gunder Frank, Walter Rodney, Samir Amin) argued that underdevelopment was not internally generated but that external domination of the Third World by capitalist countries created a global structure that prevented the possibility of independent development. Following its emergence in the Latin American and Caribbean region, dependency theory was subsequently applied to Africa and Asia.

Dependency theory has had major weaknesses; some have been addressed and some have not. It ignores changing forces that shape the relation between Western industrialized countries and the Third World. It has also been unable to give a convincing explanation for the newly industrialized countries (Taiwan, South Korea, Brazil, Singapore), which experienced considerable economic growth in the 1960s through the 1980s.

Dependency theory was modified in the 1970s with Fernando Cardoso's (1973) argument that, subject to the dictates of powerful capitalist countries, the best that a developing country can do is "dependent development". Dependency theory made important contributions to understanding African development. It showed the importance of the historical impact of colonization and economic domination. It also showed the continuous transfer of surplus from the Third World to Western industrialized countries, a process that limits the scope for indigenous industrialization and development.

Derg: (meaning "committee") Amharic name for military junta that came to power after the overthrow of the Haile Selassie regime in Ethiopia in 1974.

Economic Community of West African States (ECOWAS): an economic integration group established in 1973. The members are Benin, Burkina Faso, Cameroon, Chad, Côte d'Ivoire, Guinea, Guinea-Bissau, Liberia, Mali, Mauritania, Niger, Nigeria, Ghana, The Gambia, Senegal, and Togo.

ethnicity: refers to shared characteristics between similar individuals, including common language, common ancestors, common culture, common race, common set of religious beliefs. In Africa, ethnicity is shaped by the conflict of contending regional elites in their quest for political power. The concept of *tribalism* is often used as an alternative (a derogatory one) to ethnicity.

foreign exchange: a currency that has worldwide acceptance because of the desirability of owning that currency. U.S. dollars, French francs, German marks, Swiss francs, British pounds, and Japanese yen are examples of foreign exchange. They are also referred to as "hard currency."

Developing nations cannot purchase their imports with their weak currencies. They must use hard currency. In order to buy hard currency they must sell their products on the international market.

General Agreement on Tariffs and Trade (GATT): The agreement between member nations (over one hundred countries) to apply nondiscriminatory trade policies and liberalize international trade. Each GATT member must offer "most favored nation" status to all other GATT members. The exception is the free trade area that is allowed to discriminate in favor of its component members. In order to reduce trade barriers, GATT members organized a series of negotiating "rounds" between the signatory states (e.g., the Kennedy Round, 1963–1967; Tokyo Round, 1975–1979; and Uruguay Round, 1986–1994). The present Uruguay Round was very complex, with bitter disagreements between the United States and the EU over the latter's protectionist Common Agricultural Policy. African signatories of GATT supported the U.S. demand that the EU reduce its agricultural protectionism. Few African governments actively participated in the negotiations, which focused on North–North issues. Africa's position in GATT has not been very strong. It was unable to prevent, for example, new rules on intellectual property that would force developing nations to pay large royalties for the use of computer software. It is a matter of debate whether Africa would gain more from a free-trade world.

gross domestic product (GDP): a commonly used measure of the value of goods and services produced in a country. The GDP is a measure of the total amount of productive economic activity in a particular country. The GDP per capita is calculated by dividing the productive activities in a country by the population. The result is said to indicate the relative level of development in one country compared to others.

gross national product (GNP): The sum of the value of all goods and services produced by a country's residents in any given year. The concept of GNP and GDP are virtually the same except that GDP measures value produced in a given country, and GNP measures value produced by the factors of production of a given country, wherever they may operate in a given country or abroad. There are many reservations concerning the validity of GDP and GNP as indicators of development in the Third World. See for example Hadjor: 1993: 130–132.

guerrilla warfare: small-scale war by irregular troops against a conventional army of superior numbers and equipment. Guerrilla warfare has a long tradition in developing countries (Mexico, Cuba, El Salvador, Brazil, Colombia, Venezuela, Zimbabwe, South Africa, Mozambique, Angola, Guinea-Bissau, Namibia).

indirect rule: Technique of governance used by Britain in its African colonies. It was developed around 1900 by Lord Lugard, governor of Nigeria. It required minimal British presence in any colony and local life was barely disturbed. Through indirect rule Britain strengthened traditional authority figures, who enforced Britain's standards and orders. Indirect rule helped to preserve the power of the emirates in Northern Nigeria and the kabakaship of Buganda until independence. The idea of indirect rule was to rule the colonies as far as possible through native authorities and institutions. The belief was that the people are best ruled through conventions that they understand and the minimize cultural disruption.

International Monetary Fund (IMF): The IMF was set up to encourage international cooperation on monetary matters. In the 1970s, the Organization of Petroleum Exporting Countries' (OPEC) increase in the price of oil caused balance-of-payments problems in many non-oil-exporting developing countries. The economic crisis that ensued led a vast number of developing countries into agreements with the IMF, the bank of last resort. Since then there has been much controversy around the nature of IMF agreements, especially the claim by developing countries that the IMF does not take into account the structure of underdeveloped economies. It has a standard stabilization program for all countries regardless of the nature of their political economies. At the heart of this program is conditionality (loans issued on conditions such as currency devaluation, reduction of the public sector, increase in exports, liberalization of imports, elimination of subsidies, freezing of wages). Developing countries have argued that conditionality undermines their sovereignty. The IMF is commonly viewed in Africa as an obstacle to development. Several years ago, it was reportedly dubbed at a conference on development in Africa as the "Institute of Misery and Famine."

irredentism: term commonly used in reference to Somalia. "Somali irredentism" refers to a policy designed to unite all Somali peoples living in Kenya and Ethiopia with those in Somalia under one government.

kleptocracy: rule by stealing. In Africa this description is often applied to military governments (e.g., Ibrahim Babangida, Sani Abacha) in Nigeria and to the government of Mobutu in the former Zaire. Mobutu is said to have amassed a fortune of some US$5 billion during his thirty years in power.

legitimacy: political authority endowed on political leaders by those they rule. If political leaders act in accordance with the aspiration of those who have conferred authority on them, they enjoy legitimacy.

Maji Maji rebellion (1906): peasant rebellion against forced labor and heavy taxation under German colonial rule in Tanganyika. Germany crushed the resistance with superior military technology.

Mau Mau rebellion: common name given to the armed revolt by Kenyan peasants. The origin of the name *Mau Mau* is uncertain. The revolt broke out in 1952 against British colonialism. The rebellion was negatively portrayed as a brutal, animalistic, oath-taking people attacking Christianity and civilization. This negative portrayal was designed to convince the outside world that the rebellion by landless peasants was an irrational movement driven by lawless people. The forces of colonialism were presented as upholding freedom and democratic values. The Mau Mau rebellion gave impetus to the nationalist movement for independence and forced Britain to grant independence to Kenya much earlier than it had anticipated.

military-turned-civilian government: refers to the practice of military leaders resigning to become civilian candidates in multiparty elections held under pressure from Western governments and donors. The incumbent former military rulers would easily defeat other candidates in these multiparty elections. Examples of this phenomenon include Jerry Rawlings of Ghana, Yahya Jammeh of The Gambia, and Ibrahim Mainassara of Niger.

neoliberalism: name given to the resurgence of support since the 1980s for policies of laissez-faire. Neoliberalism advocates lower state spending, free capital movements, low taxes, decentralization, deregulation, and free trade. The International Monetary Fund and the World Bank make it the center of economic adjustment schemes. Many governments in Africa have undergone neoliberal economic reforms since the mid-1980s, but they have not solved the economic problems in these countries.

POLISARIO (Frente Popular para la Liberacion de Sakiet el Hamra y Rio de Oro): a liberation movement in the Western Sahara, a former Spanish colony, annexed to Morocco. POLISARIO was formed in 1973 by a group of Saharawi students. It called for armed struggle against Spanish colonialism. Morocco claimed Western Sahara, and Spain abandoned plans for its independence. In 1975 Spain made an agreement with Morocco and

Mauritania to share the Western Sahara between them. Mauritania abandoned all claims to Western Sahara in 1978 after POLISARIO pressure precipitated a coup d'etat there. POLISARIO has since centered on fighting Morocco. In 1984 the OAU accepted POLISARIO as a member. Morocco has been backed by the United States, whereas POLISARIO has been supported largely by Algeria. The issue has produced a split in the OAU, but the OAU still supported POLISARIO, as did seventy other countries. In 1991 the UN voted to organize a referendum in which Saharawi could decide between independence and legal incorporation into Morocco.

political liberalization: involves the expansion of public space through the recognition and protection of civil and political liberties, particularly those bearing upon the ability of citizens to engage in free political discourse to freely organize in pursuit of common interests.

populism: a political tendency that seeks to elevate and raise the status, power, and interests of those social groups located at the bottom of the social hierarchy and to assault and attack interests and groups that are highly placed at the upper end of the social hierarchy.

Sahel: a strip of land stretching across the Sahara Desert from Mauritania in the northwest to Ethiopia in the east. It is a very dry area with low rainfall. The Sahel is greatly threatened by desertification.

shadow state: Reno (1998) coined this term to describe political structures based on informal markets (e.g., Sierra Leone) such as illicit mining and exporting of diamonds. Business is done in the shadows, not in the legal realm.

Southern African Development Corporation (SADC): Comprised of Angola, Botswana, Lesotho, Malawi, Mozambique, Swaziland, Tanzania, Zambia, Zimbabwe, and South Africa. Formerly known as SADCC (Southern African Development Coordinating Conference) the group was formed in 1980 in an attempt to reduce dependence on the apartheid regime of South Africa. After the apartheid system collapsed and black majority rule was established in 1994, *SADCC* was transformed into SADC, and South Africa is now a part of the group.

Stabex and Sysmin: Export Earnings Stabilization Scheme, introduced in 1975 as part of the Lome Convention. It provides ACP countries with protection against price and production fluctuations of certain agricultural (e.g., bananas, groundnuts, tea, cocoa, cotton, coffee, coconuts, raw sisal) and mineral (e.g., iron ore) exports. The scheme provides compensation for earnings losses from export price drops.

state: a contested concept in political science. There is no agreement on its definition. In this book, I use the concept of the state to mean an institution through which the political elite enforces its interests. The African state in the postindependence period represented the narrow interests of the political elite and its allies. The main objective of those who controlled the state was to preserve the existing unequal socioeconomic relations of society.

statism: government intervention to control and regulate the economy so as to extract financial surpluses for government consumption and expansion.

Treaty of Westphalia (1648): This treaty ended the Thirty Years War in Europe. It is taken as marking the establishment of the modern European sovereign state system.

Union Douaniere et Economique de l'Afrique Central (UDEAC): an economic integration group. Members are Cameroon, Chad, Congo, the Central African Republic, Gabon, Equatorial Guinea.

Union Economique et Monetaire Ouest Africaine (UEMOA): an economic integration group. Members are Benin, Burkina Faso, Côte d'Ivoire, Mali, Niger, Senegal, and Togo. Members are all francophone African states.

ujamaa: Kiswahili word meaning "community." This word was chosen by Julius Nyerere to express the content of a socialism that he felt was deeply rooted in African tradition. *Ujamaa* villages based on cooperation, self-reliance, and socialist practices were established in Tanzania in the 1970s. Communalism from traditional African society was supposed to provide the foundation for an African socialism of the future. Building *ujamaa* villages was supposed to narrow the gap between rich and poor, eliminate exploitation, and bring about egalitarianism in Tanzania. *Ujamaa* was a practical failure; self-reliance was not achieved, and Tanzania became more dependent in the 1980s than in the 1960s. But *ujamaa* socialism did provide valuable lessons for African and other developing nations on development strategy for small agricultural countries.

World Bank (International Bank for Reconstruction and Development): The role of the World Bank is to encourage capital investment for development projects in developing countries. The World Bank's policies in developing nations are not as controversial as those of the International Monetary Fund (IMF). Its relationship with political leaders in Africa (and other Third World countries) is not as antagonistic. It is viewed by many African leaders as a partner in African development.

Sources

Mazrui, A., and M. Tidy (1984). *Nationalism and New States in Africa.* Narobi, Ibadan, and London: Heinemann.

Hadjor, Kofi B. (1987) *On Transforming Africa.* Trenton, N.J.: Africa World Press.

―――― (1992, 1993). *Dictionary of Third World Terms.* London: Penguin Books.

Bibliography

Abbink, J., and G. Hesseling (2000). *Election Observation and Democratization in Africa*. New York: St. Martin's Press.

Abernethy, D. (1983). "Bureaucratic Growth and Economic Decline in Sub-Saharan Africa." Paper presented at the annual meeting of the African Studies Association, Boston, Mass., December 1983.

Aborisade, O., and R. J. Mundt (1999). *Politics in Nigeria*. New York: Longman.

Aboyade, O. (1980). "Nigerian Public Enterprises as an Organizational Dilemma." In Paul Collins, ed., *Administration for Development in Nigeria*. Lagos: African Education Press .

Abraham, A. (1997). "War and Transition to Peace: A Study of State Conspiracy in Perpetuating Armed Conflict." *Africa Development* 22, no. 3–4, 101–116.

Abrahamsen, R. (1997). "The Victory of Popular Forces or Passive Revolution? A Neo-Gramscian Perspective on Democratization." *Journal of Modern African Studies*, 35, no. 1 (March): 129–152.

Adam, H. M. (1995). "Somalia: A Terrible Beauty Being Born?" In I. W. Zartman, ed., *Collapsed States: The Disintegration and Restoration of Legitimate Authority*. Boulder, Colo.: Lynne Rienner.

Ake, C. (1981a). *A Political Economy of Africa*. New York: Longman.

———. (1981b). "Off to a Good Start But Dangers Await." *West Africa*, May 25, 1162–1163.

Alavi, H. (1972). "The State in Post-Colonial Societies—Pakistan and Bangladesh." *New Left Review* 74 (July–August): 59–81.

Almond, G., and B. Powell (1996). *Comparative Politics: A Theoretical Framework*. New York: Harper Collins.

Annan, K. (1998). *The Causes of Conflict and the Promotion of Durable Peace and Sustainable Development in Africa*. New York: United Nations.

Apter, D. (1995). "Democracy for Uganda: A Case for Comparison." *Daedalus* 124, no.3, 155–190.

Bailey, F. G. (1971). "The Peasant View of the Life." In T. Sharin, ed., *Peasants and Peasant Society*. London: Penguin Books. 229–321.

Bakut, B. T. (2000). "The African Economic Community (AEC): A Step toward Achieving the Pan-African Ideal," In Bakut tswah Bakut and S. Dutt, eds., *Africa at the Millennium*. Houndsmill, England: Palgrave.

Bangura, Y. (1983). *Britain and Commonwealth Africa: The Politics of Economic Relations*. Manchester, England and Dover, N. H.: Manchester University Press.

Bangura, Y. (1997). "Reflections on the Abidjan Peace Accord." *Africa Development* 22, nos. 3–4, 217–241.

Barrett, D. (1982). *World Christian Encyclopedia: A Comparative Survey of Churches and Religions in the Modern World, 1900–2000*. Nairobi, Kenya: Oxford University Press.

Beck, L. (1999). "Senegal's Enlarged Presidential Majority: Deepening Democracy or Detour?" In R. Joseph, ed., *State, Conflict and Democracy in Africa*. Boulder, Colo.: Lynne Riener. 197–216.

Bienen, H. (1970). "Political Parties and Political Machines in Africa." In M. Lofchie, ed., *The State of the Nations: Constraints and Development in Independent Africa*. Berkeley: University of California Press. 195–213.

Boateng, O. (2000). "Lumumba: 'We Shall Show the World What the Black Man Can Do When He is Allowed to Work in Freedom'." *New African* (February): 22–25.

Bowen, M. (2000). *The State against the Peasantry: Rural Struggles in Colonial and Postcolonial Mozambique*. Charlottesville and London: University Press of Virginia.

Boulaga, F. E. (1993). *Les Conferences Nationales on Afrique Noire: Une Affaire à Suivre*. Paris, France: Karthala.

Bratton, M. (1994). "Economic Crisis and Political Realignment in Zambia." In J. Widner, ed., *Economic Change and Political Liberalization in Sub-Saharan Africa*. Baltimore: Johns Hopkins University Press.

———. (2000). "South Africa." In Jeffrey Kopstein and Mark Lichbach, eds., *Comparative Politics: Interests, Identities, and Institutions in a Changing Global Order*. Cambridge, England: Cambridge University Press. 381–412.

Bratton, M., and N. van de Walle (1992). "Popular Protests and Political Transition in Africa." *Comparative Politics* 24, no. 4 (July): 419–442.

———. (1994). "Neopatrimonial Regimes and Political Transitions in Africa." *World Politics* 46, no. 4 (July): 453–489.

———. (1997). *Democratic Experiments in Africa*. Cambridge, England: Cambridge University Press.

Callaghy, T. (1984). *The State-Society Struggle: Zaire in Comparative Perspective*. New York: Columbia University Press.

———. (1988). "The State and the Development of Capitalism in Africa: Regime Transition in Comparative Perspective." In D. Rothchild and Naomi Chazan, eds., *The Precarious Balance: State and Society in Africa*. Boulder, Colo.: Westview Press. 67–99.

Callaghy, T., and J. Ravenhill, eds. (1993). *Hemmed In: Responses to Africa's Economic Decline.* New York: Columbia University Press.

Chabal, P. (1992). *Power in Africa.* New York: St. Martin's Press.

Chabal, P. (1994). *Power in Africa.* 2nd ed. New York: St. Martin's Press.

Chazan, N., R. Mortimer, J. Ravenhill, and D. Rothchild, eds. (1988). *Politics and Society in Contemporary Africa.* Boulder, Colo.: Lynne Rienner.

Clapham, C. (1996). *Africa and the International System.* Cambridge, England: Cambridge University Press.

Coleman, J. (1958). *Nigeria: Background to Nationalism.* Berkeley: University of California Press.

Collier, R. B. (1982). *Regimes in Tropical Africa: Changing Forms of Supremacy, 1945–1975.* Berkeley: University of California Press.

Commodity Research Bureau (1994). *The CRB (Commodity Research Bureau) Commodity Yearbook.* New York: John Wiley.

Conteh-Morgan, E. (1997). Democratization in Africa: The Theory and Dynamics of Political Transitions. Westpoint, CT: Praeger.

Cornell, M. ed. (1981). *Europe and Africa: Issues in Post-Colonial Relations, 1980.* London: Overseas Development Institute.

Coulon, C. (1988). "Senegal: The Development and Fragility of Semi-democracy." In L. Diamond, J. Linz, S. Lipset, eds., *Democracy in Developing Countries: Africa.* Boulder, Colo.: Lynne Rienner. 141–178.

Crowder, M. (1968). *West Africa under Colonial Rule.* London: Hutchinson.

———. (1987). "Whose Dream Was It Anyway? Twenty-Five Years of African Independence." *African Affairs* 86, no. 342 (January): 7–24.

Davidson, B. (1989). *Modern Africa: A Social and Political History,* 2nd ed. London and New York: Longman.

Davis, D. (1995). "Sierra Leone: A Slow Transition," *West Africa,* Dec 6–Jan 8, 2201.

Davis, D., D. Hulme, and P. Woodhouse (1994). "Decentralization by Default: Local Government and the View from the Village in The Gambia." *Public Administration and Development* 14, 253–269.

Diamond, L. (1983). "Class, Ethnicity and the Democratic State: Nigeria, 1950–1966." *Comparative Studies in Society and History,* 25, no. 3, 459–489.

Diamond, L., J. Linz, S. Lipset, eds. (1988). *Democracy in Developing Countries: Africa.* Boulder, Colo.: Lynne Rienner Publishers.

Dupuy, A. (1997). *Haiti In The New World Order: The Limits of the Democratic Revolution.* Boulder, Colo.: Westview Press.

Edie, Carlene J. (1991). *Democracy by Default: Dependency and Clientelism in Jamaica.* Boulder, Colo.: Lynne Rienner.

———. (2000). "Democracy in The Gambia: Past, Present and Prospects for the Future." *Africa Development* xxv, nos. 3-4, 165–203.

Ellis, F. (1982). "Agriculture Price Policy in Tanzania." *World Development* 10, no. 4, 263–283.

Ephson, B. (1990). "Divestiture Problems." *West Africa*, September 3-9, 2396.

Ercolessi, M. C. (1994). "Italy's Policy in Sub-Saharan Africa." In S. Brune, J. Batz, and W. Kuhne, eds., *Africa and Europe: Relations of Two Continents in Transition*. Münster and Hamburg, Germany: Lit Verlag.

Fox, J. (1997). "The Difficult Transition from Clientelism to Citizenship: Lessons from Mexico." In D. A. Chalmers, C. M. Vilas, K. Hite, S. Martin, K. Piester, and M. Segarra, eds., *The New Politics of Inequality in Latin America: Rethinking Participation and Representation*. Oxford: Oxford University Press. 391–420.

Francis, D. (2000). "ECOMOG: A New Security Agenda in World Politics." In Bakut tswah Bakut and S. Dutt, eds., *Africa at the Millennium: An Agenda for Mature Development*. Houndsmill, England: Palgrave.

Fredland, R. (2001). *Understanding Africa: A Political Economy Perspective*. Chicago: Burnham.

Furedi, F. (1974). "The Social Composition of the Mau Mau Movement in the White Highlands." *Journal of Peasant Studies* 1, no. 4 (June): 486–505.

Gavshon, A. (1981). *Crisis in Africa: Battleground of East and West*. Middlesex, England: Penguin Books.

Girvan, N., G. Mills, A. McIntyre, A. Anderson, C. Stone, and M. Witter (1991). *Rethinking Development*. Kingston, Jamaica: Consortium Graduate School of Social Sciences, University of the West Indies.

George, S. (1993). "Uses and Abuses of African Debt." In A. Adedeji, ed., *Africa within the World: Beyond Dispossession and Dependence*. London: Zed Press. 59–72.

Glazer, A. and S. Smith (1994). *Afrique Sans Africains: Lerêve Blonc Du Continent Noir*. Paris, France: Editions Stock.

Gordon, April A., and D. L. Gordon, eds. (1996). *Understanding Contemporary Africa*. Boulder, Colo.: Lynne Rienner.

Gould, D. (1980). *Bureaucratic Corruption and Underdevelopment in the Third World: The Case of Zaire*. Elmsford, England: Pergamon Press.

Grameen Bank (1997). *Grameen Dialogue*. Dhaka, Bangladesh: Grameen Bank.

Haas, E. (1994). "Collective Conflict Management: Evidence from a New World Order." In F. Kratochwil and E. Mansfield, ed., *International Organization: A Reader*. New York and London: Harper Collins.

Hadjimichael, M. T., T. Rumbaugh, and E. Verreydt (1992). *The Gambia: Economic Adjustment in a Small Open Economy*. Washington, D.C.: International Monetary Fund.

Hadjor, K. B. (1987). *On Transforming Africa*. Trenton: Africa World Press.

———. (1993). *A Dictionary of Third World Terms*. London: Penguin Books.

Harrison, G. (1996). "Democracy in Mozambique." *Review of African Political Economy* 23, no. 67 (March): 19–34.

Herbst, J. (1989). "Political Impediments to Economic Rationality: Explaining Zimbabwe's Failure to Reform its Public Sector." *Journal of Modern African Studies*, 27, no. 1, 67–84.

Holm, J. D. (1988). "Botswana: A Paternalistic Democracy." In L. Diamond, J. Linz, S. Lipset, eds., *Democracy in Developing Countries: Africa*. Boulder, Colo.: Lynne Rienner. 179–216.

Holmquist, F., and M. Ford (1994). "Kenya: Slouching toward Democracy." *Africa Today* 39, no. 3, 97–111.

Holmquist, F., F. Weaver, and M. Ford (1994). "The Structural Development of Kenya's Political Economy." *African Studies Review* 37, no. 1 (April): 69–105.

Hopkins, A. (1973). An Economic History of West Africa. London and New York: Longman.

Howe, H. (1998). "Private Security Forces and African Stability: The Case of Executive Outcomes." *Journal of Modern African Studies*, 36, no. 2, 307–333.

Huntington, S. (1993). "Clash of Civilizations." *Foreign Affairs* 72, no. 3, 22–49.

Hutchful, E. (1996). "Ghana: 1983–1994." In P. Engberg-Pederson, P. Gibbon, P. Raikes, and L. Udsolt, eds., *Limits of Adjustment in Africa: The Effects of Economic Liberalization, 1986–1994*. Copenhagen, Denmark: Center for Development Research. 114–214.

Hyden, G. (1992). "Governance and the Study of Politics." In G. Hyden and M. Bratton, eds., *Governance and Politics in Africa*. Boulder, Colo.: Lynne Rienner.

Iyob, R. (1997). "The Eritrean Experiment: Cautious Pragmatism?" *Journal of Modern African Studies* 35, no. 4 (December): 647–676.

Jabara, C. (1994). "Structural Adjustment in a Small Open Economy: The Case of The Gambia." In David E. Sahn, ed., *Adjusting to Policy Failure in African Economies*. Ithaca, N.Y.: Cornell University Press.

Jaye, T. (2000). "ECOWAS and Liberia: Implications for Regional Intervention in Intra-State Conflicts." In Bakut tswah Bakut and S. Dutt, eds., *Africa at the Millennium*. Houndmill, England: Palgrave. 155–176.

Joseph, R. (1983). "Class, State and Prebendal Politics in Nigeria." *Journal of Commonwealth and Comparative Politics*, 21, no. 3 (November): 21–38.

———. (1991). "Africa: The Rebirth of Political Freedom." *Journal of Democracy* 2, no. 4, 11–24.

———, ed. (1999). *State, Conflict and Democracy in Africa*. Boulder, Colo., and London: Lynne Rienner.

Kaplan, R. (1994). "The Coming Anarchy." *Atlantic Monthly* 273, no. 2, (February): 44–81.

Kennedy, P. (1988). *African Capitalism: The Struggle for Ascendancy*. Cambridge: Cambridge University Press.

Khadiagala, G. (1995). "State Collapse and Reconstruction in Uganda." In I. W. Zartman, ed., *Collapsed States: The Disintegration and Restoration of Legitimate Authority*. Boulder, Colo.: Lynne Rienner. 23–48.

Khadiagala, G. (2000). "Europe in Africa's Renewal: Beyond Post-Colonialism?" In J. Harbeson and D. Rothchild, eds., *Africa in World Politics: The African System in Flux*. Boulder, Colo.: Westview Press. 83–109.

Kimuyu, P. (1999). "Regionalism in African Development." In S. Kayizzi-Mugerwa, ed., *The African Economy: Policy, Institutions and the Future*. London and New York: Routledge. 172–184.

Kok, P. (1996). "Sudan: Between Radical Restructuring and Deconstruction of State Systems." *Review of African Political Economy*, no. 70, 555–562.

Konadu-Agyemang, K. (1998). "Structural Adjustment Programs and the Perpetuating of Poverty and Underdevelopment in Africa: Ghana's Experiment." *Scandinavian Journal of Development Alternatives and Area Studies*, 17, no. 2 and 3, 127–143.

Lancaster, C. (2000). "Africa in World Affairs." In J. Harbeson and D. Rothchild, eds., *Africa in World Politics: The African State System in Flux*. Boulder, Colo.: Westview Press. 208–234.

Legum, C. (1994). "Britain's Policy in Africa." In S. Brune, J. Beyz, W. Kuhne, eds., *Africa and Europe: Relations of Two Continents in Transition*. Münster and Hamburg, Germany: Lit Verlag. 5–69.

Lemarchand, R. (1972). "Political Clientelism and Ethnicity in Tropical Africa." *American Political Science Review* 66, no. 1, 68–90.

———. (1988). "The State, the Parallel Economy and the Changing Structure of Patronage Systems." In D. Rothchild and N. Chazan, eds., *The Precarious Balance*. Boulder, Colo.: Westview Press.

———. (2000). "The Crisis in the Great Lakes." In J. Haberson and D. Rothchild, eds., *Africa in World Politics: The African State System in Flux*. Boulder, Colo.: Westview Press. 324–352.

Lewis, L. A., and L. Berry (1988). *African Environments and Resources*. Boston: Unwin Hyman.

MacGaffey, J. (1988). "Economic Disengagement and Class Formation in Zaire." In D. Rothchild and Naomi Chazan, eds., *The Precarious Balance: State and Society in Africa*. Boulder and London: Westview Press. 171–188.

Manning, C. (1999). "The Collapse of Peace in Angola." *Current History* 98, no. 628 (May): 208–212.

Marable, M. (1987). *African and Caribbean Politics: From Kwame Nkrumah to Maurice Bishop*. London: Verso.

Martin, G. (1986). "The Franc Zone: Underdevelopment and Dependency in Francophone Africa." *Third World Quarterly*, 36, no. 2, 307–331.

Martin, G. (1992). "African Regional Cooperation and Integration: Achievements, Problems and Prospects," In A. Seidman and F. Anang, eds., *21st Century Africa: Towards A New Vision of Self-Sustainable Development*. Trenton, N.J.: Africa World Press.

———. (1995a). "Continuity and Change in Franco-African Relations." *Journal of Modern African Studies*, 33, 1–20.

———. (1995b). "Francophone Africa in the Context of Franco-African Relations." In J. Harbeson and D. Rothchild, eds., *Africa in World Politics: Post-Cold War Challenges.* Boulder, Colo., Lynne Rienner. 163–188.

Martin, P. M., and P. O. O'Meara, eds. (1995). *Africa* 3rd ed. Bloomington and London: Indiana University Press.

Mazrui, A., and M. Tidy (1984). *Nationalism and New States in Africa.* Nairobi, Kenya: Heinemann.

Mbaku, J. (1994). "Military Coups as Rent-Seeking Behaviour." *Journal of Political and Military Sociology* 22 (winter): 241–284.

Mbanefo, A. C. (1975). "The Management of Public Enterprises Control and Autonomy: External and Internal Problems." In A. H. Rweyamanu and G. Hyden, eds., *A Decade of Public Administration in Africa.* Nairobi, Kenya: East African Literature Bureau. 289–299.

McNulty, M. (1999). "The Collapse of Zaire: Implosion, Revolution or External Sabotage." *Journal of Modern African Studies* 37, no. 1 (March): 53–82.

McPherson, M., and S. Radelet, eds. (1995). *Economic Recovery in The Gambia: Insights for Adjustment in Sub-Saharan Africa.* Cambridge, England: Cambridge University Press.

McQueen, M. (1998). "ACP-EU Trade Cooperation after 2000: An Assessment of Reciprocal Trade Preferences." *Journal of Modern African Studies* 36. no. 4, 660–692.

Muana, P. K. (1997). "The Kamajoi Militia: Civil War, Internal Displacement and the Politics of Counter-Insurgency." *Africa Development* 22, no. 3–4, 77–100.

Mukonoweshoro, E. (1990). "Authoritarian Reaction to Economic Crisis in Kenya." *Race and Class* 31, no. 4, 39–59.

Ndikumana, L. (2000). "Towards a Solution to Violence in Burundi: A Case for Political and Economic Liberalization." *Journal of Modern African Studies* 38, no. 3, 431–460.

———. (2001). "A Study of Central Accounts Regimes in Africa." Paper presented at the United Nations Conference on Trade and Development (UNCTAD) Workshop on "Management of Capital Flows: Comparative Experiences and Implications for Africa." Cairo, Egypt. March 20–21, 2001.

Ng, Francis, and A. J. Yeats (2000). *On the Recent Performance of Sub-Saharan African Countries: Cause for Hope or More of the Same?* Washington, D.C.: World Bank.

Nwokedi, E. (1995). *The Politics of Democratization: Changing Authoritarian Regimes in sub-Saharan Africa.* Münster and Hamburg, Germany: Lit Verlag.

Nyang, S. (1974). *The Role of the Gambian Political Parties in National Integration.* Ph.D. diss., University of Virginia.

Nyang'oro, J. (1996). "Africa's Environmental Problems." In *Understanding Contemporary Africa.* Boulder, Colo., Lynne Rienner. 195–220.

Organization For Economic Cooperation and Development (OECD) (1997). *Development Consistence Committee Report.* Paris: OECD.

Ottaway, M. (1997). *Democracy in Africa.* Boulder, Colo.: Lynne Rienner.

———. (1999a). "Ethnic Politics in Africa: Change and Continuity." In R. Joseph, ed., *State, Conflict and Democracy in Africa.* Boulder, Colo. and London: Lynne Rienner. 299–318.

———. (1999b). *Africa's New Leaders: Democracy or State Reconstruction?* Washington, D.C.: Carnegie Endowment for International Peace.

Pal, M. S. (1999). "Building African Institutions: Learning from South Asia." In S. Kayizzi-Mugerwa, ed., *The African Economy: Policy, Institutions and the Future.* London and New York: Routledge. 137–152.

Peeler, J. (1985). *Latin American Democracies.* Chapel Hill: University of North Carolina Press.

Polsky, Y. (1996.) "Russia's Policy Toward African." In M. Agonafer, ed., *Africa In The Contemporary International Disorder: Crisis and Possibilities.* Handham, MD and London, England: University Press of America. 185–202.

Powell, J. D. (1970). "Peasant Society and Clientelist Politics." *American Political Science Review* 64, no. 2, 411–425.

Radian, A. (1980). *Resource Mobilization in Poor Countries: Implementing Tax Policies.* New Brunswick, N.J.: Transaction Books.

Ravenhill, J. (1991). "Africa and Europe: The Dilution of a Special Relationship," In J. Harbeson and D. Rothchild, eds., *Africa In World Politics,* 1st ed. Boulder, Colo.: Westview Press. 179–202.

____. (1995). "Dependent by Default: Africa's Relations with the European Union." In J. Harbeson and D. Rothchild, eds., *Africa in World Politics: Post-Cold War Challenges.* Boulder, Colo., Lynne Rienner. 95–126.

Reno, W. (1998). *Warlord Politics and African States.* Boulder, Colo., and London: Lynne Rienner.

Revell, R. (1976). "The Resources Available for Agriculture." *Scientific American,* 235 (September): 165–178.

Rice, B. (1967). *Enter Gambia: The Birth of an Improbable Nation.* London: Angus and Robertson.

Rodney, W. (1972). *How Europe Underdeveloped Africa.* London: Bogle L'Ouverture.

Rothchild, D. (2000). "The Impact of U.S. Disengagement on African Intrastate Conflict Resolution." In W. Harbeson and D. Rothchild, eds., *Africa in World Politics: The African State System in Flux.* Boulder, Colo.: Westview Press.

Rothchild, D., and V. Olorunsola, eds. (1983). *State versus Ethnic Claims: African Policy Dilemmas.* Boulder, Colo.: Westview Press.

Sandbrook, R. (1993). *The Politics of Africa's Economic Recovery.* Cambridge, England: Cambridge University Press.

Sandbrook (1997). "Economic Liberalization versus Political Democratization: A Social Democratic Resolution." *Canadian Journal of African Studies,* 31, no. 3, 482–516.

Sandbrook, R., and J. Oldbaum (1997). "Reforming Dysfunctional Institutions through Democratization? Reflections on Ghana." *Journal of Modern African Studies* 35, no. 4 (December): 603–646.

Schatz, S. (1984). "The Inert Economy of Nigeria: From Nurture Capitalism to Pirate Capitalism." *Journal of Modern African Studies,* 22, no. 1 (March): 45–58.

Schraeder, P. J. (1996). "African International Relations." In D. Gordon and A. Gordon, eds., *Understanding Contemporary Africa.* Boulder, Colo., Lynne Rienner. 129–165.

Scott, J. (1972). "Patron-Client Politics and Political Change in Southeast Asia." *American Political Science Review* 66, no. 1, 91–113.

Selassie, B. (1980). *Conflict and Intervention in the Horn of Africa.* New York: Monthly Review Press.

Shain, Y., and J. Linz eds., (1995). *Between States: Interim Government and Democratic Transitions.* Cambridge, England: Cambridge University Press.

Shaw, T., and C. Newbury (1979). "Dependence or Interdependence: Africa in the Global Political Economy." In Mark Delancey, ed., *Aspects of International Relations in Africa.* Bloomington: Indiana University Press.

Shenton, R. (1987). "Nigerian Agriculture in Historical Perspective: Development and Crisis, 1900–1960." In Michael Watts, ed., *State, Oil and Agriculture in Nigeria.* Berkeley: Institute of International Studies, University of California, Berkeley. 34–57.

Sklar, R. (1963). *Nigerian Political Parties: Power in an Emergent African Nation.* Princeton: Princeton University Press.

———. (1979). "The Nature of Class Domination in Africa." *Journal of Modern African Studies,* 17, no. 4, 531–552.

———. (1983). *Nigerian Political Parties: Power in an Emergent African Nation.* 2nd ed. New York: London, Enugu, and Lagos (Nigeria) NOK Publishers.

Skoupy, J. (1988). "Developing Rangeland Resources in African Drylands." *UNEP Desertification Control Bulletin* 17, 29–40.

Stone, C. (1980a). *Democracy and Clientelism in Jamaica.* New Brunswick, N.J.: Transaction Books.

———. (1980b). *Understanding Third World Politics and Economics.* Brown's Town, Jamaica: Earle Publishers.

———. (1991). "Rethinking Development: The Role of the State in Third World Development." In N. Girvan, G. Mills, A. McIntyre, A. Anderson,

C. Stone and M. Witter eds., *Rethinking Development*. Kingston, Jamaica: Consortium Graduate School of Social Sciences, University of the West Indies. 87–100.

Strahler, A., and A. Strahler (1979). *Elements of Physical Geography*. New York: John Wiley.

Stryker, R., and S. Ndegwa, "The African Development Crisis." In P. M. Martin and P. O'Meara, eds., *Africa*, 3rd ed., Bloomington: Indiana University Press. 376.

Tangri, R. (1998). "Politics, Capital and the State in Sub-Saharan Africa." In N. Kasfir, ed., *Civil Society and Democracy in Africa*. Critical Perspectives. London: Frank Cass. 108–122.

Taylor, I. (1998). "China's Foreign Policy towards Africa in the 1990s." *Journal of Modern African Studies* 36, no. 3, 443–460.

Thomas, C. Y. (1984). *The Rise of the Authoritarian State in Peripheral Societies*. London and New York: Monthly Review Press.

Tripp, A. M. (2000). "Political Reform in Tanzania: The Struggle for Associational Autonomy." *Comparative Politics* 32, no. 2 (January): 191–214.

Umbadda, S. (1989). "Economic Crisis in the Sudan: Impact and Responses?" Paper delivered at the Conference on Economic Crisis and Third World Countries, Kingston, Jamaica, April 3–6, 1989.

United Nations (1994). *United Nations Energy Statistics Yearbook 1992*. New York: United Nations.

———. (1996). *Human and Development Index*. New York: United Nations.

United Nations Children's Fund (1993, 1994). *State of the World's Children*. Oxford: Oxford University Press.

United Nations Development Programme (1990). *Human Development Report 1990*. New York: Oxford University Press.

———. (1995). *Human Development Report 1995*. New York: Oxford University Press.

United Nations Economic Commission For Africa (1993). *Survey of Economic Conditions In Africa*. New York: United Nations.

van de Walle, N. (1991). "The Decline of the Franc Zone: Monetary Politics in Francophone Africa." *African Affairs* 90, no. 360, 383–405.

———. (1994a). "Political Liberalization and Economic Policy Reform in Africa." *World Development* 22, no. 4, 483–500.

———. (1994b). "Neopatrimonialism and Democracy in Africa with an Illustration from Cameroon." In J. Widner, ed., *Economic Change and Political Liberalization in Sub-Saharan Africa*. Baltimore: Johns Hopkins University Press. 129–157.

Wasserman, G. (1973). "The Independence Bargain: Kenya Europeans and the Land Issue, 1960–1962." *Journal of Commonwealth and Comparative Politics* 11, no. 2 (July): 99–120.

Weingrod, A. (1968). "Patrons, Patronage and Political Parties." *Comparative Studies in Society and History* 10 (July): 377–400.

Westahbe, R. (1994). "Structural Adjustment, Rent-Seeking and Liberalization in Benin." In J. Widner, ed., *Economic Change and Political Liberalization in Sub-Saharan Africa.* Baltimore: Johns Hopkins University Press. 80–100.

Whitaker, C. (1970). *The Politics of Tradition: Continuity and Change in Northern Nigeria, 1946–66.* Princeton, N.J.: Princeton University Press.

Widner, J., ed. (1994). *Economic Change and Political Liberalization in Sub-Saharan Africa.* Baltimore: Johns Hopkins University Press.

Winrow, G. M. (1990). *The Foreign Policy of the GDR in Africa.* Cambridge, England: Cambridge University Press.

Wiseman, J. (1986). "Urban Riots in West Africa, 1977–1985." *Journal of Modern African Studies* 24, 3 (September): 509–518.

———. (1990). *Democracy in Black Africa: Survival and Revival.* New York: Paragon House.

———. (1996). *The New Struggle for Democracy.* Aldershot, England: Avebury.

———. (1998). "The Gambia: From Coup to Elections." *Journal of Democracy* 9, no. 2, 64–75.

Wolf, E. (1971). "Aspects of Group Politics in a Complex Society: Mexico." In T. Sharin, ed., *Peasant and Peasant Society.* London: Penguin Books. 50–68.

Woodward, P. (1987). "Is the Sudan Governable?" *British Society for Middle Eastern Studies Bulletin* 13, no. 2, 137–149.

World Bank (1988). *Social Indicators of Development 1988.* Washington, D.C.: World Bank.

———. (1989). *SubSaharan Africa: From Crisis to Sustainable Growth.* Washington, D.C.: World Bank. ———. (1990). *World Development Report 1990.* New York: Oxford University Press.

———. (1991, 1992, 1993, 1994). *World Development Reports.* Oxford: Oxford University Press.

———. (1995a). *Toward Environmentally Sustainable Development in Sub-Saharan Africa: A World Bank Agenda.* Washington, D.C.: World Bank.

———. (1995b). *African Development Indicators 1994–1995.* Washington, D.C.: World Bank.

———. (1997). *African Development Indicators on Diskette.* Washington, D.C.: World Bank.

Wunsch, J., and D. Olowu, eds. (1990). *The Failure of the Centralized State: Institutions and Self-Governance in Africa.* Boulder, Colo., and London: Westview Press.

Young, C. (1978). "Zaire: The Unending Crisis." *Foreign Affairs,* 57, no. 1 (fall): 169–185.

Young, C. (1988). "The African State and Its Colonial Legacy." In D. Rothchild and N. Chazan, eds., *The Precarious Balance: State and Society in Africa*. Boulder, Colo.: Westview Press. 25–66.

Young, C., and T. Turner (1985). *The Rise and Decline of the Zairian State*. Madison: University of Wisconsin Press.

Young, J. (1991). "Along Ethiopia's Western Frontier." *Journal of Modern African Studies* 37, no. 2, 321–346.

Zartman, I. W. (1995a). *Collapsed States: The Disintegration and Restoration of Legitimate Authority*. Boulder, Colo.: Lynne Rienner.

———. (1995b). "Inter-African Negotiation." In J. Harbeson and D. Rothchild, eds., *Africa in World Politics: Post–Cold War Challenges*. Boulder, Colo.: Westview Press.

Index